Barnes & Noble Shakespeare

David Scott Kastan
Series Editor

BARNES & NOBLE SHAKESPEARE features newly edited texts of the plays prepared by the world's premiere Shakespeare scholars. Each edition provides new scholarship with an introduction, commentary, unusually full and informative notes, an account of the play as it would have been performed in Shakespeare's theaters, and an essay on how to read Shakespeare's language.

DAVID SCOTT KASTAN is the Old Dominion Foundation Professor in the Humanities at Columbia University and one of the world's leading authorities on Shakespeare.

Barnes & Noble Shakespeare
Published by Barnes & Noble
122 Fifth Avenue
New York, NY 10011
www.barnesandnoble.com/shakespeare

Image on page 368:
William Shakespeare, Comedies, Histories, & Tragedies, London, 1623, Bequest of Stephen Whitney Phoenix, Rare Book & Manuscript Library, Columbia University.

ISBN-13: 978-1-4114-0039-9
ISBN-10: 1-4114-0039-9

Library of Congress Cataloging-in-Publication Data

Shakespeare, William, 1564–1616.
  Othello / [William Shakespeare].
     p. cm. — (Barnes and Noble Shakespeare)
  Includes bibliographical references.
  ISBN-13: 978-1-4114-0039-9 (alk. paper)
  ISBN-10: 1-4114-0039-9 (alk. paper)
  1. Othello (Fictitious character)—Drama. 2. Interracial marriage—Drama. 3. Venice (Italy)—Drama. 4. Jealousy—Drama. 5. Muslims—Drama. I. Title. II. Series: Shakespeare, William, 1564–1616. Works. 2006.

PR2829.A1 2006
822.3'3—dc22   2006009006

Printed and bound in the United States.
1 3 5 7 9 10 8 6 4 2

OTHELLO

William

SHAKESPEARE

DANIEL VITKUS
EDITOR

Barnes & Noble Shakespeare

Contents

Introduction to *Othello*
by Daniel Vitkus

S hakespeare's *Othello* uses both realism and symbolism to produce powerful dramatic effects. On the one hand, the tragedy is a study in the psychology of deception and jealousy. The audience watches as Othello undergoes a terrible transformation: reason and love give way to wild emotion and uncontrollable hatred. The play's presentation of this process refers to the transformative reality of jealousy and its power to corrupt the mind. The play's realism is most palpable, perhaps, during the central action of the play, in Act Three, scene three, which forces the audience to watch, in frustration and suspense, as the evil Iago spins a web of lies to entrap and destroy Othello. We value the play in part because the main characters and the words they exchange seem so real and vivid, and because the simplicity and depth of their emotions make their passions still so easy to understand, four hundred years after the play was written. Love, hatred, jealousy, and revenge: these primitive motives for action are expressed with compelling eloquence by the characters that Shakespeare created. Othello, Iago, and Desdemona call for the audience to attend, sympathize, and identify with their suffering.

But what makes *Othello* an enduring work of art, appreciated by readers and playgoers from the seventeenth to the twenty-first century, is not only its realistic presentation of all-too-human passions and actions. Like all of Shakespeare's great plays, *Othello* is a drama that communicates many of its meanings on a symbolic level. Iago, Desdemona, and Othello are not only characters who come alive in a theatrical production or in the mind of the reader; they are also embodiments of larger concepts such as innocence, evil, and difference. The characters, the objects they employ on stage, and even the images conjured by the play's poetic language may function as symbols or emblems that stand for something else, or something larger. It is in this sense that we can describe Shakespearean drama as "emblematic." If we fail to heed this emblematic or symbolic level of the play's meaning, then we miss at least half of what is happening in *Othello*.

In order to appreciate the emblematic significance of this tragedy, it helps to know that *Othello*, perhaps more than any other play that Shakespeare wrote, draws upon an older dramatic tradition that was fundamentally symbolic, not realistic. Shakespeare's *Othello* is based, in part, on the popular religious drama known as the morality play, a form of drama that used personification allegory to represent a struggle between the forces of good and those of evil. In these morality plays, the protagonist is called Everyman or Mankind, and during the course of the play this representative man encounters a series of characters who urge him either to sin or to virtue. As a fallen man and an inheritor of original sin, Everyman inevitably falls into temptation. The basic dramatic structure of *Othello* is similar: the Moor is a kind of Everyman who is tempted, falls, and is judged, with the fate of his eternal soul at stake. But the Moor is an odd kind of Everyman, since his status as a Moor marks him as different, not typical, finally not Everyman at all. And it is this difference, perhaps, indicated by the symbolic color black, that prevents him from obtaining the redemption and salvation that Everyman acquires in the end. Thus, *Everyman* is a divine comedy, while *Othello* is a tragedy.

Iago is the character who is most clearly recognizable from this earlier tradition of popular religious drama, which was rooted in medieval customs and rituals. As a realistic character, Iago is Othello's hypocritical and scheming officer, third in command under Othello and Cassio, but he is also a direct descendant of the morality play figure known as the Vice. The Vice was a trickster figure who delighted in sharing his schemes with the audience as he worked to tempt and damn Everyman. His jokes and asides to the audience invoked the spectators' laughter and implicated them in his plots to bring his victim to ruin. Shakespeare's audience would have recognized Iago, in light of that earlier tradition, as a figure who represents evil itself, evil in its seductive and intrusive form as a force that strives in the world to persuade human beings to commit sin and be damned. He represents that demonic power that preys on our weaknesses in order to turn us against those we love.

The issue of realism versus symbolism must also be considered if we want to understand a central issue in the play—the blackness of Othello and what that blackness meant for Shakespeare and his audience. At the present historical moment, *Othello* is the object of great cultural interest in large part because it presents an interracial couple and explores the situation of a black Moor, a member of a minority group, who has acquired a position of power and authority in white Venice. Today's concern with racial difference has been an inspiration for stage and screen versions of *Othello*, but if we wish to understand Shakespeare's text properly we cannot assume that the play's portrayal of blackness and whiteness is consistent with current definitions of racial identity. When Shakespeare's *Othello* first appeared on the London stage, audiences there had had little direct contact with Moors or with any dark-skinned people from Africa. There was, however, a long-standing tradition in England of actors and entertainers (including local folk performers and dancers called mummers or morris dancers) who put on blackface makeup, usually made from soot or coal, in order to impersonate Moors, Turks, or Saracens. There were also stage Moors (like Shakespeare's Aaron in *Titus Andronicus*) who were more fully fleshed out as characters, but whose blackface appearance was meant to be an external sign of their essentially evil nature.

When *Othello* was first performed, many of the spectators would not see the actor in blackface as a lifelike impersonation of a real human being. Made up in black, the actor appeared unreal, even monstrous. In part, they would be drawn into the realistic fiction that presented the story of Othello the Moor of Venice, but at the same time that black skin color would also convey an emblematic meaning. For Shakespeare's audience, stage blackness was largely symbolic, a coded color that stood for evil, damnation, and ignorance. By contrast, Western audiences today often see Othello played by an African or African-American, and they understand Iago, Brabantio, and Roderigo's remarks about Othello (calling him "the thick-lips" at 1.1.66, and "an old black ram" at 1.1.88, etc.) to be the result of a racism that really came much later, when slavery and colonization became important systems supporting the British economy. But in Shakespeare's England, there was already a color prejudice that would provide a basis for later assumptions of white superiority, and we need to keep in mind that color prejudice was exacerbated, not created, by slavery and colonial relations.

Early modern Europeans did not believe that physical difference, including skin color, was determined by heredity, genetics, or evolutionary development—these were concepts that were not yet known. In English society during Shakespeare's lifetime, without the notions of race that would arise later in Europe, black skin color was understood (or misunderstood) primarily within a symbolic logic that associated external differences with an internal condition of the spirit or mind. Descriptions of black-skinned "Moors" existed (in printed travel tales, for example), but in Shakespeare's culture what we call race was defined according to two theories: on the one hand, the climatic theory, which attributed darker skin color to the sun's rays or to the heat of the local climate; and on the other, a Christian myth of origins. In his *Pseudodoxia Epidemica* (1646), when Sir Thomas Browne posed the question, "Why some men, yea and they a mighty and considerable part of mankind, should first acquire and still retain the gloss and tincture of blackness," he answered that "the causes generally received . . . are but two in number. The heat and scorch of the sun, or the curse of God on Cham and his posterity" (232–233). This second explanation relies upon the biblical story of Noah and the belief that Noah's son Cham (or Ham) was punished by God because he violated the command of his father, Noah, who said that while they remained in the ark, all of Noah's family should abstain from sexual relations. According to George Best's version of this myth, printed in 1578, "all of [Cham's] posterity after him should be so black and loathsome that it might remain a spectacle of disobedience to all the world. And of this black and cursed Chus [Cham's first son] came all these black Moors which are in Africa. . . ."

This was the myth of blackness known to Shakespeare and his contemporaries, but what about more accurate ethnographic information? Or even direct contact with African peoples? Were there any "real" Moors in England during Shakespeare's day? What did Othello's black presence signify to playgoers in Shakespeare's London? Did they perceive the white actor in blackface as a representational mirror of African or Moorish identity? Scholars have searched carefully for evidence of Moors and Africans in Shakespeare's England, but there are few traces of an African presence in London before the beginning of the seventeenth century. Much has been made of two items: first, in 1596 and 1601 Queen Elizabeth issued proclamations calling for the deportation of "blackamoors" from England; and second, in the winter of 1600–1601, an embassy of "noble Moors" from Morocco made an extended visit to the English court. These two indicators of an African or Moorish presence within England's borders have received so much notice because there is little else in the archive that indicates a significant presence at this time. What these findings do suggest is that the appearance of Moors or Africans in Shakespeare's England was seen as contaminating and threatening, or interesting and exotic, because it was so rare. English subjects knew about the large-scale enslavement of sub-Saharan Africans by Spanish and Portuguese masters, and they also knew about the existence of slavery in the Mediterranean, Africa, and the New World; but in 1603 when Shakespeare wrote *Othello*, Englishmen were much more likely to become slaves than to own slaves. Some playgoers were well educated enough to know that Moors came from North Africa (what was called Barbary), but even these people would be likely to associate Moorishness with certain stereotypical characteristics. They might, for example, be aware of what Leo Africanus, the most authoritative Renaissance writer on Africa, said about the "Moors of Barbary": "no nation in the world is so subject unto jealousy; for they will rather lose their lives, than put up any disgrace in behalf of their women."

Older conceptions of blackness, fostered through a long tradition of popular performance, were more prevalent than any tendency to make direct associations between a stage Moor and real Moors living in Algiers or Tunis. Stage blackness was primarily (though not exclusively) symbolic, emblematic, and nonnaturalistic. In Shakespeare's theater, audiences would have been far more likely to comprehend blackface performance according to a longstanding tradition that associated blackness with sin or damnation than to see it as an exploration of social problems or possibilities.

Today's typical approach to theatrical performance sometimes makes difficult a proper historical understanding of exotic characters, like Othello, who strut the stage like allegorical things more than as representations of something fully human. Early modern actors did not attempt, like Laurence Olivier buffing his mock-Moorish makeup to a high polish, to create the effect of a "real live" Moor on stage. Instead, they put on blackface in order to become a ritually disfigured body—a figure of whiteness obscured. This was not just a matter of stage makeup. It was something akin to the symbolic face painting practiced as a part of myth-reenactment ceremonies among traditional peoples. At the time that Shakespeare wrote, there was still some confusion as to whether Moors were human beings or monsters.

For medieval and early modern audiences, the cosmetic trick of blackface performance was the sign of something unnatural, or something perverse. Audiences saw the actor playing the Moor as a natural-born white man who had covered his whiteness. Blackface performance was therefore a kind of cross-dressing that invoked a set of preestablished emblematic meanings: the performative significance of blackness was founded upon a range of conventional characteristics—evil, sin, barbarity, infidelity, misfortune, ignorance, contamination, and so on. These associations constitute a prejudicial framework into which the black character enters and through which (or perhaps against which) the actor in blackface then speaks as an individual character. In the culture of early modern England, the term _Moor_ was used to describe native inhabitants of India, North America, Indonesia, North Africa, sub-Saharan Africa, and the Arab world. On stage, black characters were marked as different, but any distinct ethnographic details were usually obscured by a more basic sense of difference. Most of the people in Shakespeare's audience would not know to make distinctions among darker-skinned people: Moor, Arab, Turk, what they called _Mahometan_ (i.e., Muslim)—all were confused and lumped together as radically "other." This dispersal of specific geographic associations only served to strengthen what audiences perceived to be the universal meaning of blackness.

In his 1584 _Discoverie of Witchcraft_, Reginald Scott reports that "A damned soul may and doth take the shape of a black Moor." In late medieval miracle plays and sometimes later, damned souls were represented by actors who painted their bodies black or wore black costumes. In late medieval drama, stage devils and demons were dressed in black clothes, sometimes with black leather fittings over their limbs, or wearing a black cape draped over their body and black hose on their legs, and sporting black-feathered wings. Their faces were colored black, too. And they had horns, like Othello's self-image, the monstrous cuckold-beast.

The early scenes of *Othello* reaffirm the conventional association of black skin with devils and damnation. In the play's second scene, for example, Brabantio refers to Othello when he says, "Damned as thou art" (1.2.65). Shakespeare's play repeatedly encourages the audience to read blackness as a symbol of sin: this occurs, for instance, when Othello himself says that Desdemona's "name, that was as fresh / As Dian's visage, is now begrimed and black / As mine own face" (3.3.390–392). In the play's final scene, Othello's damnation is explicitly announced. In the words of Emilia, Othello's blackness is again the mark of a devil damned: "Oh, the more angel she, and you the blacker devil!" (5.2.129).

Rather than isolating or separating the symbolic from the realistic in Shakespeare's drama, it might be more helpful to see them as operating simultaneously in a kind of discrepant awareness or dual consciousness. The stage Moor was a symbolic devil-figure, but at the same time represented more specific ethnographic identities and individual character traits. *Othello* draws upon the religious drama, but it also panders to English culture's newly stimulated curiosity about exotic peoples. Playwrights like Shakespeare led the way as English drama shifted from the allegorical personifications of the medieval morality play toward a more realistic staging of individual character psychology.

Othello is perhaps Shakespeare's most tightly focused play. It takes the metaphysical issues of damnation and salvation and places them within a human, domestic framework. Its plot is centered in a tense little knot of characters—Iago, Desdemona, and Othello. This triangle forms the basic structure that organizes the play's action, and that action works to accelerate time itself, rushing Othello toward the murder of Desdemona. The audience gets caught up in Iago's plot to transform Othello, and the play begins to function in what has been called "double time." There is no time for Cassio and Desdemona to have committed "the act of shame / A thousand times" (5.2.208–209), but the audience, along with Othello, is swept along by the relentless persuasions of Iago. After the initial excitement and urgency of the Venetian response to the Turkish attack on Cyprus, the scope of the play shrinks and contracts from the wide Mediterranean Sea to the fatal, claustrophobic bedroom where Othello kills Desdemona. The play, which began as a grand romance in a time of war, ends up as a domestic tragedy.

The play's first scene invokes the traditional meaning of stage blackness when Iago describes Othello as a "devil" (1.1.91) and "a lascivious Moor" (1.1.127), but when Othello makes his first entrance, he does not seem to fit the stereotype of barbarism, lust, evil, and treachery. Rather, he speaks eloquently and behaves with dignity and decorum. Already, the audience is shown that they should not judge a person by external appearance. Instead, the example of Desdemona and Othello's mutual love illustrates that physical or cultural differences do not ensure incompatibility or opposition of mind. Desdemona explains that she "saw Othello's visage in his mind" (1.3.251). At this point, Othello's blackness violates convention and expectation. The text makes clear that Othello is, after all, a Christian—but for Shakespeare's audience there is a nagging sense, encouraged by Iago, that the Christian Moor might retain the taint of Islamic savagery.

Shakespeare's play turns on the question of identity—and on the mistaken identity of Iago and Desdemona. Othello thinks Iago is "honest," and his faith in Iago's honesty leads him to believe that Desdemona is a devil. The hypocrisy of Iago, and Othello's inability to perceive Iago's evil until it is too late—these are the dramatic elements that support the play's complex unfolding of the appearance-reality theme. The idea of judging by appearances is carefully developed through the language and imagery of the play, which is organized by means of a series of binary oppositions: seeming versus being; words versus deeds; words versus thoughts; public, external reputation (honor or shame) versus a private, internal state of mind or condition of the spirit; thinking something is so, as opposed to knowing that it is so. For Othello, seeing is believing, and he never fully appreciates the degree to which appearances can be deceiving. The key terms here are *show, see, sight, to think, to know, to seem/seeming*, and the verb *to be*.

Love and *honesty* are also important words and concepts that make up the verbal trap set by Iago for Othello. Both of these words change their meanings, depending on whether they refer to the love or honesty of a man—or that of a woman. A sexist double standard, one that prevailed in Shakespeare's society, produces these gendered differences in meaning. *Honesty* for women was primarily a sexual honesty: in this sense, Othello demands of Desdemona, "Swear thou art honest!" (4.2.40). On the other hand, *honesty* for men was a question of truth telling, of keeping one's word pure, not one's body. Similarly, *love* between a man and a woman usually implied physical affection and romantic passion, while *love* between men (in the early modern sense) has a much broader meaning, including male bonding, loyalty, service, and friendship—and not usually sex.

The text employs the concepts of love and honesty in order to explore the gap between perception and truth. Consider the following three examples:

Iago to Cassio: "I think you think I love you." (2.3.295)

Othello to Iago: "If thou dost love me, / Show me thy thought."
(3.3.118–119)

Othello: "This honest creature doubtless / Sees and knows more, much more, than he unfolds." (3.3.248–249)

In each case, thought is hidden from view, and a mistaken interpretation of what someone is thinking leads to trouble. These exchanges between Iago and the other characters serve to raise larger questions of identity: Who are we? What everyone else thinks we are? What we think we are? Where does real identity lie? In the eye of the beholder? Or in some internal essence that cannot be known?

This concern with identity and its potential slipperiness begins with Iago's declaration in the first scene, "I am not what I am" (1.1.65) and ends with Othello's plea, "Speak of me as I am" (5.2.341). "Men should be what they seem" (3.3.130) says Iago, and Othello echoes him in assent. "Certain, men should be what they seem" (3.3.132) mutters Othello, already confused and stunned by Iago's implication that Cassio, who has all the appearance of honor—in fact, *is* honorable—is not honest.

The question of identity is a source of deep anxiety for Othello because he is divided from the Italian characters by his appearance as a dark-skinned Moor—his physical difference—but at the same time he has assimilated by adopting the identity of the noble, honorable Christian soldier, the defender of Cyprus against Muslims and Turks. Religious identity is crucial in *Othello*, not only in terms of Christian versus Turkish infidel, but even more importantly in terms of salvation and damnation, Heaven and Hell, angels and devils. Iago, who invokes "all the tribe of Hell" (1.3.352) is the white devil, while Desdemona is a pure angel, but Othello calls Desdemona a "fair devil" (3.3.481). Religious and sexual language were closely linked in Shakespeare's society and in the play. When Othello asks Desdemona, "Are you not a strumpet?", she answers, "No, as I am a Christian" (4.2.85–86). He persists: "What, not a whore?" "No, as I shall be saved" is her response (4.2.90). The view of women as devilish, damned whores by nature was a part of the patriarchal, misogynist thinking that dominated in Shakespeare's society. Demonizing myths about women developed in sexist societies in order to maintain and

justify male power over women, and to give vent to masculine anxieties
about the control of procreation, sexual behavior, and the getting of
legitimate heirs. That a woman may seem to be one thing (a pure, beautiful angel) and yet be another (a whore) comes to signify, in the mind of
Othello, the very nature of womankind. He becomes a jealous husband
because he trusts in this patriarchal myth: that women are either pure,
virtuous angels or damned whores, and nothing in between. Othello
can only turn against Desdemona on such slim evidence because he is
preconditioned to suspect her of adultery—and also because he values
his love of Iago more than he values his love for any woman.

Othello says to Iago: "I think my wife be honest and think
she is not. / I think that thou art just and think thou art not" (3.3.388–
389). Driven to extreme passion by this conflict, Othello ultimately
takes the word of a soldier and friend whom he loves over his true love
Desdemona. Othello is an exemplar of the most radical version of
patriarchy—the system of male, military honor, and male bonding
through violence and war. The play's sexual tension is connected to
the threat of violence and death; it is set "in a town of war / Yet wild,
the people's hearts brimful of fear" (2.3.199–200) on Cyprus, Venus's
island, under martial law.

Othello uses the military logic of irrefutable command and
absolute obedience—simplistic, inflexible, extreme. He is an absolutist in love and war: friend or foe, victory or defeat, all or nothing,
black or white, love and hate, saint and whore. He thinks in grand
opposites (for example, when he tells Desdemona at 3.3.90–91, "I do
love thee! And when I love thee not, / Chaos is come again"), but this
kind of inflexible, binary logic is inadequate to cope with the complex
world of Iago. Othello is also limited because he has no sense of humor or irony—he is deadly serious. He lacks the capacity to see things
from different sides. Othello uses words like bricks with dictionary
definitions printed on them—he is an absolutist with words, insensi-
tive to the multiple meanings and instabilities inherent in language

itself. Absolutists can never be certain enough of the absolute—it is their only means of support. When Othello says, "If it were now to die, / 'Twere now to be most happy, for I fear / My soul hath her content so absolute / That not another comfort like to this / Succeeds in unknown fate" (2.1.186–190), it is an ominous irony of which the audience is aware, but not Othello.

Othello's language is single minded, forceful, and inflexible. His vocabulary is lofty but limited; it does not include the domestic or the intimate, and this makes him vulnerable. Iago truly knows Othello and his limitations, and Iago's evil feeds the sexual Puritanism that he recognizes in Othello. He plays on Othello's disgust with the idea of Desdemona's sleeping with Cassio—a repugnance that rapidly overwhelms Othello's mind. Iago works his victim with consummate skill, relentlessly. Iago exhausts Othello in Act Three, scene three, as the Moor holds the stage for over 450 lines. At the beginning of the scene, he is a noble lover who tells his wife, "I will deny thee nothing!" (3.3.82); by the end he has been transformed into a jealous monster who swears he will "tear her all to pieces" (3.3.435). Iago's vertiginous rhetorical spinning is too much for the "free and open" (1.3.391) Moor who "thinks men honest that but seem to be so" (1.3.392). Iago's words disorient him, insinuating being where there is only seeming, confusing appearance and reality. Dazzled thus, Othello is "led by th' nose / As asses are" (1.3.393–394). By Act Four, scene one, Iago is able to induce Othello's "trance," and Iago stands in triumph over the Moor's prostrate body.

The key to Iago's victory is his awareness that Othello cannot endure instability, inconsistency, or uncertainty. For Othello, all must be fixed, certain, known, proven. And Othello is honorable to the point of stubbornness; he cannot go back on his word. He is a military commander who cannot undermine his authority by admitting that he has made a huge mistake. This mentality leads him to make illogical pronouncements like, "To be once in doubt / Is to be resolved" (3.3.183–184) or "I'll see before I doubt; when I doubt, prove" (3.3.194). Once Iago has Othello convinced, Iago seals the deal by immediately making the unbearable suggestion that "Your mind may change" (3.3.455). This use of reverse psychology provokes an instant response: "Never, Iago" (3.3.456).

The brilliant representation of psychological realism in Act Three, scene three shifts, at the very end of the scene, back into the symbolic mode. Iago and Othello kneel together to pronounce what is both a mock marriage vow and a diabolical compact. Othello tells Iago, with dreadful finality, "I am bound to thee forever" (3.3.218); and in the last, crowning line of this great scene, Iago responds with "I am your own forever" (3.3.482). The bargain is sealed: Iago owns Othello's soul in return for Iago's satanic service. This is confirmed in the play's final scene when Othello looks "down towards [Iago's] feet" (5.2.283), almost expecting to see the devil's cloven hooves. We know that Othello has lost his former identity—his essence and soul—when Lodovico asks, "Where is this rash and most unfortunate man?" and Othello can only reply, "That's he that was Othello. Here I am" (5.2.280–281).

Othello's pathetic claim, "naught I did in hate, but all in honor" (5.2.292) does not excuse his deadly error. In the end, Othello fails to sustain the role of virtue, honor, and nobility and becomes the "malignant . . . Turk" (5.2.352), the enemy of Venice who must be killed once more. He has converted to the ugly stereotype of the jealous, sex-obsessed Moor and the cruel, violent Turk. The only honorable thing left to do is to compensate for his crimes by killing the thing he has become.

What then does Shakespeare's play, _Othello_, say to us today? It is a cautionary tale about jealousy, envy, suspicion, and a portrait of evil and hypocrisy—a warning to beware the Iagos of the world. Furthermore, we are cautioned not to define our judgments in terms of absolute, binary oppositions. Perhaps what Shakespeare's play is

telling us is that the world is not a world of black and white opposites—of good versus evil, honest versus dishonest, true versus false,
virgins and whores, angels and devils. Or of rigid stereotypes. Those
who read the world in this way may end up like Othello, destroying
the things they love.

Instead of falling into the error of Othello, perhaps what we
need to do is to combine honorable intentions with a sophisticated,
flexible ability to interpret what we see and what we are told. Another
way of putting it: being a good soldier is not enough—dealing
with the ironies, ambiguities, moral complexities, difficult decisions,
and contradictory signals that confront us will require the use of a
critical analysis that looks carefully at the facts on the ground and
demands more than just the superficial "ocular proof" (3.3.364) of
video imagery presented by our own Iago-like spin doctors.
Skepticism is essential (the intelligent doubt that Othello could not
endure), and most of all—compromise and negotiation. These are
abilities that the "unbookish" mercenary Othello lacks (4.1.101).
"Men should be what they seem," says Iago (3.3.130), but the central
message of the play is found in its insistence that external appearance
or spoken word do not correspond to internal thoughts or motives.

As a realistic character, Othello elicits our sympathy
because he is a noble and well-intentioned man who speaks with
passion and eloquence, but falls victim nonetheless to Iago's careful
manipulation. We watch, in suspense, as Othello descends from the
height of a love that was achieved in spite of racial prejudice, to a pro-
found failure of judgment, and finally, a giving way to bestial passion.
We all wonder whether we might be susceptible to the machinations
of an Iago who knows us well enough to attack where we are most
vulnerable. At the same time, Othello's tragedy expresses a symbolic
meaning that supplements our identification with his plight. The
blackness of Othello, coupled with the terrible silence of Iago at the
end, expresses a symbolic sense of evil's deadly power and stubborn

persistence. The blackness painted on the actor's face marks him with the sign of that evil, which may arise even from love itself. At the end of the play, Othello's blackness takes on the traditional association with death, Hell, and damnation. Finally, the symbolic meaning of blackness overtakes the sense of Othello as a real man: Othello's monstrous error, conveyed by Shakespeare's poetry and lamented in high tragic terms, carries the character of Othello beyond the level of realism. His suicide and his dying kiss are gestures that speak in powerful images of blood and death, and they conclude the play in a symbolic ritual that defines a violent place where the extreme passions of love and revenge meet in death.

Shakespeare and His England
by David Scott Kastan

hakespeare is a household name, one of those few that don't need a first name to be instantly recognized. His first name was, of course, William, and he (and it, in its Latin form, *Gulielmus*) first came to public notice on April 26, 1564, when his baptism was recorded in the parish church of Stratford-upon-Avon, a small market town about ninety miles northwest of London. It isn't known exactly when he was born, although traditionally his birthday is taken to be April 23. It is a convenient date (perhaps too convenient) because that was the date of his death in 1616, as well as the date of St. George's Day, the annual feast day of England's patron saint. It is possible Shakespeare was born on the 23rd; no doubt he was born within a day or two of that date. In a time of high rates of infant mortality, parents would not wait long after a baby's birth for the baptism. Twenty percent of all children would die before their first birthday.

Life in 1564, not just for infants, was conspicuously vulnerable. If one lived to age fifteen, one was likely to live into one's fifties, but probably no more than sixty percent of those born lived past their mid-teens. Whole towns could be ravaged by epidemic disease. In 1563, the year before Shakespeare was born, an outbreak of plague claimed over one third of the population of London. Fire, too, was a constant threat; the thatched roofs of many houses were highly flammable, as well as offering handy nesting places for insects and rats. Serious crop failures in several years of the decade of the 1560s created food shortages, severe enough in many cases to lead to the starvation of the elderly and the infirm, and lowering the resistances of many others so that between 1536 and 1560 influenza claimed over 200,000 lives.

Shakespeare's own family in many ways reflected these unsettling realities. He was one of eight children, two of whom did not survive their first year, one of whom died at age eight; one lived to twenty-seven, while the four surviving siblings died at ages ranging from Edmund's thirty-nine to William's own fifty-two years. William married at an unusually early age. He was only eighteen, though his wife was twenty-six, almost exactly the norm of the day for women, though men normally married also in their mid- to late twenties. Shakespeare's wife Anne was already pregnant at the time that the marriage was formally confirmed, and a daughter, Susanna, was born six months later, in May 1583. Two years later, she gave birth to twins, Hamnet and Judith. Hamnet would die in his eleventh year.

If life was always at risk from what Shakespeare would later call "the thousand natural shocks / That flesh is heir to" (*Hamlet*, 3.1.62–63), the incessant threats to peace were no less unnerving, if usually less immediately life threatening. There were almost daily rumors of foreign invasion and civil war as the Protestant Queen Elizabeth assumed the crown in 1558 upon the death of her Catholic half sister, Mary. Mary's reign had been marked by the public burnings of Protestant "heretics," by the seeming subordination of England to Spain, and by a commitment to a ruinous war with France, that, among its other effects, fueled inflation and encouraged a debasing of the currency. If, for many, Elizabeth represented the hopes for a peaceful and prosperous Protestant future, it seemed unlikely in the early days of her rule that the young monarch could hold her England together against the twin menace of the powerful Catholic monarchies of Europe and the significant part of her own population who were reluctant to give up their old faith. No wonder the Queen's principal secretary saw England in the early years of Elizabeth's rule as a land surrounded by "perils many, great and imminent."

In Stratford-upon-Avon, it might often have been easy to forget what threatened from without. The simple rural life, shared by about ninety percent of the English populace, had its reassuring natural rhythms and delights. Life was structured by the daily rising and setting of the sun, and by the change of seasons. Crops were planted and harvested; livestock was bred, its young delivered; sheep were sheared, some livestock slaughtered. Market days and fairs saw the produce and crafts of the town arrayed as people came to sell and shop—and be entertained by musicians, dancers, and troupes of actors. But even in Stratford, the lurking tensions and dangers could be daily sensed. A few months before Shakespeare was born, there had been a shocking "defacing" of images in the church, as workmen, not content merely to whitewash over the religious paintings decorating the interior as they were ordered, gouged large holes in those felt to be too "Catholic"; a few months after Shakespeare's birth, the register of the same church records another deadly outbreak of plague. The sleepy market town on the northern bank of the gently flowing river Avon was not immune from the menace of the world that surrounded it.

This was the world into which Shakespeare was born. England at his birth was still poor and backward, a fringe nation on the periphery of Europe. English itself was a minor language, hardly spoken outside of the country's borders. Religious tension was inescapable, as the old Catholic faith was trying determinedly to hold on, even as Protestantism was once again anxiously trying to establish itself as the national religion. The country knew itself vulnerable to serious threats both from without and from within. In 1562, the young Queen, upon whom so many people's hopes rested, almost fell victim to smallpox, and in 1569 a revolt of the Northern earls tried to remove her from power and restore Catholicism as the national religion. The following year, Pope

Pius V pronounced the excommunication of "Elizabeth, the pretended queen of England" and forbade Catholic subjects obedience to the monarch on pain of their own excommunication. "Now we are in an evil way and going to the devil," wrote one clergyman, "and have all nations in our necks."

It was a world of dearth, danger, and domestic unrest. Yet it would soon dramatically change, and Shakespeare's literary contribution would, for future generations, come to be seen as a significant measure of England's remarkable transformation. In the course of Shakespeare's life, England, hitherto an unsophisticated and underdeveloped backwater acting as a bit player in the momentous political dramas taking place on the European continent, became a confident, prosperous, global presence. But this new world was only accidentally, as it is often known today, "The Age of Shakespeare." To the degree that historical change rests in the hands of any individual, credit must be given to the Queen. This new world arguably was "The Age of Elizabeth," even if it was not the Elizabethan Golden Age, as it has often been portrayed.

The young Queen quickly imposed her personality upon the nation. She had talented councilors around her, all with strong ties to her of friendship or blood, but the direction of government was her own. She was strong willed and cautious, certain of her right to rule and convinced that stability was her greatest responsibility. The result may very well have been, as historians have often charged, that important issues facing England were never dealt with head-on and left to her successors to settle, but it meant also that she was able to keep her England unified and for the most part at peace.

Religion posed her greatest challenge, though it is important to keep in mind that in this period, as an official at Elizabeth's court said, "Religion and the commonwealth cannot be parted asunder." Faith then was not the largely voluntary commitment it is today, nor was there any idea of some separation of church and state. Religion was literally a matter of life and death, of salvation and damnation, and the Church was the Church of England. Obedience to it was not only a matter of conscience but also of law. It was the single issue on which the nation was most likely to be torn apart.

Elizabeth's great achievement was that she was successful in ensuring that the Church of England became formally a Protestant Church, but she did so without either driving most of her Catholic subjects to sedition or alienating the more radical Protestant community. The so-called "Elizabethan Settlement" forged a broad Christian community of what has been called prayer-book Protestantism, even as many of its practitioners retained, as a clergyman said, "still a smack and savor of popish principles." If there were forces on both sides who were uncomfortable with the Settlement—committed Protestants, who wanted to do away with all vestiges of the old faith, and convinced Catholics, who continued to swear their allegiance to Rome—the majority of the country, as she hoped, found ways to live comfortably both within the law and within their faith. In 1571, she wrote to the Duke of Anjou that the forms of worship she recommended would "not properly compel any man to alter his opinion in the great matters now in controversy in the Church." The official toleration of religious ambiguity, as well as the familiar experience of an official change of state religion accompanying the crowning of a new monarch, produced a world where the familiar labels of Protestant and Catholic failed to define the forms of faith that most English people practiced. But for Elizabeth, most matters of faith could be left to individuals, as long as the Church itself, and Elizabeth's position at its head, would remain unchallenged.

In international affairs, she was no less successful with her pragmatism and willingness to pursue limited goals. A complex mix of prudential concerns about religion, the economy, and national security drove her foreign policy. She did not have imperial ambitions; in the main, she wanted only to be sure there would be no invasion of England and to encourage English trade. In the event, both goals brought England into conflict with Spain, determining the increasingly anti-Catholic tendencies of English foreign policy and, almost accidentally, England's emergence as a world power. When Elizabeth came to the throne, England was in many ways a mere satellite nation to the Netherlands, which was part of the Hapsburg Empire that the Catholic Philip II (who had briefly and unhappily been married to her predecessor and half sister, Queen Mary) ruled from Spain; by the end of her reign England was Spain's most bitter rival.

The transformation of Spain from ally to enemy came in a series of small steps (or missteps), no one of which was intended to produce what in the end came to pass. A series of posturings and provocations on both sides led to the rupture. In 1568, things moved to their breaking point, as the English confiscated a large shipment of gold that the Spanish were sending to their troops in the Netherlands. The following year saw the revolt of the Catholic earls in northern England, followed by the papal excommunication of the Queen in 1570, both of which were by many in England assumed to be at the initiative, or at very least with the tacit support, of Philip. In fact he was not involved, but England under Elizabeth would never again think of Spain as a loyal friend or reliable ally. Indeed, Spain quickly became its mortal enemy. Protestant Dutch rebels had been opposing the Spanish domination of the Netherlands since the early 1560s but, other than periodic financial support, Elizabeth had done little to encourage them. But in 1585, she sent troops under the command of the Earl of Leicester to support the Dutch rebels against the Spanish. Philip decided then to launch a full-scale attack on England, with the aim of deposing Elizabeth and restoring the Catholic faith. An English assault on Cadiz in 1587 destroyed a number of Spanish ships, postponing Philip's plans, but in the summer of 1588 the mightiest navy in the world, Philip's grand armada, with 132 ships and 30,493 sailors and troops, sailed for England.

By all rights, it should have been a successful invasion, but a combination of questionable Spanish tactics and a fortunate shift of wind resulted in one of England's greatest victories. The English had twice failed to intercept the armada off the coast of Portugal, and the Spanish fleet made its way to England, almost catching the English ships resupplying in Plymouth. The English navy was on its heels, when conveniently the Spanish admiral decided to anchor in the English Channel off the French port of Calais to wait for additional troops coming from the Netherlands. The English attacked with fireships, sinking four Spanish galleons, and strong winds from the south prevented an effective counterattack from the Spanish. The Spanish fleet was pushed into the North Sea, where it regrouped and decided its safest course was to attempt the difficult voyage home around Scotland and Ireland, losing almost half its ships on the way. For many in England the improbable victory was a miracle, evidence of God's favor for Elizabeth and the Protestant nation. Though war with Spain would not end for another fifteen years, the victory over the armada turned England almost overnight into a major world power, buoyed by confidence that they were chosen by God and, more tangibly, by a navy that could compete for control of the seas.

From a backward and insignificant Hapsburg satellite, Elizabeth's England had become, almost by accident, the leader of Protestant Europe. But if the victory over the armada signaled England's new place in the world, it hardly marked the end of England's travails. The economy, which initially was fueled by the military buildup, in the early 1590s fell victim to inflation, heavy taxation to support the war with Spain, the inevitable wartime disruptions of trade, as well as crop failures and a general economic downturn in Europe. Ireland, over which England had been attempting to impose its rule since 1168, continued to be a source of trouble and great expense (in some years costing the crown nearly one fifth of its total revenues). Even when the most organized of the rebellions, begun in 1594 and led by Hugh O'Neill, Earl of Tyrone, formally ended in 1603, peace and stability had not been achieved.

But perhaps the greatest instability came from the uncertainty over the succession, an uncertainty that marked Elizabeth's reign from its beginning. Her near death from smallpox in 1562 reminded the nation that an unmarried queen could not insure the succession, and Elizabeth was under constant pressure to marry and produce an heir. She was always aware of and deeply resented the pressure, announcing as early as 1559: "this shall be for me sufficient that a marble stone shall declare that a queen, having reigned such a time, lived and died a virgin." If, however, it was for her "sufficient," it was not so for her advisors and for much of the nation, who hoped she would wed. Arguably Elizabeth was the wiser, knowing that her unmarried hand was a political advantage, allowing her to diffuse threats or create alliances with the seeming possibility of a match. But as with so much in her reign, the strategy bought temporary stability at the price of longer-term solutions.

By the mid 1590s, it was clear that she would die unmarried and without an heir, and various candidates were positioning themselves to succeed her. Enough anxiety was produced that all published debate about the succession was forbidden by law. There was no direct descendant of the English crown to claim rule, and all the claimants had to reach well back into their family history to find some legitimacy. The best genealogical claim belonged to King James VI of Scotland. His mother, Mary, Queen of Scots, was the granddaughter of James IV of Scotland and Margaret Tudor, sister to Elizabeth's father, Henry VIII. Though James had right on his side, he was, it must be remembered, a foreigner. Scotland shared the island with England but was a separate nation. Great Britain, the union of England and Scotland, would not exist formally until 1707, but with Elizabeth's death early in the morning of March 24, 1603, surprisingly uneventfully the thirty-seven-year-old James succeeded to the English throne. Two nations, one king: King James VI of Scotland, King James I of England.

Most of his English subjects initially greeted the announcement of their new monarch with delight, relieved that the crown had successfully been transferred without any major disruption and reassured that the new King was married with two living sons. However, quickly many became disenchanted with a foreign King who spoke

English with a heavy accent, and dismayed even further by the influx of Scots in positions of power. Nonetheless, the new King's greatest political liability may well have been less a matter of nationality than of temperament: he had none of Elizabeth's skill and ease in publicly wooing her subjects. The Venetian ambassador wrote back to the doge that the new King was unwilling to "caress the people, nor make them that good cheer the late Queen did, whereby she won their loves."

He was aloof and largely uninterested in the daily activities of governing, but he was interested in political theory and strongly committed to the cause of peace. Although a steadfast Protestant, he lacked the reflexive anti-Catholicism of many of his subjects. In England, he achieved a broadly consensual community of Protestants. The so-called King James Bible, the famous translation published first in 1611, was the result of a widespread desire to have an English Bible that spoke to all the nation, transcending the religious divisions that had placed three different translations in the hands of his subjects. Internationally, he styled himself *Rex Pacificus* (the peace-loving king). In 1604, the Treaty of London brought Elizabeth's war with Spain formally to an end, and over the next decade he worked to bring about political marriages that might cement stable alliances. In 1613, he married his daughter to the leader of the German Protestants, while the following year he began discussions with Catholic Spain to marry his son to the Infanta Maria. After some ten years of negotiations, James's hopes for what was known as the Spanish match were finally abandoned, much to the delight of the nation, whose long-felt fear and hatred for Spain outweighed the subtle political logic behind the plan.

But if James sought stability and peace, and for the most part succeeded in his aims (at least until 1618, when the bitter religio-political conflicts on the European continent swirled well out of the King's control), he never really achieved concord and cohesion. He ruled over two kingdoms that did not know, like, or even want to understand one another, and his rule did little to bring them closer together. His England remained separate from his Scotland, even as he ruled over both. And even his England remained self divided, as in truth it always was under Elizabeth, ever more a nation of prosperity and influence but still one forged out of deep-rooted divisions of means, faiths, and allegiances that made the very nature of English identity a matter of confusion and concern. Arguably this is the very condition of great drama—sufficient peace and prosperity to support a theater industry and sufficient provocation in the troubling uncertainties about what the nation was and what fundamentally mattered to its people to inspire plays that would offer tentative solutions or at the very least make the troubling questions articulate and moving.

Nine years before James would die in 1625, Shakespeare died, having returned from London to the small market town in which he was born. If London, now a thriving modern metropolis of well over 200,000 people, had, like the nation itself, been transformed in the course of his life, the Warwickshire market town still was much the same. The house in which Shakespeare was born still stood, as did the church in which he was baptized and the school in which he learned to read and write. The river Avon still ran slowly along the town's southern limits. What had changed was that Shakespeare was now its most famous citizen, and, although it would take more than another 100 years to fully achieve this, he would in time become England's, for having turned the great ethical, social, and political issues of his own age into plays that would live forever.

William Shakespeare:
A Chronology

1558	**November 17: Queen Elizabeth crowned**
1564	April 26: Shakespeare baptized, third child born to John Shakespeare and Mary Arden
1564	**May 27: Death of Jean Calvin in Geneva**
1565	John Shakespeare elected alderman in Stratford-upon-Avon
1568	**Publication of the Bishops' Bible**
1568	September 4: John Shakespeare elected Bailiff of Stratford-upon-Avon
1569	**Northern Rebellion**
1570	**Queen Elizabeth excommunicated by the pope**
1572	**August 24: St. Bartholomew's Day Massacre in Paris**
1577–1580	**Sir Francis Drake sails around the world**
1582	November 27: Shakespeare and Anne Hathaway married (Shakespeare is 18)
1583	Queen's Men formed
1583	May 26: Shakespeare's daughter, Susanna, baptized
1584	**Failure of the Virginia Colony**
1585	February 2: Twins, Hamnet and Judith, baptized (Shakespeare is 20)

1586   **Babington Plot to dethrone Elizabeth and replace her with Mary, Queen of Scots**

1587   **February 8: Execution of Mary, Queen of Scots**

1587   **Rose Theatre built**

1588   **August: Defeat of the Spanish armada** (Shakespeare is 24)

1588   **September 4: Death of Robert Dudley, Earl of Leicester**

1590   **First three books of Spenser's *Faerie Queene* published; Marlowe's *Tamburlaine* published**

1592   March 3: *Henry VI, Part One* performed at the Rose Theatre (Shakespeare is 27)

1593   **February–November: Theaters closed because of plague**

1593   Publication of *Venus and Adonis*

1594   Publication of *Titus Andronicus*, first play by Shakespeare to appear in print (though anonymously)

1594   Lord Chamberlain's Men formed

1595   March 15: Payment made to Shakespeare, Will Kemp, and Richard Burbage for performances at court in December, 1594

1595   **Swan Theatre built**

1596   **Books 4–6 of *The Faerie Queene* published**

1596   August 11: Burial of Shakespeare's son, Hamnet (Shakespeare is 32)

1596–1599   Shakespeare living in St. Helen's, Bishopsgate, London

1596   October 20: Grant of Arms to John Shakespeare

1597   May 4: Shakespeare purchases New Place, one of the two largest houses in Stratford (Shakespeare is 33)

1598   Publication of *Love's Labor's Lost*, first extant play with Shakespeare's name on the title page

1598   Publication of Francis Meres's *Palladis Tamia*, citing Shakespeare as "the best for Comedy and Tragedy" among English writers

1599   **Opening of the Globe Theatre**

1601   **February 7: Lord Chamberlain's Men paid 40 shillings to play *Richard II* by supporters of the Earl of Essex, the day before his abortive rebellion**

1601   **February 17: Execution of Robert Devereaux, Earl of Essex**

1601   September 8: Burial of John Shakespeare

1602   May 1: Shakespeare buys 107 acres of farmland in Stratford

1603   **March 24: Queen Elizabeth dies; James VI of Scotland succeeds as James I of England** (Shakespeare is 39)

1603   May 19: Lord Chamberlain's Men reformed as the King's Men

1604   Shakespeare living with the Mountjoys, a French Huguenot family, in Cripplegate, London

1604   **First edition of Marlowe's *Dr. Faustus* published (written c. 1589)**

1604   March 15: Shakespeare named among "players" given scarlet cloth to wear at royal procession of King James

1604   Publication of authorized version of *Hamlet* (Shakespeare is 40)

1605   **Gunpowder Plot**

1605   June 5: Marriage of Susanna Shakespeare to John Hall

1608   Publication of *King Lear* (Shakespeare is 44)

1608–1609   Acquisition of indoor Blackfriars Theatre by King's Men

1609   *Sonnets* published

1611   **King James Bible published** (Shakespeare is 47)

1612   November 6: Death of Henry, eldest son of King James

1613   February 14: Marriage of King James's daughter Elizabeth to Frederick, the Elector Palatine

1613   March 10: Shakespeare, with some associates, buys gatehouse in Blackfriars, London

1613   June 29: Fire burns the Globe Theatre

1614   Rebuilt Globe reopens

1616   February 10: Marriage of Judith Shakespeare to Thomas Quiney

1615   March 25: Shakespeare's will signed

1616   April 23: Shakespeare dies (age 52)

1616   April 23: Cervantes dies in Madrid

1616   April 25: Shakespeare buried in Holy Trinity Church in Stratford-upon-Avon

1623   October: King James returns from Madrid, having failed to marry his son Charles to Maria Anna, Infanta of Spain

1623   August 6: Death of Anne Shakespeare

1623   First Folio published with 36 plays (18 never previously published)

Words, Words, Words: Understanding Shakespeare's Language
by David Scott Kastan

t is silly to pretend that it is easy to read Shakespeare. Reading Shakespeare isn't like picking up a copy of *USA Today* or *The New Yorker*, or even F. Scott Fitzgerald's *Great Gatsby* or Toni Morrison's *Beloved*. It is hard work, because the language is often unfamiliar to us and because it is more concentrated than we are used to. In the theater it is usually a bit easier. Actors can clarify meanings with gestures and actions, allowing us to get the general sense of what is going on, if not every nuance of the language that is spoken. "Action is eloquence," as Volumnia puts it in *Coriolanus*, "and the eyes of th' ignorant / More learnèd than the ears" (3.276–277). Yet the real greatness of Shakespeare rests not on "the general sense" of his plays but on the specificity and suggestiveness of the words in which they are written. It is through language that the plays' full dramatic power is realized, and it is that rich and robust language, often pushed by Shakespeare to the very limits of intelligibility, that we must learn to understand. But we can come to understand it (and enjoy it), and this essay is designed to help.

Even experienced readers and playgoers need help. They often find that his words are difficult to comprehend. Shakespeare sometimes uses words no longer current in English or with meanings that have changed. He regularly multiplies words where seemingly one might do as well or even better. He characteristically writes sentences that are syntactically complicated and imaginatively dense. And it isn't just we, removed by some 400 years from his world, who find him difficult to read; in his own time, his friends and fellow actors knew Shakespeare was hard. As two of them, John Hemings and Henry Condell, put it in their prefatory remarks to Shakespeare's First Folio in 1623, "read him, therefore, and again and again; and if then you do not like him, surely you are in some manifest danger not to understand him."

From the very beginning, then, it was obvious that the plays both deserve and demand not only careful reading but continued re-reading—and that not to read Shakespeare with all the attention a reader can bring to bear on the language is almost to guarantee that a reader will not "understand him" and remain among those who "do not like him." But Shakespeare's colleagues were nonetheless confident that the plays exerted an attraction strong enough to ensure and reward the concentration of their readers, confident, as they say, that in them "you will find enough, both to draw and hold you." The plays do exert a kind of magnetic pull, and have successfully drawn in and held readers for over 400 years.

Once we are drawn in, we confront a world of words that does not always immediately yield its delights; but it will—once we learn to see what is demanded of us. Words in Shakespeare do a lot, arguably more than anyone else has ever asked them to do. In part, it is because he needed his words to do many things at once. His stage had no sets and few props, so his words are all we have to enable us to imagine what his characters see. And they also allow us to see what the characters don't see, especially about themselves. The words are vivid and immediate, as well as complexly layered and psychologically suggestive. The difficulties they pose are not the "thee's" and "thou's" or "prithee's" and "doth's" that obviously mark the chronological distance between Shakespeare and us. When Gertrude says to Hamlet, "thou hast thy father much offended"

(3.4.8), we have no difficulty understanding her chiding, though we might miss that her use of the "thou" form of the pronoun expresses an intimacy that Hamlet pointedly refuses with his reply: "Mother, *you* have my father much offended" (3.4.9; italics mine).

Most deceptive are words that look the same as words we know but now mean something different. Words often change meanings over time. When Horatio and the soldiers try to stop Hamlet as he chases after the Ghost, Hamlet pushes past them and says, "I'll make a ghost of him that lets me" (1.4.85). It seems an odd thing to say. Why should he threaten someone who "lets" him do what he wants to do? But here "let" means "hinder," not, as it does today, "allow" (although the older meaning of the word still survives, for example, in tennis, where a "let serve" is one that is hindered by the net on its way across). There are many words that can, like this, mislead us: "his" sometimes means "its," "an" often means "if," "envy" means something more like "malice," "cousin" means more generally "kinsman," and there are others, though all are easily defined. The difficulty is that we may not stop to look thinking we already know what the word means, but in this edition a ° following the word alerts a reader that there is a gloss in the left margin, and quickly readers get used to these older meanings.

Then, of course, there is the intimidation factor—strange, polysyllabic, or Latinate words that not only are foreign to us but also must have sounded strange even to Shakespeare's audiences. When Macbeth wonders whether all the water in all the oceans of the world will be able to clean his bloody hands after the murder of Duncan, he concludes: "No; this my hand will rather / The multitudinous seas incarnadine, / Making the green one red" (2.2.64–66). Duncan's blood staining Macbeth's murderous hand is so offensive that, not merely does it resist being washed off in water, but it will "the multitudinous seas incarnadine": that is, turn the sea-green oceans blood-red. Notes will easily clarify the meaning of the two odd words, but it is worth observing that they would have been as odd to Shakespeare's readers as they are to us. The *Oxford English Dictionary* (*OED*) shows no use of "multitudinous" before this, and it records no use of "incarnadine" before 1591 (*Macbeth* was written about 1606). Both are new words, coined from the Latin, part of a process in Shakespeare's time where English adopted many Latinate words as a mark of its own emergence as an important vernacular language. Here they are used to express the magnitude of Macbeth's offense, a crime not only against the civil law but also against the cosmic order, and then the simple monosyllables of turning "the green one red" provide an immediate (and needed) paraphrase and register his own, sickening awareness of the true hideousness of his deed.

As with "multitudinous" in *Macbeth*, Shakespeare is the source of a great many words in English. Sometimes he coined them himself, or, if he didn't invent them, he was the first person whose writing of them has survived. Some of these words have become part of our language, so common that it is hard to imagine they were not always part of it: for example, "assassination" (*Macbeth*, 1.7.2), "bedroom" (*A Midsummer Night's Dream*, 2.2.51), "countless" (*Titus Andronicus*, 5.3.59), "fashionable" (*Troilus and Cressida*, 3.3.165), "frugal" (*The Merry Wives of Windsor*, 2.1.28), "laughable" (*The Merchant of Venice*, 1.1.56), "lonely" (*Coriolanus*, 4.1.30), and "useful" (*King John*, 5.2.81). But other words that he originated were not as, to use yet another Shakespearean coinage, "successful" (*Titus Andronicus*, 1.1.66). Words like "crimeless" (*Henry VI, Part Two*, 2.4.63, meaning "innocent"), "facinorous" (*All's Well That Ends Well*, 2.3.30, meaning "extremely wicked"), and "recountment" (*As You Like It*, 4.3.141, meaning "narrative" or "account") have, without much resistance, slipped into oblivion. Clearly Shakespeare liked words, even unwieldy ones. His working vocabulary, about 18,000 words, is staggering, larger than almost any other English writer, and he seems to be the first person to use in print about 1,000 of these. Whether he coined the new words himself or was intrigued by the new words he heard in the streets of London doesn't really matter; the point is that he was remarkably alert to and engaged with a dynamic language that was expanding in response to England's own expanding contact with the world around it.

But it is neither new words nor old ones that are the source of the greatest difficulty of Shakespeare's language. The real difficulty (and the real delight) comes in trying to see how he uses the words, how he endows them with more than their denotative meanings. Why, for example, does Macbeth say that he hopes that the "sure and firm-set earth" (2.1.56) will not hear his steps as he goes forward to murder Duncan? Here "sure" and "firm-set" mean virtually the same thing: stable, secure, fixed. Why use two words? If this were a student paper, no doubt the teacher would circle one of them and write "redundant." But the redundancy is exactly what Shakespeare wants. One word would do if the purpose were to describe the solidity of the earth, but here the redundancy points to something different. It reveals something about Macbeth's mind, betraying through the doubling how deep is his awareness of the world of stable values that the terrible act he is about to commit must unsettle.

Shakespeare's words usually work this way: in part describing what the characters see and as often betraying what they feel. The example from *Macbeth* is a simple example of how this works. Shakespeare's words are carefully patterned. How one says something is every bit as important as what is said, and the conspicuous patterns that are created alert us to the fact that something more than the words' lexical sense has been put into play. Words can be coupled, as in the example above, or knit into even denser metaphorical constellations to reveal something about the speaker (which often the speaker does not know), as in Prince Hal's promise to his father that he will outdo the rebels' hero, Henry Percy (Hotspur):

Percy is but my factor, good my lord,

To engross up glorious deeds on my behalf,

And I will call him to so strict account

That he shall render every glory up,

Yea, even the slightest worship of his time,

Or I will tear the reckoning from his heart.

(Henry IV, Part One, 3.2.147–152)

The Prince expresses his confidence that he will defeat Hotspur, but revealingly in a reiterated language of commercial exchange ("factor," "engross," "account," "render," "reckoning") that tells us something important both about the Prince and the ways in which he understands his world. In a play filled with references to coins and counterfeiting, the speech demonstrates not only that Hal has committed himself to the business at hand, repudiating his earlier, irresponsible tavern self, but also that he knows it is a business rather than a glorious world of chivalric achievement; he inhabits a world in which value (political as well as economic) is not intrinsic but determined by what people are willing to invest, and he proves himself a master of producing desire for what he has to offer.

Or sometimes it is not the network of imagery but the very syntax that speaks, as when Claudius announces his marriage to Hamlet's mother:

Therefore our sometime sister, now our Queen,

Th' imperial jointress to this warlike state,

Have we—as 'twere with a defeated joy,

With an auspicious and a dropping eye,

With mirth in funeral and with dole in marriage,

In equal scale weighing delight and dole—

Taken to wife.

(Hamlet, 1.2.8–14)

All he really wants to say here is that he has married Gertrude, his former sister-in-law: "Therefore our sometime sister . . . Have we . . . Taken to wife." But the straightforward sentence gets interrupted and complicated, revealing his own discomfort with the announcement. His elaborations and intensifications of Gertrude's role ("sometime sister," "Queen," "imperial jointress"), the self-conscious rhetorical balancing of the middle three lines (indeed "in equal scale weighing delight and dole"), all declare by the all-too obvious artifice how desperate he is to hide the awkward facts behind a veneer of normalcy and propriety. The very unnaturalness of the sentence is what alerts us that we are meant to understand more than the simple relation of fact.

Why doesn't Shakespeare just say what he means? Well, he does—exactly what he means. In the example from *Hamlet* just above, Shakespeare shows us something about Claudius that Claudius doesn't know himself. Always Shakespeare's words will offer us an immediate sense of what is happening, allowing us to follow the action, but they also offer us a counterplot, pointing us to what might be behind the action, confirming or contradicting what the characters say. It is a language that shimmers with promise and possibility, opening the characters' hearts and minds to our view—and all we have to do is learn to pay attention to what is there before us.

Shakespeare's Verse

Another distinctive feature of Shakespeare's dramatic language is that much of it is in verse. Almost all of the plays mix poetry and prose, but the poetry dominates. *The Merry Wives of Windsor* has the lowest percentage (only about 13 percent verse), while *Richard II* and *King John* are written entirely in verse (the only examples, although *Henry VI, Part One* and *Part Three* have only a very few prose lines). In most of the plays, about seventy percent of the lines are written in verse.

Shakespeare's characteristic verse line is a non-rhyming iambic pentameter ("blank verse"), ten syllables with every second one stressed. In *A Midsummer Night's Dream*, Titania comes to her senses after a magic potion has led her to fall in love with an ass-headed Bottom: "Methought I was enamored of an ass" (4.1.77). Similarly, in *Romeo and Juliet*, Romeo gazes up at Juliet's window: "But soft, what light through yonder window breaks" (2.2.2). In both these examples, the line has ten syllables organized into five regular beats (each beat consisting of the stress on the second syllable of a pair, as in "But soft," the da-dum rhythm forming an "iamb"). Still, we don't hear these lines as jingles; they seem natural enough, in large part because this dominant pattern is varied in the surrounding lines.

The play of stresses indeed becomes another key to meaning, as Shakespeare alerts us to what is important. In *Measure for Measure*, Lucio urges Isabella to plead for her brother's life: "Oh, to him, to him, wench! He will relent" (2.2.129). The iambic norm (unstressed-stressed) tells us (and an actor) that the emphasis at the beginning of the line is on "to" not "him"—it is the action not the object that is being emphasized—and at the end of the line the stress falls on "will." Alternatively, the line can play against the established norm. In *Hamlet*, Claudius corrects Polonius's idea of what is bothering the Prince: "Love? His affections do not that way tend" (3.1.161). The iambic norm forces the emphasis onto "that" ("do not *that* way tend"), while the syntax forces an unexpected stress on the opening word, "Love." In the famous line, "The course of true love never did run smooth" (*A Midsummer Night's Dream*, 1.1.134), the iambic expectation is varied in both the middle and at the end of the line. Both "love" and the first syllable of "never" are stressed, as are both syllables at the end: "run smooth," creating a metrical foot in which both syllables are stressed (called a "spondee"). The point to notice is that the "da-dum, da-dum, da-dum, da-dum, da-dum" line is not inevitable; it merely sets an expectation against which many variations can be heard.

In fact, even the ten-syllable norm can be varied. Shakespeare sometimes writes lines with fewer or more syllables. Often there is an extra, unstressed syllable at the end of a line (a so-called "feminine ending"); sometimes there are verse lines with only nine. In *Henry IV, Part One*, King Henry replies incredulously to the rebel Worcester's claim that he hadn't "sought" the confrontation with the King: "You have not sought it? How comes it then?" (5.1.27). There are only nine syllables here (some earlier editors, seeking to "correct" the verse, added the word "sir" after the first question to regularize the line). But the pause where one expects a stressed syllable is dramatically effective, allowing the King's anger to be powerfully present in the silence.

As even these few examples show, Shakespeare's verse is unusually flexible, allowing a range of rhythmical effects. It should not be understood as a set of strict rules but as a flexible set of practices rooted in dramatic necessity. It is designed to highlight ideas and emotions, and it is based less upon rigid syllable counts than on an arrangement of stresses within an understood temporal norm, as one might expect from a poetry written to be heard in the theater rather than read on the page.

Here Follows Prose

Although the plays are dominated by verse, prose plays a significant role. Shakespeare's prose has its own rhythms, but it lacks the formal patterning of verse, and so is printed without line breaks and without the capitals that mark the beginning of a verse line. Like many of his fellow dramatists, Shakespeare tended to use prose for comic scenes, the shift from verse serving, especially in his early plays, as a social marker. Upper-class characters speak in verse; lower-class characters speak in prose. Thus, in *A Midsummer Night's Dream*, the Athenians of the court, as well as the fairies, all speak in verse, but the "rude mechanicals," Bottom and his artisan friends, all speak in prose, except for the comic verse they speak in their performance of "Pyramis and Thisbe."

As Shakespeare grew in experience, he became more flexible about the shifts from verse to prose, letting it, among other things, mark genre rather than class and measure various kinds of intensity. Prose becomes in the main the medium of comedy. The great comedies, like *Much Ado About Nothing, Twelfth Night*, and *As You Like It*, are all more than fifty percent prose. But even in comedy, shifts between verse and prose may be used to measure subtle emotional changes. In Act One, scene three of *The Merchant of Venice*, Shylock and Bassanio begin the scene speaking of matters of business in prose, but when Antonio enters and the deep conflict between the Christian and the Jew becomes evident, the scene shifts to verse. But prose may itself serve in moments of emotional intensity. Shylock's famous speech in Act Three, scene one, "Hath not a Jew eyes . . ." is all in prose, as is Hamlet's expression of disgust at the world ("I have of late—but wherefore I know not—lost all my mirth . . .") at 3.1.261–276. Shakespeare comes to use prose to vary the tone of a scene, as the shift from verse subtly alerts an audience or a reader to some new emotional register.

Prose becomes, as Shakespeare's art matures, not inevitably the mark of the lower classes but the mark of a salutary daily-ness. It is appropriately the medium in which letters are written, and it is the medium of a common sense that will at least challenge the potential self-deceptions of grandiloquent speech. When Rosalind mocks the excesses and artifice of Orlando's wooing in Act Four, scene one of *As You Like It*, it is in prose that she seeks something genuine in the expression of love:

The poor world is almost six thousand years old, and in all this time there was not any man died in his own person, *videlicit* [i.e., namely], in a love cause . . . . Men have died from time to time, and worms have eaten them, but not for love.

Here the prose becomes the sound of common sense, an effective foil to the affectation of pinning poems to trees and thinking that it is real love.

It is not that prose is artless; Shakespeare's prose is no less self-conscious than his verse. The artfulness of his prose is different, of course. The seeming ordinariness of his prose is no less an effect of his artistry than is the more obvious patterning of his verse. Prose is no less serious, compressed, or indeed figurative. As with his verse, Shakespeare's prose performs numerous tasks and displays various, subtle formal qualities; and recognizing the possibilities of what it can achieve is still another way of seeing what Shakespeare puts right before us to show us what he has hidden.

Further Reading

N.F. Blake, *Shakespeare's Language*: An Introduction (New York: St. Martin's Press, 1983).

Jonathan Hope, *Shakespeare's Grammar* (London: Thomson, 2003).

Sister Miriam Joseph, *Shakespeare's Use of the Arts of Language* (New York: Columbia University Press, 1947).

M. M. Mahood, *Shakespeare's Wordplay* (London: Methuen, 1957).

Russ McDonald, *Shakespeare and the Arts of Language* (Oxford: Oxford University Press, 2001).

Brian Vickers, *The Artistry of Shakespeare's Prose* (London: Methuen, 1968).

George T. Wright, *Shakespeare's Metrical Art* (University of California Press, 1991).

Key to the Play Text

Symbols

∘   Indicates an explanation or definition in the left-hand margin.

1   Indicates a gloss on the page facing the play text.

[ ]   Indicates something added or changed by the editors (i.e., not in the early printed text that this edition of the play is based on).

Terms

F, Folio, or *First Folio*   The first collected edition of Shakespeare's plays, published in 1623.

Q1, Q2, or *Quarto*   *Quarto* refers to a small, inexpensive format in which individual play books were usually published. *Othello* was published in quarto in 1622 (Q1) and again in 1630 (Q2), although this edition is based on the Folio text of 1623.

Othello

William Shakespeare

List of Roles

Othello	*a Moorish general*
Desdemona	*his wife, a Venetian lady*
Brabantio	*her father, a Venetian senator*
Iago	*Othello's ensign*
Emilia	*Iago's wife and Desdemona's waiting woman*
Cassio	*Othello's lieutenant*
Roderigo	*suitor of Desdemona, a Venetian gentleman*
Bianca	*a courtesan in Cyprus in love with Cassio*
Duke of Venice	
Senators	
Montano	*a Venetian official in Cyprus*
Gratiano	*Brabantio's brother*
Lodovico	*Brabantio's kinsman*
Clown	*servant to Othello and Desdemona*
Officers	
Gentlemen	
Sailor	
Messenger	
Herald	

Officers, soldiers, servants, attendants, musicians, torchbearers

1   *Tush*

A dismissive interjection (omitted
from the 1623 Folio as a profanity)

2   *Never tell me.*

I don't believe you.

3   *I take it much unkindly*

I am very displeased.

4   *had my purse*

Access to my money

5   *'Sblood*

Short for *God's blood*. An emphatic
oath, used here to express
exasperation (and, like *Tush*, also
omitted from the Folio text, along
with other profanities)

6   *lieutenant*

Second in command

7   *Off-capped*

Took their hats off (in respect)

8   *Nonsuits my mediators*

Rejects the suit of my supporters

9   *arithmetician*

I.e., one whose military knowledge
is derived from books, rather than
from experience on the battlefield.

10   *(A fellow almost damned in a fair wife)*

The meaning of this line is obscure;
nowhere else in the play is it implied
that Cassio has a wife. The line may
be a mocking reference to Cassio's
reputation as a ladies' man, or it may
represent a holdover from
Shakespeare's source (Giraldi
Cinthio's *Hecatommithi*, 1565), in
which the Cassio figure is married. It
is also possible that Shakespeare
originally intended for Cassio to be
married, then dropped the idea and
neglected to delete this reference.

11   *Nor the division of a battle knows / More
than a spinster*

Who knows no more about
deploying troops than a woman
who spins thread

12   *toga'd*

Wearing togas (like Roman consuls
and senators). This is the reading
of the 1622 Quarto; the 1623 Folio
prints "tongued," probably an
error but possibly suggesting that
the consuls merely talk.

en medias res
(In the middle of things)

Act 1, Scene 1

*Enter **Roderigo** and **Iago**.*

Roderigo

Tush![1] Never tell me.[2] I take it much unkindly[3]

That thou, Iago, who hast had my purse[4]

purse strings As if the strings° were thine, shouldst know of this.

Iago

listen to 'Sblood,[5] but you'll not hear° me! If ever I did dream

Of such a matter, abhor me.

Roderigo

Thou told'st me 5

Thou didst hold him in thy hate.

Iago

Despise me

men If I do not. Three great ones° of the city,

petition In personal suit° to make me his lieutenant,[6]

Off-capped[7] to him, and, by the faith of man,

I know my price; I am worth no worse a place. 10

But he (as loving his own pride and purposes)

bombastic / verbosity Evades them with a bombast° circumstance°

expressions Horribly stuffed with epithets° of war,

and, in conclusion,

The fact is Nonsuits my mediators.[8] For "Certes,"° says he, 15

"I have already chose my officer."

And what was he?

Indeed Forsooth,° a great arithmetician,[9]

i.e., a foreigner (from Florence) One Michael Cassio, a Florentine°

(A fellow almost damned in a fair wife)[10] 20

That never set a squadron in the field,

Nor the division of a battle knows

theory More than a spinster[11]—unless the bookish theoric,°

speak about Wherein the toga'd[12] consuls can propose°

1   *prattle without practice*

Empty talk without practical experience

2   *of whom his eyes had seen the proof*

Whose merit in battle Othello himself witnessed

3   *be-leed and calmed*

Cut off from the wind and thus becalmed and brought to a standstill

4   *By debitor and creditor*

I.e., by a mere accountant. The phrase *by debitor and creditor* refers to the then-novel method of double-column bookkeeping—one column reserved for debit, one for credit—which was thought to have originated in Venice.

5   *in good time*

Literally, the expression means "soon"; here, said with sarcasm, it means something like "believe it or not."

6   *God bless the mark*

A sarcastic exclamation. The phrase was usually offered as an apology for having mentioned something horrible or indecent.

7   *his Moorship's*

A coinage formed on the analogy of "his worship's"

8   *ancient*

The word meant (and was pronounced like) "ensign." An *ensign*, in Elizabethan terms, was a standard-bearer, the lowest ranking commissioned officer.

9   *by letter and affection*

By letters of support and the good will of friends (i.e., by favoritism)

10   *old gradation*

The traditional practice of promotion according to seniority

11   *content you*

Be content.

12   *serve my turn upon him*

Use him for my own ends

13   *(doting on his own obsequious bondage)*

I.e., pathetically grateful for his position in someone else's service

14   *For naught but provender*

Thinking of no more than his daily bread (*provender* literally means "animal feed")

15   *Whip me*

I would whip (*Me* here is an obsolete form, the ethical dative, and means "for me" or "as far as I'm concerned").

16   *forms and visages of duty*

Manners and expressions that profess loyalty

As masterly as he. Mere prattle without practice [1]   25
preference Is all his soldiership. But he, sir, had th' election,°
And I, of whom his eyes had seen the proof [2]
battlegrounds At Rhodes, at Cyprus, and on other grounds°
Christened and heathen, must be be-leed and calmed [3]
number cruncher By debitor and creditor. [4] This counter-caster°   30
He, in good time, [5] must his lieutenant be
And I, God bless the mark, [6] his Moorship's [7] ancient. [8]

Roderigo

By Heaven, I rather would have been his hangman.

Iago

Why, there's no remedy. 'Tis the curse of service.
Promotion Preferment° goes by letter and affection, [9]   35
And not by old gradation, [10] where each second
Stood heir to th' first. Now, sir, be judge yourself,
sense / obliged Whether I in any just term° am affined°
To love the Moor.

Roderigo

serve I would not follow° him then.   40

Iago

Oh, sir, content you. [11]
I follow him to serve my turn upon him. [12]
We cannot all be masters, nor all masters
loyally / observe Cannot be truly° followed. You shall mark°
bowing Many a duteous and knee-crooking° knave   45
That (doting on his own obsequious bondage [13])
life Wears out his time,° much like his master's ass,
dismissed For naught but provender, [14] and, when he's old, cashiered.°
Whip me [15] such honest knaves. Others there are
adorned Who, trimmed° in forms and visages of duty, [16]   50
Keep yet their hearts attending on themselves
bestowing And, throwing° but shows of service on their lords,

1   *Do well thrive by them*

Manage to profit by them

2   *Do themselves homage*

Become their own masters

3   *not I for*

I don't act out of

4   *peculiar end*

Personal reasons

5   *compliment extern*

Outward show

6   *I am not what I am.*

At one level, this is merely another way for Iago to declare that he is not what he seems to be. But those who are familiar with the Bible would immediately recognize this as a blasphemous, parodic allusion to Exodus 3:14, where Moses asks God for his name and God replies, "I am that I am." Thus Iago asserts his own identity in terms of a negation and a hidden, diabolical evil that stands in contrast to God's presence.

7   *thick-lips*

A noun formed from the stereotypical racial characteristic (pointing to the unthinking racism of Roderigo)

8   *Though that his joy be joy*

Even if his happiness is real

9   *like timorous accent*

A similarly terrifying tone

Do well thrive by them [1] and, when they have lined

i.e., pockets   their coats,°

spirit   Do themselves homage. [2] These fellows have some soul,°

claim to be   And such a one do I profess° myself. For, sir,   55

It is as sure as you are Roderigo,

choose to be   Were I the Moor, I would not be° Iago:

In following him I follow but myself.

Heaven is my judge, not I for [3] love and duty,

only seem   But seeming° so for my peculiar end, [4]   60

reveal   For when my outward action doth demonstrate°

instinctive / nature   The native° act and figure° of my heart

In compliment extern, [5] 'tis not long after

But I will wear my heart upon my sleeve

small crows   For daws° to peck at. I am not what I am. [6]   65

Roderigo

own   What a full fortune does the thick-lips [7] owe°

it off   If he can carry 't° thus!

Iago

                                   Call up her father.

Go / i.e., Othello   Rouse him. Make° after him,° poison his delight,

Proclaim him in the streets, incense her kinsmen,

And, though he in a fertile climate dwell,   70

Torment   Plague° him with flies. Though that his joy be joy, [8]

possibilities   Yet throw such chances° of vexation on 't,

i.e., delight   As it may lose some color.°

Roderigo

Here is her father's house; I'll call aloud.

Iago

Do, with like timorous accent [9] and dire yell   75

As when, by night and negligence, the fire

Is spied in populous cities.

Roderigo

What, ho, Brabantio! Signior Brabantio, ho!

1   above

In Elizabethan outdoor theaters
such as the Globe, Brabantio
would have appeared *above* the
stage in a gallery that was used to
represent windows, balconies, and
other elevated locations. In the
Folio, "*Bra Above.*" appears as the
speech prefix.

2   *Zounds*

A strong oath, a colloquial form of
"by God's wounds"

3   *ram*

Like the goat, the *ram* was
proverbially associated with
lechery.

4   *tupping*

Copulating with. (The word was
ordinarily used of animals rather
than people.)

5   *white*

Undefiled (but also with racial
overtones)

Iago

Awake! What, ho, Brabantio! Thieves! Thieves!

money bags   Look to your house, your daughter, and your bags!°   80

Thieves, thieves!

[*Enter*] **Brabantio**, *above*. [1]

Brabantio

What is the reason of this terrible summons?

What is the matter there?

Roderigo

Signior, is all your family within?

Iago

Are your doors locked?

Brabantio

Why   Why? Wherefore° ask you this?   85

Iago

Zounds,[2] sir, you're robbed! For shame, put on your

    gown.

broken   Your heart is burst;° you have lost half your soul:

Even now, now, very now, an old black ram[3]

Is tupping[4] your white[5] ewe. Arise, arise,

snoring / alarm   Awake the snorting° citizens with the bell,°   90

Or else the devil will make a grandsire of you.

Arise, I say!

Brabantio

                 What, have you lost your wits?

Roderigo

Most reverend signior, do you know my voice?

Brabantio

Not I. What are you?

Roderigo

My name is Roderigo.   95

1   *Upon malicious knavery*

    For the purpose of making trouble

2   *But thou must needs be sure*

    Make no mistake

3   *grange*

    An isolated farmhouse (and
    therefore vulnerable to
    housebreakers)

4   *In simple and pure soul*

    With honest and innocent
    intentions

5   *covered*

    Like *tupping, covered* denotes the act
    of copulation and is usually used
    in reference to mating animals.

6   *you'll have your daughter covered with a Bar-*
    bary horse. You'll have your nephews neigh at
    you. You'll have coursers for cousins and gennets
    for germans.

    Like the earlier image of the *old black*
    ram ... tupping your white ewe, (lines 88–
    89), these lines imagine sex between
    the newlywed Othello and Desde-
    mona as animal copulation. This is
    part of the text's pattern of bestial
    imagery, culminating in Othello's
    Goats and monkeys (4.1.263), as Iago
    turns Othello from a romantic
    conception of love toward a degraded
    idea of it as mere animal lust. *Barbary*
    horse puns on "barbarian" and alludes
    to thoroughbred horses from North
    Africa, famous for their speed and
    strength, as well as to Othello's
    origins in North Africa, or Barbary.

According to Iago, the marriage of
Othello and Desdemona is
monstrous miscegenation and will
lead to the begetting of an extended
family of half beasts. In early modern
parlance, *nephews* and *cousins* had less
precise meanings than today, along
with *germans*, refer generally to close
relatives or descendants. Iago's
mocking alliteration suggests the
braying noises of horses or animals
(In his 1997 edition of *Othello*, E. A. J.
Honigmann cites Jeremiah 5:8: "In
the desire of uncleanly lust they are
become like the stoned horse, every
man neigheth at his neighbor's
wife").

Brabantio

The worser welcome.

I have charged thee not to haunt about my doors.

In honest plainness thou hast heard me say

My daughter is not for thee. And now in madness,

intoxicating / drinks Being full of supper and distempering° drafts,°   100

Upon malicious knavery¹ dost thou come

disturb To start° my quiet?

Roderigo

Sir, sir, sir—

Brabantio

But thou must needs be sure²

temperament / rank My spirits° and my place° have in their power   105

To make this bitter to thee.

Roderigo

                                                    Patience, good sir.

Brabantio

What tell'st thou me of robbing? This is Venice;

My house is not a grange.³

Roderigo

revered   Most grave° Brabantio,

In simple and pure soul⁴ I come to you—

Iago

Zounds, sir, you are one of those that will not serve   110

God if the devil bid you. Because we come to do you

service and you think we are ruffians, you'll have your

North African daughter covered⁵ with a Barbary° horse. You'll have

relatives your nephews° neigh to you. You'll have coursers for

small Spanish horses cousins and gennets° for germans.⁶   115

Brabantio

foul-mouthed What profane° wretch art thou?

1 *making the beast with two backs*

I.e., copulating

2 *Thou*

Brabantio insultingly uses the
familiar form of address, here and
in line 120, while Iago and
Roderigo use the more respectful
you.

3 *As partly I find it is*

As almost seems to be the case

4 *odd-even*

I.e., late, around midnight (neither
night nor day)

5 *Transported with no worse nor better
guard / But with a knave of common
hire, a gondolier*

I.e., carried (to Othello) by no
better a companion than a
gondolier, a lowly servant who could
be hired by anyone

6 *your wrong rebuke*

Been unfairly rebuked

7 *extravagant and wheeling*

Vagrant and irresponsible. Othello
is a mercenary soldier of no fixed
nationality (i.e., *of here and
everywhere* in line 138), a fact that
Iago attempts to use against him.

8 *Straight satisfy yourself.*

Go at once to find out.

9 *Strike on the tinder*

Get me a light (*tinder* is readily
flammable material)

Iago

I am one, sir, that comes to tell you your daughter and
the Moor are making the beast with two backs. [1]

Brabantio

lowlife   Thou[2] art a villain!°

Iago

                  You are a senator!

Brabantio

answer for   This thou shalt answer.° I know thee, Roderigo.   120

Roderigo

Sir, I will answer anything. But, I beseech you,
If 't be your pleasure and most wise consent—
As partly I find it is [3]—that your fair daughter
sleepy   At this odd-even [4] and dull° watch o' th' night,
Transported with no worse nor better guard   125
But with a knave of common hire, a gondolier, [5]
embraces   To the gross clasps° of a lascivious Moor—
approval   If this be known to you and your allowance,°
insolent   We then have done you bold and saucy° wrongs.
But if you know not this, my manners tell me   130
We have your wrong rebuke. [6] Do not believe
against   That from° the sense of all civility
I thus would play and trifle with your reverence.
Your daughter—if you have not given her leave—
flagrant   I say again, hath made a gross° revolt,   135
Tying her duty, beauty, wit, and fortunes
To   In° an extravagant and wheeling [7] stranger
Of here and everywhere. Straight satisfy yourself. [8]
If she be in her chamber or your house,
Let loose on me the justice of the state   140
For thus deluding you.

Brabantio

                  Strike on the tinder, [9] ho!

1   *to my place*

I.e., for someone in my position
(as Othello's ensign)

2   *Which even now stands in act*

Which are in progress; despite the
plural form, *wars* is the subject of
stands (as well as the antecedent of
Which)

3   *for their souls*

Even if they sold their souls

4   *In which regard*

And therefore

5   *for necessity of present life*

Because my livelihood
depends on it

6   *That you shall surely find him, / Lead to
the Sagittary the raisèd search*

To be sure that you find Othello,
lead those who have been
awakened to search (for
Desdemona) to the Sagittary, (an
inn named after Sagittarius, the
Centaur, one of the signs of the
zodiac.)

candle   Give me a taper!° Call up all my people!
incident   This accident° is not unlike my dream;

Belief of it oppresses me already.

Light, I say, light!   *He exits*.

Iago

           [*to* **Roderigo**] Farewell, for I must leave you.   145

proper / healthy   It seems not meet° nor wholesome° to my place[1]
produced as a witness   To be producted°—as, if I stay, I shall—

Against the Moor. For I do know the state,

delay / rebuke   However this may gall° him with some check,°
dismiss   Cannot with safety cast° him, for he's embarked   150
pressing   With such loud° reason to the Cyprus wars—

Which even now stands in act[2]—that, for their souls,[3]

capability   Another of his fathom° they have none

To lead their business. In which regard,[4]

Though I do hate him as I do Hell-pains,   155

Yet for necessity of present life[5]

I must show out a flag and sign of love,

pretence / So that   Which is indeed but sign.° That° you shall surely find him,

Lead to the Sagittary the raisèd search,[6]

And there will I be with him. So farewell.   *He exits*.   160

Enter **Brabantio**, *with servants and torches*.

Brabantio

It is too true an evil: gone she is.

life   And what's to come of my despisèd time°

Is naught but bitterness. Now, Roderigo,

unlucky   Where didst thou see her?—Oh, unhappy° girl!—

With the Moor, say'st thou? Who would be a father?   165

How didst thou know 'twas she?—Oh, she deceives me

all understanding   Past thought!°—What said she to you?—Get more tapers;

Raise all my kindred. —Are they married, think you?

1   *treason of the blood*

   Brabantio implies either that
Desdemona has betrayed her
family or that she herself has been
betrayed by her own passions.

2   *Some one way, some another.*

   A command addressed to
Brabantio's men, telling them to
go off looking for Desdemona in
separate directions.

Roderigo

Truly, I think they are.

Brabantio

Oh, Heaven, how got she out? Oh, treason of the blood! [1]   170

this time on   Fathers, from hence° trust not your daughters' minds

Are / magical powers   By what you see them act. Is° there not charms°

essential nature   By which the property° of youth and maidhood

corrupted   May be abused?° Have you not read, Roderigo,

Of some such thing?

Roderigo

                    Yes, sir, I have indeed.   175

Brabantio

i.e., Roderigo   Call up my brother—Oh, would you° had had her!

—Some one way, some another. [2]—Do you know

Where we may apprehend her and the Moor?

Roderigo

find   I think I can discover° him, if you please

To get good guard and go along with me.   180

Brabantio

Pray you lead on. At every house I'll call.

expect help   I may command° at most.—Get weapons, ho!

And raise some special officers of night.

repay   —On, good Roderigo. I will deserve° your pains.

                              They exit.

1   *I lack iniquity / Sometime to do*
    me service.
    I lack the sinful nature that is
    sometimes necessary to
    accomplish what I want.

2   *I did full hard forbear him*
    With great difficulty I kept myself
    from hurting him

3   *But, I pray you, sir, / Are you fast*
    married?
    Iago may be asking whether the
    wedding ceremony has been
    performed or whether the
    marriage has been consummated
    sexually (since if it hasn't, the
    marriage can be annulled).

4   *hath in his effect a voice potential / As*
    double as the Duke's
    Has influence that is potentially as
    great as the Duke's (which is held
    to be double that of any senator)

5   *signiory*
    Government of Venice

6   *out-tongue*
    Speak more eloquently than

7   *my demerits / May speak unbonneted to*
    as proud a fortune / As this that I have
    reached
    My merits can freely testify that I
    deserve as great a destiny as that
    which I have now attained (by
    marrying Desdemona). *Unbonneted*
    means "without undue humility"
    (literally, "without having to
    remove my hat," as one should do
    when encountering superiors).

Act 1, Scene 2

Enter **Othello**, **Iago**, [*and*] *attendants with torches.*

Iago

business Though in the trade° of war I have slain men,

essence Yet do I hold it very stuff° o' th' conscience

deliberate To do no contrived° murder. I lack iniquity

  Sometime to do me service. [1] Nine or ten times

struck I had thought t' have yerked° him here under the ribs.

Othello

  'Tis better as it is.

Iago

chattered   Nay, but he prated°

insulting And spoke such scurvy° and provoking terms

  Against your honor

  That, with the little godliness I have,

  I did full hard forbear him. [2] But, I pray you, sir,   10

securely Are you fast° married? [3] Be assured of this:

i.e., Brabantio That the magnifico° is much beloved

  And hath in his effect a voice potential

  As double as the Duke's. [4] He will divorce you,

punishment Or put upon you what restraint or grievance°   15

  The law, with all his might to enforce it on,

scope Will give him cable.°

Othello

worst   Let him do his spite.°

  My services which I have done the signiory [5]

be made known Shall out-tongue [6] his complaints. 'Tis yet to know°—

  Which, when I know that boasting is an honor,   20

proclaim / derive I shall promulgate°—I fetch° my life and being

standing / merits From men of royal siege,° and my demerits°

  May speak unbonneted to as proud a fortune

  As this that I have reached. [7] For know, Iago,

1   *For the sea's worth*
    For all the treasure in the sea

2   *manifest me rightly*
    **Allow me to be truly seen
    for what I am**

3   *Janus*
    **Roman god of doorways,
    beginnings, and endings, usually
    depicted with two faces**

Except	But° that I love the gentle Desdemona,
unconfined	I would not my unhousèd,° free condition
restraint / confinement	Put into circumscription° and confine°
	For the sea's worth. [1] But look, what lights come yond?

[handwritten: If Othello didn't love Desd. the he wouldn't have married her]

25

Enter **Cassio**, *with [officers and] torches.*

Iago

awakened	Those are the raisèd° father and his friends.
	You were best go in.

[handwritten: Bar. walks in w/ friends]

Othello

               Not I, I must be found.

qualities / innocent	My parts,° my title, and my perfect° soul
	Shall manifest me rightly. [2] Is it they?

30

[handwritten: His reputation will protect them]

Iago

By Janus, [3] I think no.

Othello

The servants of the Duke and my lieutenant?
The goodness of the night upon you, friends!
What is the news?

35

Cassio

immediate	The Duke does greet you, General,
	And he requires your haste-post-haste° appearance,
	Even on the instant.

Othello

business at hand	What is the matter,° think you?

Cassio

guess	Something from Cyprus, as I may divine.°
urgency	It is a business of some heat.° The galleys
successive	Have sent a dozen sequent° messengers
	This very night at one another's heels,
senators	And many of the consuls,° raised and met,
urgently	Are at the Duke's already. You have been hotly° called for.

40

[handwritten: warships have been sending messages and Othello is ready]

45

1   *makes he*

   Is he doing

2   *boarded a land carrack*

   **Boarded a galleon or merchant
   ship (with sexual implications)**

3   *lawful prize*

   **Legitimately won booty (i.e., if
   Othello and Desdemona's
   wedding was legally binding)**

4   *Marry*

   **I.e., by the Virgin Mary (a common
   exclamation used for emphasis)**

5   *Have with you.*

   Let's go.

At which point   When,° being not at your lodging to be found,
separate / search parties   The Senate hath sent about three several° quests°
To search you out.

Othello
                        'Tis well I am found by you.
speak   I will but spend° a word here in the house
And go with you.   [*He exits.*]

Cassio
                     Ancient, what makes he [1] here?   50

Iago
Faith, he tonight hath boarded a land carrack; [2]
If it prove lawful prize, [3] he's made forever.

Cassio
I do not understand.

Tonight he boarded a treasure ship and if he stays he can keep it

Iago
                     He's married.

Cassio
                           To who?

Iago
Marry, [4] to—

       [*Enter **Othello**.*]

                 Come, captain, will you go?

Othello
Have with you. [5]   55

Cassio
Here comes another troop to seek for you.

      Enter **Brabantio**, **Roderigo**, *with officers and torches.*

Now othello is going to be confronted by Brab.

1 *You, Roderigo? Come, sir; I am for you.*

   Iago pretends to attack Roderigo
   to disguise their relationship.

2 *refer me*

   Appeal; submit my case

3 *things of sense*

   Sensible creatures (i.e., human
   beings)

4 *fair*

   (1) attractive; (2) chaste;
   (3) fair-skinned

5 *a general mock*

   Everyone's ridicule

6 *Judge me the world if 'tis not gross in
   sense*

   Let the world judge ill of me if it is
   not completely obvious

7 *Abused*

   Taken advantage of

8 *disputed on*

   Investigated

Iago

It is Brabantio. General, be advised,

with a He comes to° bad intent.

Othello

Stop Holla! Stand° there!

Roderigo

Signior, it is the Moor.

Brabantio

Down with him, thief!

[*They draw their swords.*]

Iago

You, Roderigo? Come, sir; I am for you.[1] 60

Othello

Put Keep° up your bright swords, for the dew will rust them.

[*to* **Brabantio**] Good signior, you shall more command
   with years
Than with your weapons.

Brabantio

hidden O thou foul thief, where hast thou stowed° my daughter?

bewitched Damned as thou art, thou hast enchanted° her, 65

For I'll refer me[2] to all things of sense,[3]

If she in chains of magic were not bound,

delicate Whether a maid so tender,° fair,[4] and happy,

opposed So opposite° to marriage that she shunned

well groomed The wealthy, curlèd° darlings of our nation, 70

Would ever have, t' incur a general mock,[5]

guardians Run from her guardage° to the sooty bosom

Of such a thing as thou—to fear, not to delight.

Judge me the world if 'tis not gross in sense[6]

manipulated That thou hast practiced° on her with foul charms, 75

Abused[7] her delicate youth with drugs or minerals

the will That weakens motion.° I'll have 't disputed on.[8]

'Tis probable and palpable to thinking.

[Handwritten annotations:]
Iago already knows what will happen

Iago wants to hide their relat.

Says that his age + status inspire more than

Barb accuses Othello of black majic

1   *I therefore apprehend and do attach thee / For an abuser of the world, a practicer / Of arts inhibited and out of warrant.*

Here Brabantio accuses Othello of using black magic to win Desdemona, the implication being that otherwise she would not naturally be attracted *to the sooty bosom / Of such a thing* (1.2.72–73). In England, Parliament had passed an "Act Against Conjurations, Enchantments and Witchcrafts" in 1563 (hence this is *out of warrant*, i.e., forbidden by law); and in Shakespeare's day, it was still widely believed that love could be induced through magical charms or potions. In Shakespeare's *A Midsummer Night's Dream*, another thwarted patriarch, Egeus, accuses the young lover Lysander of having *bewitched the bosom* (1.1.27) of his daughter Hermia by using love charms. The accusation of erotic enchantment would seem even more plausible, however, to an audience that associated African or Moorish exoticism with superstition, idol worship, and the forbidden arts. The orientalist correlation of Moors with magic is confirmed when Othello describes *the magic in the web* of his mother's handkerchief, which was fashioned by the sibyl and *dyed in mummy which the skillful / Conserved of maidens' hearts* (3.4.64–70).

2   *fit time / Of law and course of direct session*

The regular schedule and process of the law courts

3   *brothers of the state*

Fellow senators

4   *have passage free*

Be generally accepted

arrest   I therefore apprehend and do attach° thee

As / corrupter   For° an abuser° of the world, a practicer   80

prohibited   Of arts inhibited° and out of warrant. [1]

   —Lay hold upon him. If he do resist,   *Barab. tells them*

   Subdue him at his peril!   *to arrest Othello*

Othello

Don't move   Hold° your hands,

faction; followers   Both you of my inclining° and the rest.

   Were it my cue to fight, I should have known it   85

Where / wish   Without a prompter. —Whither° will° you that I go

   To answer this your charge?   *You have charged*

              me serious crimes,

Brabantio   *where will I serve*

             To prison, till fit time

   Of law and course of direct session [2]

   Call thee to answer.

Othello

             What if I do obey?

   How may the Duke be therewith satisfied,   *The Duke will*

                                       90

   Whose messengers are here about my side   *not be*

immediate   Upon some present° business of the state   *satisfied*

   To bring me to him?   *b/c he needs a*

              meeting

Officer

             'Tis true, most worthy signior.

   The Duke's in council, and your noble self,

   I am sure, is sent for.   *Brab, too*

Brabantio

             How? The Duke in council?   *If this*   95

along   In this time of the night? Bring him away.°   *crime isn't*

trivial   Mine's not an idle° cause. The Duke himself,   *punished,*

   Or any of my brothers of the state, [3]   *slaves will*

as if   Cannot but feel this wrong as° 'twere their own.   *run the*

   For if such actions may have passage free, [4]   *world*   100

   Bond-slaves and pagans shall our statesmen be.   101

saying that the law is   *They exit.*

on Brab side

1   *As in these cases, where the aim reports /*
      'Tis oft with difference

      **As can happen in these cases, when
reports are based on guesswork
there are often inconsistencies.**

2   *to judgment*

      Upon reflection

3   *I do not so secure me in the error, / But
the main article I do approve / In fearful
sense.*

      **I.e., the inaccuracy doesn't reassure
me; I do believe the gist of the report
and fear its implications.**

Act 1, Scene 3

Enter **Duke**, **Senators**, *and* **Officers**.

Duke

consistency   There's no composition° in this news

credibility   That gives them credit.°

First Senator

contradictory   Indeed, they are disproportioned.°

My letters say a hundred and seven galleys.

Duke

And mine a hundred forty.

Second Senator

                  And mine, two hundred.   5

agree / exact   But though they jump° not on a just° account—

estimate   As in these cases, where the aim° reports

'Tis oft with difference [1]—yet do they all confirm

heading   A Turkish fleet, and bearing° up to Cyprus.

Duke

Nay, it is possible enough to judgment. [2]   10

I do not so secure me in the error,

But the main article I do approve

In fearful sense. [3]

Sailor

[*within*] What, ho, what, ho, what, ho!

Officer

A messenger from the galleys.

    Enter **Sailor**.

Duke

                Now? What's the business?   15

1 *How say you by this change?*
   What do you make of this
   development?

2 *keep us in false gaze*
   Distract us from the real target

3 *When we consider / Th' importancy of*
   Cyprus to the Turk, / And let ourselves
   again but understand / That, as as it more
   concerns the Turk than Rhodes
   When Shakespeare wrote *Othello*, the
   Turks were a regional superpower
   that posed a threat to Christian
   rulers in Europe and the
   Mediterranean. Both Rhodes and
   Cyprus were (and are) islands located
   near the Turkish coast but inhabited
   by a majority population of Greek
   Christians. The military scenario
   constructed in *Othello* is not,
   however, historically accurate. In
   fact, both Rhodes and Cyprus had
   been conquered by the Ottoman
   Turks long before Shakespeare
   wrote his play. This passage's
   allusion to the *warlike brace* (line 26)
   of Rhodes and the greater
   vulnerability of Cyprus to attack
   reflect Shakespeare's knowledge
   that, at one time, Rhodes had been
   strongly fortified by the Knights
   Hospitalers, a crusading religious
   order who held Cyprus as their
   feudal possession before
   surrendering to the Turkish Sultan
   Suleiman I in 1523. Cyprus was a
   Venetian possession when it was
   invaded and conquered by the Turks
   in 1571. At the beginning of Act Two,
   the sudden drowning of the Turks
   (see 2.1.20: *Our wars are done*) is
   therefore a rewriting of history that
   reverses historical reality. This
   fantasy is a reworking of the English
   Protestant victory over the Spanish
   Armada in 1588, a triumph that was
   greatly aided by storms at sea (a
   commemorative medal was minted
   by Elizabeth I with an inscription
   declaring "God breathed and they
   were scattered").

4 *as it more concerns the Turk than Rhodes, /*
   So may he with more facile question bear it
   The Turks are more concerned with
   Cyprus than with Rhodes, and in
   addition they can capture Cyprus
   more easily.

5 *warlike brace*
   State of military readiness

6 *Neglecting an attempt of ease and gain*
   Passing up an easy and profitable
   opportunity

7 *reverend and gracious*
   Addressed to the senators (i.e.,
   reverend and gracious gentlemen)

Sailor

The Turkish preparation makes for Rhodes;
So was I bid report here to the state
By Signior Angelo.

Duke

—How say you by this change? [1]

First Senator

                    This cannot be,

test / diversion   By no assay° of reason. 'Tis a pageant°   20
To keep us in false gaze. [2] When we consider
Th' importancy of Cyprus to the Turk,
only   And let ourselves again but° understand
i.e., Cyprus   That, as it° more concerns the Turk than Rhodes, [3]
So may he with more facile question bear it, [4]   25
On account of the fact   For° that it stands not in such warlike brace [5]
military power   But altogether lacks th' abilities°
equipped   That Rhodes is dressed° in. If we make thought of this,
We must not think the Turk is so unskillful
for last   To leave that latest° which concerns him first,   30
Neglecting an attempt of ease and gain [6]
gamble on   To wake and wage° a danger profitless.

Duke

certainty / i.e., the Turk is   Nay, in all confidence,° he's° not for Rhodes.

Officer

Here is more news.

Enter a **Messenger**.

Messenger

Turks   The Ottomites,° reverend and gracious, [7]   35
Steering with due course toward the isle of Rhodes,
joined up / additional   Have there injointed° them with an after° fleet.

1   *re-stem / Their backward course*

    Sail back the way they came

2   *bearing with frank appearance*

    Making no attempt to disguise

3   *recommends*

    Reports to

4   *Marcus Luccicos*

    An otherwise unknown name, perhaps a misreading of the manuscript

5   *general*

    Common to all (i.e., all Christian nations)

6   *aught I heard of business*

    Anything I heard of recent events

7   *general care*

    Public interest

First Senator

Ay, so I thought. How many, as you guess?

Messenger

Of thirty sail. And now they do re-stem

Their backward course,[1] bearing with frank appearance[2]   40

intentions   Their purposes° toward Cyprus. Signior Montano,

servant   Your trusty and most valiant servitor,°

freely given   With his free° duty, recommends[3] you thus

And prays you to believe him.

Duke

'Tis certain then for Cyprus.   45

Marcus Luccicos,[4] is not he in town?

First Senator

He's now in Florence.

Duke

immediately / Hurry   Write from us to him, post-post-haste.° Dispatch.°

First Senator

Here comes Brabantio and the valiant Moor.

Enter **Brabantio**, **Othello**, **Cassio**, **Iago**,
Roderigo, *and officers*.

Duke

immediately   Valiant Othello, we must straight° employ you   50

Against the general[5] enemy Ottoman.

noble   [*to* **Brabantio**] I did not see you. Welcome, gentle°

signior.

missed   We lacked° your counsel and your help tonight.

Brabantio

So did I yours. Good your Grace, pardon me;

position (as senator)   Neither my place° nor aught I heard of business[6]   55

Hath raised me from my bed, nor doth the general care[7]

personal   Take hold on me, for my particular° grief

1   *For nature so prepost'rously to err, /*
    Being not deficient, blind, or lame of
    sense, / Sans witchcraft could not

    For nature to make such a
    monstrous error—being neither
    mentally deficient, blind, nor
    stupid—would be impossible
    without the aid of witchcraft.

2   *the bloody book of law / You shall*
    yourself read in the bitter letter, /
    After your own sense

    I.e., You shall pronounce the
    sentence according to the strictest
    sense (*the bitter letter*) of the harsh
    law (*the bloody book of law*).
    Witchcraft was punishable by
    death in Shakepeare's England.

3   *Stood in your action*

    Were the one accused

torrential / overwhelming   Is of so flood-gate° and o'erbearing° nature

consumes   That it engluts° and swallows other sorrows

And it is still itself.   *His problem is worse*

Duke   *than everything else*

Why? What's the matter?   60

Brabantio

My daughter! Oh, my daughter!

All

Dead?

Brabantio

Ay, to me.

deceived   She is abused,° stol'n from me, and corrupted

itinerant drug sellers   By spells and med'cines bought of mountebanks;°

For nature so prepost'rously to err,   *says that*

Being not deficient, blind, or lame of sense   *only drugs*   65

Sans witchcraft could not. [1]   *or witchcraft could make his daughter do this*

Duke

Whoe'er he be that in this foul proceeding

out of   Hath thus beguiled your daughter of° herself

And you of her, the bloody book of law

You shall yourself read in the bitter letter,   70

own   After your own sense, [2] yea, though our proper° son

Stood in your action. [3]   *I will acuse anyone*

Brabantio

Humbly I thank your Grace.

Here is the man, this Moor, whom now it seems

Your special mandate for the state affairs

Hath hither brought.

All

We are very sorry for 't.   75

Duke

[*to* **Othello**] What in your own part can you say to this?

1   *very head and front*
    Full extent

2   *since these arms of mine had seven years'*
    pith / Till now some nine moons wasted
    I.e., from the time I was seven years
    old until nine months ago

3   *that her motion / Blushed at herself*
    That she blushed at her own
    impulses

4   *in spite of*
    Despite differences in

5   *That will confess perfection so could err /*
    Against all rules of nature
    That perfection itself (i.e.,
    Desdemona) could so stray from
    the laws of nature.

6   *and must be driven / To find out practices*
    of cunning Hell / Why this should be
    And therefore (judgment) is forced
    to seek the explanation in
    diabolical deceptions.

Brabantio

Nothing, but this is so.

Othello

Most potent, grave, and reverend signiors,

My very noble and approved good masters,

That I have ta'en away this old man's daughter, 80

It is most true; true, I have married her.

The very head and front[1] of my offending

Unrefined   Hath this extent, no more. Rude° am I in my speech,

language   And little blessed with the soft phrase° of peace,

strength   For, since these arms of mine had seven years' pith° 85

months   Till now some nine moons° wasted,[2] they have used

most worthy / battlefield   Their dearest° action in the tented field,°

And little of this great world can I speak

than what / conflicts   More than° pertains to feats of broils° and battle,

benefit   And therefore little shall I grace° my cause 90

In speaking for myself. Yet, by your gracious patience,

plain   I will a round,° unvarnished tale deliver

with what   Of my whole course of love: what° drugs, what charms,

What conjuration, and what mighty magic—

behavior / with   For such proceeding° I am charged withal°— 95

I won his daughter.

Brabantio

A maiden never bold,

subdued   Of spirit so still° and quiet that her motion

Blushed at herself,[3] and she, in spite of[4] nature,

reputation   Of years, of country, credit,° everything,

To fall in love with what she feared to look on? 100

It is a judgment maimed and most imperfect

That will confess perfection so could err

Against all rules of nature,[5] and must be driven

To find out practices of cunning Hell

assert   Why this should be.[6] I therefore vouch° again 105

1 *mixtures powerful o'er the blood*

Potions that have power to affect the passions

2 *dram, conjured to this effect*

Small amount of medicine, magically concocted for this purpose

3 *thin habits and poor likelihoods / Of modern seeming do prefer against him*

Flimsy evidence (literally, threadbare clothing) and unreliable suggestions based on stereotypical assumptions can bring against him

4 *indirect and forcèd courses*

Devious or coercive means

That with some mixtures powerful o'er the blood [1]
Or with some dram, conjured to this effect, [2]
He wrought upon her.

Duke *Only spells could do this*

                        To vouch this is no proof

extensive / proof   Without more wider° and more overt test°
appearances   Than these thin habits° and poor likelihoods *you need*
                    Of modern seeming do prefer against him. [3] *proof*

First Senator

But, Othello, speak.

Did you by indirect and forcèd courses [4]

corrupt   Subdue and poison° this young maid's affections?
conversation   Or came it by request and such fair question°   115
can offer   As soul to soul affordeth?°

Othello

                        I do beseech you,

Send for the lady to the Sagittary,

And let her speak of me before her father.

false, guilty   If you do find me foul° in her report,

The trust, the office I do hold of you,   120

Not only take away but let your sentence

Even fall upon my life.

Duke

                        Fetch Desdemona hither.

Othello

Ancient, conduct them. You best know the place.

                        [**Iago** *and attendants exit.*]

And till she come, as truly as to Heaven

desire   I do confess the vices of my blood,°   125

truthfully   So justly° to your grave ears I'll present

How I did thrive in this fair lady's love,

And she in mine.

1 *i' th' imminent deadly breach*
**Through breaches in fortifications
(*deadly* is a displaced modifier
referring to the dangers he escapes
from)**

2 *Anthropophagi*
Literally, "man-eaters" (Greek)

3 *These things to hear*
In order to hear these things better

4 *intentively*
With steady attention

5 *beguile her of*
Draw out of her

Duke

Say it, Othello.

Othello

Her father loved me, oft invited me,

Continually Still° questioned me the story of my life   130

From year to year: the battles, sieges, fortunes,

experienced That I have passed.°

I ran it through, even from my boyish days

To th' very moment that he bade me tell it,

occurrences Wherein I spoke of most disastrous chances,°   135

events / sea Of moving accidents° by flood° and field,

escapes Of hair-breadth 'scapes° i' th' imminent deadly breach, [1]

Of being taken by the insolent foe

ransom And sold to slavery, of my redemption° thence

behavior And portance° in my traveler's history,   140

caves / barren Wherein of antres° vast and deserts idle,°

Rough quarries, rocks, hills whose heads touch Heaven,

opportunity / story It was my hint° to speak—such was my process°—

And of the cannibals that each other eat,

The Anthropophagi, [2] and men whose heads   145

Do grow beneath their shoulders. These things to hear [3]

Would Desdemona seriously incline;

always But still° the house affairs would draw her hence,

complete Which ever as she could with haste dispatch°

eager She'd come again, and with a greedy° ear   150

Devour up my discourse, which I, observing,

opportune Took once a pliant° hour and found good means

To draw from her a prayer of earnest heart

relate That I would all my pilgrimage dilate,°

pieces Whereof by parcels° she had something heard   155

But not intentively. [4] I did consent,

And often did beguile her of [5] her tears

injury When I did speak of some distressful stroke°

1   *kisses*

The 1622 Quarto prints "sighs,"
which many editors prefer, but
kisses is not impossible, if a bit
forward as an expression of
sympathy (though clearly
Desdemona is not as passive as her
father imagines her, and *kisses*,
while signs of some intimacy, need
not be passionate).

2   *made her such a man*

Either (1) made her into such a
man; or (2) created such a man for
her (to marry)

3   *take up this mangled matter at the best*

Make the best of a bad situation

4   *Destruction on my head if my bad blame /
Light on the man*

May destruction fall on my head if I
have erroneously accused him.

_i.e., I in my_   That my° youth suffered. My story being done,

She gave me for my pains a world of kisses. [1]   160

exceedingly   She swore, in faith, "'twas strange, 'twas passing° strange;

'Twas pitiful, 'twas wondrous pitiful."

She wished she had not heard it, yet she wished

That Heaven had made her such a man. [2] She thanked me

And bade me, if I had a friend that loved her,   165

merely   I should but° teach him how to tell my story

And that would woo her. Upon this hint I spake.

experienced   She loved me for the dangers I had passed,°

And I loved her that she did pity them.

This only is the witchcraft I have used.   170

confirm   Here comes the lady. Let her witness° it.

Enter **Desdemona**, **Iago**, [and] _attendants._

Duke

I think this tale would win my daughter too.

Good Brabantio, take up this mangled matter at the best. [3]

Men do their broken weapons rather use

Than their bare hands.

Brabantio

                I pray you, hear her speak.   175

If she confess that she was half the wooer,

mistaken   Destruction on my head if my bad° blame

Light on the man. [4]—Come hither, gentle mistress.

Do you perceive in all this noble company

Where most you owe obedience?

Desdemona

                My noble father,   180

I do perceive here a divided duty.

To you I am bound for life and education.

teach   My life and education both do learn° me

1   *I here do give thee that with all my heart /*
Which, but thou hast already, with all
my heart / I would keep from thee.

I hearby give you happily that
which, if you didn't already have it,
I would most passionately hope to
keep from you.

2   *For your sake*

Because of you

3   *teach me tyranny / To hang clogs on*
them

Make me sufficiently tyrannical to
attach blocks of wood to their legs
(to prevent their escape)

4   *lay a sentence*

Speak a truth

5   *When remedies are past, the griefs are*
ended / By seeing the worst, which late
on hopes depended

I.e., when there is no way to fix a
situation, there is no point in
grieving once the outcome is
known, however much you had
hoped for better.

6   *What cannot be preserved when fortune*
takes, / Patience her injury a mock'ry
makes.

What fortune steals from us is
gone, but bearing the loss
patiently turns fortune's insult
back against her.

7   *So let the Turk of Cyprus us beguile: / We*
lose it not, so long as we can smile.

Then let's let the Ottoman Empire
steal Cyprus away from us: (by your
logic) as long as we keep smiling,
we won't have lost it.

	How to respect you: you are the lord of duty.	
to this extent	I am hitherto° your daughter, but here's my husband,	185
	And so much duty as my mother showed	
	To you, preferring you before her father,	
claim	So much I challenge° that I may profess	
	Due to the Moor my lord.	

Brabantio

God be with you. I have done.

	Please it your Grace, on to the state affairs.	190
beget	I had rather to adopt a child than get° it.	
	—Come hither, Moor.	
	I here do give thee that with all my heart	
	Which, but thou hast already, with all my heart	
	I would keep from thee.[1] [*to* **Desdemona**] For your	
	sake,[2] jewel,	195
	I am glad at soul I have no other child,	
elopement	For thy escape° would teach me tyranny	
	To hang clogs on them.[3]—I have done, my lord.	

Duke

for	Let me speak like° yourself and lay a sentence[4]	
stair	Which, as a grece° or step, may help these lovers:	200
	When remedies are past, the griefs are ended	
recently	By seeing the worst, which late ° on hopes depended.[5]	
misfortune	To mourn a mischief ° that is past and gone	
surest	Is the next° way to draw new mischief on.	
	What cannot be preserved when fortune takes,	205
	Patience her injury a mock'ry makes.[6]	
	The robbed that smiles steals something from the thief;	
useless	He robs himself that spends a bootless° grief.	

Brabantio

	So let the Turk of Cyprus us beguile:	
	We lose it not, so long as we can smile.[7]	210

1 *He bears the sentence well that nothing bears / But the free comfort which from thence he hears, / But he bears both the sentence and the sorrow / That, to pay grief, must of poor patience borrow.*

It's easy to follow such advice if you have nothing to endure except the offered consolation, but it costs the man twice as much if you require him also to bear the grief itself. (I.e., Brabantio suffers doubly to bear both his grief and the Duke's platitudes.)

2 *These sentences to sugar or to gall, / Being strong on both sides, are equivocal.*

I.e., the Duke's maxims are so widely applicable as to lack any moral force or comfort.

3 *piercèd*

Lancing was a common medical treatment for infected wounds; Brabantio is saying that words of comfort are as ineffective in taking away heartfelt grief as lancing would be in healing some serious wound.

4 *most allowed sufficiency*

Fully recognized ability

5 *opinion, a more sovereign mistress of effects, throws a more safer voice on you*

Popular opinion, which has more power to affect our decisions, recommends you as the more reliable man for the job.

6 *stubborn and boisterous expedition*

Difficult and dangerous enterprise

7 *The tyrant custom*

A proverbial identification of *custom*, i.e., habit, as an oppressive and domineering force. Over time, force of habit has made Othello comfortable with the hard life of a warrior.

8 *flinty and steel couch of war*

I.e., sleeping in armor on the hard ground

9 *thrice-driven bed of down*

Mattress stuffed with the softest goose down, which has been sifted over and over to winnow out the coarse feathers

10 *Due reference of place, and exhibition*

Appropriate recognition of her status, and financial support

He bears the sentence well that nothing bears
But the free comfort which from thence he hears,
But he bears both the sentence and the sorrow
That, to pay grief, must of poor patience borrow. [1]
bitterness   These sentences to sugar or to gall,°   215
Being strong on both sides, are equivocal. [2]
But words are words. I never yet did hear
injured   That the bruised° heart was piercèd [3] through the ears.
I humbly beseech you, proceed to th' affairs of state.
Duke
military force   The Turk with a most mighty preparation° makes for   220
strength   Cyprus. Othello, the fortitude° of the place is best
deputy   known to you, and, though we have there a substitute° of
most allowed sufficiency, [4] yet opinion, a more sovereign
mistress of effects, throws a more safer voice on you. [5]
tarnish / brightness   You must therefore be content to slubber° the gloss° of   225
your new fortunes with this more stubborn and
boisterous expedition. [6]
Othello
The tyrant custom, [7] most grave senators,
Hath made the flinty and steel couch of war [8]
acknowledge   My thrice-driven bed of down. [9] I do agnize°   230
innate / enthusiasm   A natural° and prompt alacrity°
hardship / take charge of   I find in hardness,° and do undertake°
This present wars against the Ottomites.
authority   Most humbly, therefore, bending to your state,°
arrangements   I crave fit disposition° for my wife,   235
Due reference of place, and exhibition, [10]
companions   With such accommodation and besort°
accords   As levels° with her breeding.
Duke
Why, at her father's.

1   *a charter in your voice*

    Permission in your judgment

2   *downright violence*

    Radical break (with convention)

3   *storm*

    **The 1622 Quarto's "scorn" is a
    plausible reading, since both "scorn"
    of fortunes" and *storm of fortunes* were
    common expressions, and each
    could easily be misread as the other.**

4   *very quality*

    True nature

5   *I saw Othello's visage in his mind*

    **I.e., it was the quality of his mind
    that determined my sense of who
    Othello was; often a troublesome
    line to modern readers, as
    Desdemona seems to be suggesting
    that there is something inherently
    wrong with Othello's *visage*, a
    prejudice that would have been
    quite common in Shakespeare's day.**

6   *moth*

    **The meaning here is unclear:
    either the *moth* is an insignificant
    creature; or perhaps a weak one,
    unable to be drawn from the warm
    flame of domestic *peace* into the
    dark uncertainties of war; or
    perhaps an idler who stays at home
    to cause domestic ruin (eating
    away at valuable cloth and
    textiles).**

7   *rites*

    **Both marriage *rites* and the
    "rights" of a wife**

8   *support / By*

    Endure through

9   *To please the palate of my appetite*

    For my own personal pleasure

10 *comply with heat*

    Submit to sexual desire

11 *young affects*

    Youthful appetites

12 *But to be free and bounteous to her mind*

    **I.e., but out of respect for
    Desdemona's feeling and ideas**

Brabantio

          I will not have it so.

Othello

Nor I.   240

Desdemona

Nor would I there reside,

To put my father in impatient thoughts

sight   By being in his eye.° Most gracious Duke,

proposal / sympathetic   To my unfolding° lend your prosperous° ear

And let me find a charter in your voice [1]   245

T' assist my simpleness.

Duke

wish   What would° you, Desdemona?

Desdemona

That I did love the Moor to live with him,

My downright violence [2] and storm [3] of fortunes

proclaim   May trumpet° to the world. My heart's subdued

Even to the very quality [4] of my lord.   250

I saw Othello's visage in his mind, [5]

qualities   And to his honors and his valiant parts°

Did I my soul and fortunes consecrate,

noble   So that, dear° lords, if I be left behind

A moth [6] of peace, and he go to the war,   255

taken from The rites [7] for why I love him are bereft° me,

sad   And I a heavy° interim shall support

painful   By [8] his dear° absence. Let me go with him.

Othello

consent   Let her have your voice.°

Bear witness Vouch° with me, Heaven, I therefore beg it not   260

To please the palate of my appetite, [9]

Nor to comply with heat [10]—the young affects [11]

In me defunct—and proper satisfaction,

But to be free and bounteous to her mind; [12]

1   *light-winged toys*

    Trifling erotic delights

2   *feathered Cupid*

    Cupid, the Roman god of love, was usually depicted as a young winged boy.

3   *speculative and officed instrument*

    Eyes and other faculties of perception and judgment

4   *That my disports corrupt and taint my business*

    That my amorous activities might endanger or discredit my mission

5   *Let housewives make a skillet of my helm*

    Let my helmet be melted down and made into cookware for *housewives*.

6   *Make head against my estimation*

    Rise up to attack my reputation

7   *And such things else of quality and respect / As doth import you*

    Along with any other matters that might be of importance or relevance to you

should suspect	And Heaven defend your good souls that you think° 265
neglect	I will your serious and great business scant°
	When she is with me. No, when light-winged toys [1]
close / lustful	Of feathered Cupid [2] seel° with wanton° dullness
	My speculative and officed instrument, [3]
	That my disports corrupt and taint my business, [4] 270
	Let housewives make a skillet of my helm, [5]
undignified	And all indign° and base adversities
	Make head against my estimation. [6]

Duke

Be it as you shall privately determine,

begs for Either for her stay or going. Th' affair cries° haste, 275
And speed must answer it.

First Senator

You must away tonight.

Othello

               With all my heart.

Duke

At nine i' th' morning here we'll meet again.
—Othello, leave some officer behind,
And he shall our commission bring to you, 280
And such things else of quality and respect
As doth import you. [7]

Othello

           So please your Grace, my ancient;
A man he is of honesty and trust.

escort To his conveyance° I assign my wife,
With what else needful your good Grace shall think 285
To be sent after me.

Duke

          Let it be so.
Good night to every one. [*to* **Brabantio**] And, noble
    signior,

1 *Look to her*

Watch her (see also 3.3.210–212)

2 *My life upon her faith!*

I'd stake my life upon her fidelity.

3 *attend on her*

Act as her waiting woman

4 *in the best advantage*

At the most favorable opportunity

5 *of worldly matter and direction*

Of practical business and
instructions

delightful If virtue no delighted° beauty lack,

Your son-in-law is far more fair than black.

First Senator

Treat Adieu, brave Moor. Use° Desdemona well.   290

Brabantio

Look to her, ¹ Moor, if thou hast eyes to see;

may deceive She has deceived her father, and may° thee.

He exits [with **Duke**, **Cassio**, **Senators**,

and officers] .

Othello

My life upon her faith! ²—Honest Iago,

My Desdemona must I leave to thee.

I prithee, let thy wife attend on her, ³   295

And bring them after in the best advantage. ⁴

—Come, Desdemona, I have but an hour

Of love, of worldly matter and direction, ⁵

To spend with thee. We must obey the time.

He [and **Desdemona**] *exit.*

Roderigo

Iago.   300

Iago

What say'st thou, noble heart?

Roderigo

What will I do, think'st thou?

Iago

Why, go to bed and sleep.

Roderigo

immediately I will incontinently° drown myself.

Iago

If thou dost, I shall never love thee after. Why, thou   305

silly gentleman?

1 *guinea hen*

A female guinea fowl, though the term is also slang for "prostitute"

2 *A fig!*

A contemptuous interjection, often accompanied by a rude gesture (the thumb inserted between the first and second fingers in a fist)

3 *nettles . . . lettuce . . . hyssop . . . thyme*

Iago's horticulture examples are obscure, but the point is to pair opposites: *nettles* and *lettuce*, like *hyssop* and *thyme*, were thought to be of opposite natures, "one being dry, the other moist," as a 16th -century herbalist wrote. The phrase *weed up* means "free from weeds" to allow growth.

4 *sterile with idleness*

Barren (because untilled)

5 *power and corrigible authority*

Ability to control and improve

6 *If the beam of our lives had not one scale of reason to poise another of sensuality*

The image is of life as a scale balancing reason on one side with sensuality on the other.

7 *blood*

Appetitive or lustful part of our nature

8 *sect or scion*

These are words from gardening meaning "cutting" and "offshoot" (Iago has gone back to the horticultural metaphor with which he began).

Roderigo

It is silliness to live when to live is torment, and then have
we a prescription to die when death is our physician.

Iago

Oh, villainous! I have looked upon the world for four times
seven years, and, since I could distinguish betwixt a   310
benefit and an injury, I never found man that knew
how to love himself. Ere I would say I would drown

exchange   myself for the love of a guinea hen, [1] I would change°
my humanity with a baboon.

Roderigo

What should I do? I confess it is my shame to be so   315

infatuated / character   fond,° but it is not in my virtue° to amend it.

Iago

Virtue? A fig! [2] 'Tis in ourselves that we are thus or thus.
Our bodies are our gardens, to the which our wills are

plant   gardeners; so that if we will plant nettles or sow° lettuce,
set hyssop and weed up thyme, [3] supply it with one   320

kind / divide   gender° of herbs or distract° it with many—either to have
it sterile with idleness[4] or manured with industry—why,
the power and corrigible authority[5] of this lies in our wills.

balance   If the beam° of our lives had not one scale of reason to
poise another of sensuality, [6] the blood [7] and baseness of   325
our natures would conduct us to most preposterous

outcomes   conclusions.° But we have reason to cool our raging

emotions / unbridled   motions,° our carnal stings, our unbitted° lusts, whereof
I take this that you call love to be a sect or scion. [8]

Roderigo

It cannot be.   330

Iago

permissiveness   It is merely a lust of the blood and a permission° of the
will. Come; be a man. Drown thyself? Drown cats and

i.e., newborn / myself   blind° puppies! I have professed me° thy friend, and I

joined   confess me knit° to thy deserving with cables of perdu-

1   *cables of perdurable toughness*

    Bonds of everlasting strength

2   *Put money in thy purse.*

    I.e., sell your assets to have cash on
    hand.

3   *Follow thou the wars*

    Become a mercenary

4   *defeat thy favor with an usurped beard*

    Disguise your appearance with a
    false beard.

5   *thou shalt see an answerable*
    sequestration

    You will see that the separation will
    be correspondingly sudden.

6   *locusts*

    The sweet fruit of the carob tree

7   *coloquintida*

    Bitter apple (used as a purgative)

8   *She must change for youth.*

    I.e., she will opt for a younger man.

9   *wilt needs*

    Must

10 *sanctimony and a frail vow*

    Pretended piety and a meaningless
    promise

11 *super-subtle Venetian*

    I.e., Desdemona (in early modern
    England, Venice and Venetians
    were often associated with both
    sophistication and depravity)

12 *A pox of*

    A dismissive expression,
    comparable to "To Hell with . . . "

13 *It is clean out of the way.*

    It is completely inappropriate.

14 *hanged in compassing thy joy*

    I.e., executed for obtaining your
    desire

15 *If thou canst cuckold him, thou dost*
    thyself a pleasure, me a sport.

    If you can make him a *cuckold* (by
    seducing his wife), you'll give
    yourself *pleasure* and me
    amusement.

16 *Traverse*

    Meaning obscure, though
    evidently a military command such
    as "about-face"

help	rable toughness. [1] I could never better stead° thee than now. *335*
—	Put money in thy purse. [2] Follow thou the wars; [3] defeat thy
	favor with an usurped beard. [4] I say, put money in thy purse.
	It cannot be long that Desdemona should continue her love
	to the Moor—put money in thy purse—nor he his to her
sudden	It was a violent° commencement in her, and thou shalt *340*
	see an answerable sequestration [5]—put but money in
	thy purse. These Moors are changeable in their
desires	wills°—fill thy purse with money. The food that to him
	now is as luscious as locusts [6] shall be to him shortly as
	bitter as coloquintida. [7] She must change for youth. [8] *345*
	When she is sated with his body she will find the errors
	of her choice. Therefore, put money in thy purse
	If thou wilt needs [9] damn thyself, do it a more
elegant	delicate° way than drowning. Make all the money thou
blundering; wandering	canst. If sanctimony and a frail vow [10] betwixt an erring° *350*
	barbarian and super-subtle Venetian [11] be not too hard
population	for my wits and all the tribe° of Hell, thou shalt enjoy
	her. Therefore make money. A pox of [12] drowning thy-
	self! It is clean out of the way. [13] Seek thou rather to be
	hanged in compassing thy joy [14] than to be drowned *355*
	and go without her.

Roderigo

committed / outcome	Wilt thou be fast° to my hopes if I depend on the issue?°

Iago

can be	Thou art° sure of me. Go; make money. I have told thee
	often, and I re-tell thee again and again, I hate the
heartfelt	Moor. My cause is hearted;° thine hath no less reason. *360*
united	Let us be conjunctive° in our revenge against him. If
	thou canst cuckold him, thou dost thyself a pleasure,
	me a sport. [15] There are many events in the womb of
brought to fruition	time which will be delivered.° Traverse, [16] go, provide
	thy money. We will have more of this tomorrow. Adieu. *365*

1 *snipe*
   First recorded instance of the word
   to mean "fool" or "gull" (its literal
   meaning, "a long-billed marsh
   bird," was considerably older)

2 *it is thought abroad*
   It is generally rumored

3 *in that kind*
   Of that fact

4 *do as if for surety*
   Act as though it were a certainty

5 *his place*
   I.e., his position as Othello's
   lieutenant

6 *plume up my will*
   Gratify my desire

Roderigo

Where shall we meet i' th' morning?

Iago

At my lodging.

Roderigo

early   I'll be with thee betimes.°

Iago

Go to, farewell. Do you hear, Roderigo?

Roderigo

What say you?   370

Iago

No more of drowning, do you hear?

Roderigo

persuaded   I am changed.°

Iago

Go to, farewell. Put money enough in your purse.

Roderigo

I'll sell all my land.   *He exits.*

Iago

always   Thus do I ever° make my fool my purse,   375
hard won / abuse For I mine own gained° knowledge should profane°
waste   If I would time expend° with such a snipe[1]
Except   But° for my sport and profit. I hate the Moor,
                And it is thought abroad[2] that 'twixt my sheets
duty   He's done my office.° I know not if 't be true,   380
                But I, for mere suspicion in that kind,[3]
in high regard Will do as if for surety.[4] He holds me well;°
                The better shall my purpose work on him.
handsome   Cassio's a proper° man. Let me see now:
                To get his place[5] and to plume up my will[6]   385
                In double knavery. How? How—Let's see—

1   *He hath a person and a smooth dispose*

     **He has a (pleasing) physical
     appearance and a pleasant
     disposition.**

2   *engendered*

     **Conceived (with a pun on the
     obstetrical meaning carried out in
     the next line)**

After some time, to abuse Othello's ears

i.e., Cassio / i.e., Othello's   That he° is too familiar with his° wife?

i.e., Cassio   He° hath a person and a smooth dispose [1]

created / unfaithful   To be suspected, framed° to make women false.°   390

generous   The Moor is of a free° and open nature

merely   That thinks men honest that but° seem to be so,

easily   And will as tenderly° be led by th' nose

As asses are.

I have 't! It is engendered! [2] Hell and night   395

Must bring this monstrous birth to the world's light.

[He exits.]

— Lets us know how
far Iago is willing to
go for what he wants
— Lays out a blueprint
for the rest of the
book

1   *What ribs of oak, when mountains melt*
    on them, / Can hold the mortise?

    What ship (with *ribs of oak*), when
    mountainous waves crash upon it,
    can keep its *mortise* (joints) from
    splitting apart?

2   *The chidden billow seems to pelt the*
    clouds

    The waves, *chidden* (rebuked) by the
    wind, seem to pummel the *clouds*.

3   *the burning bear*

    The constellation Ursa Minor

4   *the guards of th' ever-fixèd pole*

    The polestar is the brightest star in
    the constellation Ursa Minor. The
    guards are the constellation's two
    next brightest stars, Dubhe and
    Merak.

5   *I never did like molestation view*

    I never saw such turbulence

6   *they . . . bear it out*

    They will survive it.

Act 2, Scene 1

Enter **Montano** *and two* **Gentlemen**.

Montano

promontory What from the cape° can you discern at sea?

First Gentleman

turbulent / sea Nothing at all. It is a high-wrought° flood.°
sky / ocean I cannot 'twixt the heaven° and the main°
Perceive Descry° a sail.

Montano

Methinks the wind hath spoke aloud at land: 5
A fuller blast ne'er shook our battlements.
raged If it hath ruffianed° so upon the sea,
What ribs of oak, when mountains melt on them,
Can hold the mortise?[1] What shall we hear of this?

Second Gentleman

breaking up A segregation° of the Turkish fleet. 10
If you do For do° but stand upon the foaming shore,
The chidden billow seems to pelt the clouds;[2]
swells of the sea The wind-shaked surge,° with high and monstrous mane,
Seems to cast water on the burning bear[3]
And quench the guards of th' ever-fixèd pole.[4] 15
I never did like molestation view[5]
angry On the enchafèd° flood.

Montano

it turns out that   If that° the Turkish fleet
in a bay Be not ensheltered and embayed,° they are drowned;
It is impossible to bear it out.[6]

Enter a [**Third**] **Gentleman**.

Third Gentleman

News, lads: our wars are done! 20

1 *in full commission here*

   Sent here with complete authority

2 *though he speak of comfort / Touching*
   the Turkish loss

   Though he brings us comforting
   news of the Turks' *loss* (of their
   ships)

3 *throw out our eyes for*

   Watch for

4 *Even till we make the main and th' aerial*
   blue / An indistinct regard

   Even if we have to keep watch until
   the blue sea and blue sky become
   indistinguishable from one
   another (from staring out so long)

5 *is expectancy / Of more arrivance*

   Brings the hope of more arrivals

The desperate tempest hath so banged the Turks

undertaking That their designment° halts. A noble ship of Venice

destruction / damage Hath seen a grievous wrack° and sufferance°

the greater part On most° part of their fleet.

Montano

How? Is this true?

Third Gentleman

The ship is here put in,   25

i.e., a ship from Verona A Veronesa;° Michael Cassio,

Lieutenant to the warlike Moor Othello,

Is come on shore; the Moor himself at sea

And is in full commission here[1] for Cyprus.

Montano

I am glad on 't. 'Tis a worthy governor.   30

Third Gentleman

But this same Cassio, though he speak of comfort

soberly Touching the Turkish loss,[2] yet he looks sadly°

And prays the Moor be safe, for they were parted

By With° foul and violent tempest.

Montano

i.e., be safe   Pray heavens he be,°

For I have served him, and the man commands   35

ideal Like a full° soldier. Let's to the seaside, ho!——

much As well° to see the vessel that's come in

As to throw out our eyes for[3] brave Othello,

Even till we make the main and th' aerial blue

An indistinct regard.[4]

Third Gentleman

Come, let's do so,   40

For every minute is expectancy

Of more arrivance.[5]

Enter **Cassio**.

1   *well shipped*
    Equipped with a seaworthy vessel

2   *approved allowance*
    Proven reputation

3   *my hopes, not surfeited to death, / Stand
    in bold cure*
    I.e., *my hopes* (for Othello's safe
    arrival) are not unhealthily
    optimistic but indeed seem likely
    to be fulfilled.

4   *My hopes do shape him for*
    I imagine it is

5   *shot of courtesy*
    Volley from a ship's cannon
    intended as a friendly salute

6   *give truth*
    Report back

Cassio

valiant men   Thanks, you the valiant° of this warlike isle

praise   That so approve° the Moor. Oh, let the heavens

                Give him defense against the elements,   45

                For I have lost him on a dangerous sea.

Montano

                Is he well shipped?¹

Cassio

ship   His bark° is stoutly timbered, and his pilot

                Of very expert and approved allowance.²

                Therefore my hopes, not surfeited to death,   50

                Stand in bold cure.³

A Voice

                (*within*) A sail, a sail, a sail!

Cassio

                What noise?

Second Gentleman

cliff looking out   The town is empty. On the brow° o' th' sea

                Stand ranks of people, and they cry "A sail!"   55

Cassio

                My hopes do shape him for⁴ the governor.

                                        [*a shot fired within*]

Second Gentleman

                They do discharge their shot of courtesy:⁵

                Our friends at least.

Cassio

                                I pray you, sir, go forth

                And give truth⁶ who 'tis that is arrived.

Second Gentleman

                                I shall.   *He exits.*

1   *wild fame*

     Excited rumor

2   *quirks of blazoning pens*

     **Extravagant verbal displays of
     poets who meticulously describe
     the beauties of a woman**

3   *And in th' essential vesture of creation /
     Does tire the ingener*

     **(1) and with the natural beauty of
     her form, she exhausts the poet's
     ability to describe her; (2) in
     creating her, God (the divine
     ingener) has exhausted his own
     capabilities. *Essential vesture of
     creation* means "the clothing she
     was dressed in by nature" (i.e., her
     body); *ingener* is like our modern
     "engineer," meaning "designer" or
     "inventor," though here is
     accented on the first syllable.**

4   *ensteeped*

     **Hidden below the surface of the
     sea**

5   *enclog the guiltless keel*

     Wreck innocent ships

6   *As having sense of beauty, do omit /
     Their mortal natures, letting go safely by /
     The divine Desdemona*

     **Having an appreciation for beauty,
     act against their deadly natures
     and allow the divine Desdemona
     to pass unharmed**

7   *anticipates our thoughts / A se'nnight's
     speed*

     **Has come about a week before we
     expected (a *se'nnight* being a
     contraction of "seven-night")**

Montano

married   But good lieutenant, is your General wived?°   60

Cassio

won   Most fortunately. He hath achieved° a maid

surpasses   That paragons° description and wild fame, [1]

One that excels the quirks of blazoning pens, [2]

And in th' essential vesture of creation

Does tire the ingener. [3]

Enter [**Second**] **Gentleman**.

How now? Who has put in?   65

Second Gentleman

ensign   'Tis one Iago, ancient° to the General.

Cassio

fortunate   He's had most favorable and happy° speed.

Tempests themselves, high seas and howling winds,

jagged / shoals   The guttered° rocks and congregated sands,°

Traitors ensteeped [4] to enclog the guiltless keel, [5]   70

As having sense of beauty, do omit

Their mortal natures, letting go safely by

The divine Desdemona. [6]

Montano

What is she?

Cassio

She that I spake of, our great captain's captain,

protection   Left in the conduct° of the bold Iago,   75

disembarking   Whose footing° here anticipates our thoughts

A se'nnight's speed. [7] Great Jove, Othello guard

And swell his sail with thine own powerful breath,

That he may bless this bay with his tall ship,

Make love's quick pants in Desdemona's arms,   80

extinguished   Give renewed fire to our extincted° spirits

1 *let her have your knees*
   Kneel to her

2 *Enwheel thee round*
   Surround you

3 *how lost you company*
   **How did you come to be
   separated?**

4 *The great contention of sea and skies /
   Parted our fellowship.*
   I.e., the storm separated our ships.

And bring all Cyprus comfort!

Enter **Desdemona**, **Iago**, **Roderigo**, *and* **Emilia**.

                     Oh, behold,
The riches of the ship is come on shore!
You men of Cyprus, let her have your knees. [1]
Hail to thee, lady—and the grace of Heaven,   85
Before, behind thee, and on every hand
Enwheel thee round! [2]

Desdemona

                  I thank you, valiant Cassio.
What tidings can you tell me of my lord?

Cassio

He is not yet arrived, nor know I aught
But that he's well and will be shortly here.   90

Desdemona

Oh, but I fear—how lost you company? [3]

Cassio

The great contention of sea and skies
Parted our fellowship. [4]

A Voice

[*within*] A sail, a sail!

Cassio

But, hark, a sail.   95

                       [*a shot fired within*]

Second Gentleman

They give their greeting to the citadel:
This likewise is a friend.

Cassio

               See for the news.

           [**Second Gentleman** *exits.*]

1   *'Tis my breeding / That gives me this bold show of courtesy.*

When a gentleman greeted a lady in early modern England, he would bow, and then, if he were romantically inclined, he might attempt to kiss the lady's hand, first offering his hand, palm facing down. If the lady welcomed the kiss, she would place her fingers lightly on top of his hand. Then the gentleman would lightly kiss the lady's middle finger, between the first and second knuckle, making sure to maintain eye contact. The performance of this ritual act was, as Cassio indicates, a sign of upper-class breeding and would never be attempted by a social inferior. This exchange highlights the class difference between the courtly Cassio and the soldier Iago, who sees this as foppish (see lines 171–173).

2   *has no speech*

Desdemona may either mean that Emilia is speechless at Iago's ill-natured quip, or that (contrary to Iago's joke) she is a woman of few words.

3   *Marry*

A mild oath (see p. 68, note 4)

4   *She puts tongue a little in her heart / And chides with thinking*

She holds her tongue and chides only in her thoughts.

5   *You are pictures out of doors, bells in your parlors, wild-cats in your kitchens, saints in your injuries, devils being offended, players in your housewifery, and housewives in your beds.*

You (women) seem perfect in public, noisy when gabbing with your friends, wild and fierce in your own kitchens, self-righteous martyrs when you've been wronged, furious devils when you've been offended, frivolous in your domestic duties, and hussies in your beds. Iago's playful remarks exemplify a deeply seated tradition of misogyny or anti-feminism in English culture. Though he may be joking, his comments suggest the image of Venetian women as hypocritical "white devils," prone to deception and sexual infidelity. Here he says that outside the house, women like Emilia appear to be silent and obedient, but at home they reveal their true nature. In private, he quips, they are busier in bed than with the housework. The idea of unruly or idle women posing as hard-working household managers is compressed in the double sense of the word "huswives" (the spelling of *housewives* in the Folio), which could mean both "housewives" and "hussies."

Good ancient, you are welcome.—Welcome, mistress.

[*He kisses* **Emilia**.]

vex   Let it not gall° your patience, good Iago,

That I extend my manners. 'Tis my breeding   *100*

That gives me this bold show of courtesy. [1]

Iago

Sir, would she give you so much of her lips

i.e., scolding words   As of her tongue° she oft bestows on me,

You would have enough.

Desdemona

Alas, she has no speech! [2]

Iago

                     In faith, too much.   *105*

always / opportunity   I find it still,° when I have leave° to sleep.

Marry, [3] before your Ladyship, I grant,

She puts her tongue a little in her heart

And chides with thinking. [4]

Emilia

                 You have little cause to say so.

Iago

You women   Come on, come on. You° are pictures out of door, bells   *110*

in your parlors, wild-cats in your kitchens, saints in

your injuries, devils being offended, players in your

housewifery, and housewives in your beds. [5]

Desdemona

Oh, fie upon thee, slanderer!

Iago

Nay, it is true, or else I am a Turk: *115*

You rise to play and go to bed to work.

Emilia

You shall not write my praise.

Iago

                 No, let me not.

1 *There's one gone to the harbor?*

Before engaging in the teasing with Iago, Desdemona ensures that someone has gone to keep an eye out for Othello.

2 *Come, how wouldst thou praise me?*

Desdemona challenges Iago to improvise a witty poem on the subject of her virtues.

3 *as birdlime does from frieze*

I.e., slowly and with great difficulty. *Birdlime* was a sticky substance applied to tree branches for the purpose of catching birds; *frieze* was a type of coarse, woolen cloth, which could not be unstuck from birdlime without pulling out the threads.

4 *my muse labors, / And thus she is delivered*

I.e., my creativity has gone into labor, and this is the child to which it has given birth.

5 *fair*

The word had a wide range of meanings, among them: fair-haired (the primary meaning here), fair-skinned, beautiful, fortunate, honest, chaste, and unsoiled. All of these meanings could and probably should be taken into account.

6 *The one's for use, the other useth it*

I.e., the first was made to be used, the second was made to use the first (for her own purposes).

7 *black*

Dark-haired (though in this play the racial sense must inevitably creep in, as Iago's reply makes clear)

8 *white*

A complicated pun; a *wight* was an old-fashioned (from Middle English) word for "fellow" (see 2.3.84), but *white* refers to the racial identification central to the play, and could also refer to the white bull's-eye at the center of an archery target.

9 *helped her to an heir*

Led her to become pregnant (or possibly "helped her find a rich heir to marry")

Desdemona

What wouldst write of me if thou shouldst
    praise me?

Iago

i.e., the test   O gentle lady, do not put me to 't,°

For I am nothing if not critical.   120

Desdemona

try   Come on; assay.° There's one gone to the harbor?[1]

Iago

Ay, madam.

Desdemona

disguise   [*aside*] I am not merry, but I do beguile°

The thing I am by seeming otherwise.

[*to* **Iago**] Come, how wouldst thou praise me?[2]   125

Iago

working on   I am about° it, but indeed my invention

head   Comes from my pate° as birdlime does from frieze:[3]

It plucks out brains and all. But my muse labors,

And thus she is delivered:[4]

intelligence   If she be fair[5] and wise, fairness and wit,°   130

The one's for use, the other useth it.[6]

Desdemona

Well praised! How if she be black[7] and witty?

Iago

in addition   If she be black, and thereto° have a wit,

She'll find a white[8] that shall her blackness fit.

Desdemona

Worse and worse!   135

Emilia

How if fair and foolish?

Iago

She never yet was foolish that was fair,

For even her folly helped her to an heir.[9]

1   *But does foul pranks*

    Who doesn't engage in sexual acts

2   *a deserving woman indeed*

    A truly deserving woman

3   *put on the vouch of very malice*

    Condone the most malicious testimony against her

4   *Had tongue at will*

    Was never at a loss for words

5   *Fled from her wish and yet said "Now I may"*

    I.e., refrained from indulging her desires even when she had a chance to satisfy them

6   *her revenge being nigh, / Bade her wrong stay and her displeasure fly*

    Her opportunity for revenge being present, she restrained her sense of wrong and let her anger dissipate.

7   *change the cod's head for the salmon's tail*

    I.e., mistake the worthless for the edible part of the fish

8   *To suckle fools and chronicle small beer.*

    To nurse children and keep track of insignificant household matters

Desdemona

foolish   These are old fond° paradoxes to make fools laugh i' th'
                  alehouse. What miserable praise hast thou for her   *140*
unattractive   that's foul° and foolish?

Iago

besides   There's none so foul and foolish thereunto°
                  But does foul pranks[1] which fair and wise ones do.

Desdemona

overwhelming   O heavy° ignorance! Thou praisest the worst best. But
                  what praise couldst thou bestow on a deserving   *145*
certainty   woman indeed,[2] one that in the authority° of her merit
                  did justly put on the vouch of very malice itself?[3]

Iago

always   She that was ever° fair and never proud,
                  Had tongue at will[4] and yet was never loud,
extravagantly dressed   Never lacked gold and yet went never gay,°   *150*
                  Fled from her wish and yet said "Now I may";[5]
                  She that being angered, her revenge being nigh,
Commanded   Bade° her wrong stay and her displeasure fly;[6]
                  She that in wisdom never was so frail
                  To change the cod's head for the salmon's tail;[7]   *155*
                  She that could think and ne'er disclose her mind,
                  See suitors following and not look behind,
person   She was a wight,° if ever such wights were—

Desdemona

                  To do what?

Iago

                  To suckle fools and chronicle small beer.[8]   *160*

Desdemona

                  Oh, most lame and impotent conclusion! Do not learn
from   of° him, Emilia, though he be thy husband. How say
blasphemous / licentious you, Cassio? Is he not a most profane° and liberal°
i.e., teacher   counselor?°

1   *kissed your three fingers*

    **An extravagant courtly gesture,
which Iago mocks for its
foppishness (see p. 118, note 1)**

2   *clyster-pipes*

    **Tubes used to insert rectal
suppositories or administer
enemas**

3   *It gives me wonder great as my content*

    I'm as surprised as I am delighted

Cassio

to the point / appreciate He speaks home,° madam; you may relish° him more   165
in the role of in° the soldier than in the scholar.

[**Cassio** *and* **Desdemona** *clasp hands.*]

Iago

[*aside*] He takes her by the palm. Ay, well said; whisper!
insubstantial With as little° a web as this will I ensnare as great a fly as
ensnare Cassio. Ay, smile upon her; do. I will gyve° thee in thine
own courtship. You say true; 'tis so indeed. If such   170
lieutenancy tricks as these strip you out of your lieutenantry,° it had
if you been better you° had not kissed your three fingers¹ so
gallant oft, which now again you are most apt to play the sir°
in. Very good, well kissed, and excellent courtesy! 'Tis
so, indeed! Yet again your fingers to your lips? Would   175
they were clyster-pipes² for your sake!—

[*trumpet sounds within*]

The Moor! I know his trumpet.

Cassio

'Tis truly so.

Desdemona

welcome Let's meet him and receive° him.

Cassio

Lo, where he comes!

Enter **Othello** *and attendants.*

Othello

O my fair warrior!

Desdemona

My dear Othello!

Othello

It gives me wonder great as my content³   180
To see you here before me. O my soul's joy!

1   *Olympus-high*

  As high as Mount Olympus (in
  Greek mythology, the dwelling
  place of the gods)

2   *If it were now to die, / 'Twere now to be*
  most happy

  If it were my fate to die now, I
  would die completely happy.

3   *Succeeds in unknown fate*

  Can follow in our uncertain future

4   *And this, and this, the greatest discords*
  be / That e'er our hearts shall make!

  Presumably *this, and this* refers to
  the light kisses he offers her on
  each cheek, and then with mild
  irony says that these should be the
  greatest *discords* they ever
  encounter, with a musical pun that
  Iago picks up in his next speech.

5   *set down the pegs*

  Untune the instrument by
  loosening the *pegs* (which control
  the pitch), thereby destroying your
  harmony.

6   *prattle out of fashion*

  Chatter inappropriately

7   *dote / In mine own comforts*

  Behave foolishly because of my
  great happiness

If after every tempest come such calms,

May the winds blow till they have wakened death,

ship / waves And let the laboring bark° climb hills° of seas

Olympus-high [1] and duck again as low   185

Hell is As Hell's° from Heaven! If it were now to die,

'Twere now to be most happy, [2] for I fear

contentment My soul hath her content° so absolute

That not another comfort like to this

Succeeds in unknown fate. [3]

Desdemona

                          The heavens forbid   190

Anything other than But° that our loves and comforts should increase

Even as our days do grow.

Othello

                         Amen to that, sweet powers!

I cannot speak enough of this content.

It stops me here; it is too much of joy.

And this, and this, the greatest discords be   195

That e'er our hearts shall make! [4]

Iago

in harmony [*aside*] Oh, you are well-tuned° now,

But I'll set down the pegs [5] that make this music,

As honest as I am.

Othello

Come, let us to the castle.   200

News, friends! Our wars are done; the Turks are drowned.

i.e., Montano How does my old acquaintance° of this isle?

received —Honey, you shall be well desired° in Cyprus;

I have found great love amongst them. O my sweet,

I prattle out of fashion, [6] and I dote   205

In mine own comforts. [7]—I prithee, good Iago,

unload Go to the bay and disembark° my coffers.

captain Bring thou the master° to the citadel.

1 *Do thou meet me*

I.e., meet me; "do thou" and "do you" were regularly used to introduce an imperative in early modern English, not a question (as also in line 264).

2 *court of guard*

Guardhouse or watchpost

3 *Lay thy finger thus*

I.e., lay your finger on your lips (a gesture to be silent).

4 *prating*

Talking like a fool

5 *sympathy in years*

Closeness in age

6 *required conveniences*

Necessary points of similarity

7 *heave the gorge*

Vomit

8 *Very nature*

Nature itself

9 *voluble*

The word can mean both "glib" and "inconstant"

He is a good one, and his worthiness
Does challenge° much respect.—Come, Desdemona,   210
Once more, well met at Cyprus.

                 Othello, **Desdemona**, [*and attendants*] *exit.*

Iago

[*calling to an attendant*] Do thou meet me [1] presently at the
harbor. [*to* **Roderigo**] Come hither. If thou be'st valiant,
as they say base men being in love have then a nobility in
their natures more than is native° to them, list° me.   215
The lieutenant tonight watches° on the court of guard. [2]
First, I must tell thee this: Desdemona is directly° in
love with him. *Iago says Desd. is in*

Roderigo *love with Cassio*

With him? Why, 'tis not possible.

Iago

Lay thy finger thus, [3] and let thy soul be instructed: mark   220
me with what violence° she first loved the Moor, but°
for bragging and telling her fantastical lies. To love
him still for prating? [4] Let not thy discreet° heart think
it. Her eye must be fed, and what delight shall she have
to look on the devil? When the blood° is made dull   225
with the act of sport,° there should be, again to inflame
it, and to give satiety° a fresh appetite, loveliness in
favor,° sympathy in years, [5] manners and beauties—all
which the Moor is defective in. Now for want° of these
required conveniences, [6] her delicate tenderness° will   230
find itself abused,° begin to heave the gorge, [7] disrelish°
and abhor the Moor. Very nature [8] will instruct her in it
and compel her to some second choice. Now, sir, this
granted—as it is a most pregnant° and unforced° position
—who stands so eminent in the degree of this fortune   235
as Cassio does? A knave very voluble, [9] no further
conscionable than in putting on the mere form of civil

Margin glosses (left column):
command
natural / listen to
stands watch
clearly
suddenness / merely
discerning
desire
lovemaking
exhausted satisfaction
appearance
lack
youthfulness
cheated / dislike
obvious / natural

1 *no further conscionable than in putting on the mere form of civil and humane seeming, for the better compass of his salt and most hidden loose affection*
  With no more conscience than (it takes) to adopt the mere appearance of refinement and courtesy, the better to achieve his secret lecherous desires

2 *that has an eye can stamp and counterfeit advantages, though true advantage never present itself*
  Who has the vision to create dishonest opportunities when no honest ones present themselves

3 *Blessed fig's-end*
  I.e., *blessed* my foot; don't be ridiculous (but see 1.3.317 and note).

4 *The wine she drinks is made of grapes.*
  I.e., she is no better than anyone else.

5 *an index and obscure prologue to the history of lust and foul thoughts*
  Iago compares the courtly intimacies exchanged between Cassio and Desdemona to the table of contents (*index*) and preface of a dirty book, which leads the way to a lustful and lascivious *history* (tale).

6 *hard at hand*
  A moment later

7 *master and main exercise*
  Paramount and principal activity

[Handwritten note:] Lines 220-246 Iago basically says that Desdemona's loves will not last forever and she needs a very handsome guy because Othello is old and ugly and he is trying to get Rodrigo to figh Cassio

and humane seeming, for the better compass of his
salt and most hidden loose affection.[1] Why none,
slippery / cunning why none! A slipper° and subtle° knave, a finder of   240
opportunity occasion,° that has an eye can stamp and counterfeit
advantages, though true advantage never present
itself.[2] A devilish knave. Besides, the knave is handsome, young, and hath all those requisites in him
inexperienced / for that folly and green° minds look after.° A pestilent,   245
complete knave, and the woman hath found him
already.

Roderigo

I cannot believe that in her. She's full of most blessed
condition.

Iago

Blessed fig's-end![3] The wine she drinks is made of grapes.[4]   250
If she had been blessed, she would never have loved
the Moor. Blessed pudding! Didst thou not see her
play paddle° with the palm of his hand? Didst not mark that?

Roderigo

Yes, that I did; but that was but courtesy.

Iago

Lechery, by this hand, an index and obscure prologue   255
to the history of lust and foul thoughts![5] They met so
near with their lips that their breaths embraced
together. Villainous thoughts, Roderigo! When these
intimacies / point mutualities° so marshal° the way, hard at hand[6] comes
i.e., sexual the master and main exercise,[7] th' incorporate°   260
conclusion. Pish! But, sir, be you ruled by me. I have
brought you from Venice. Watch you tonight. For the
command, I'll lay 't upon you. Cassio knows you not.
I'll not be far from you. Do you find some occasion
to anger Cassio, either by speaking too loud, or   265

Iago says that the two are soon
to be lovers

1   *whose qualification shall come into no*
    true taste again but by the displanting of
    Cassio
    Who will not behave normally
    again unless Cassio is removed
    from his office.

2   *bring it to any opportunity*
    Arrange it somehow

3   *A most dear husband*
    ***Dear* could mean "expensive," so**
    Iago's observation here is
    characteristically double edged:
    Othello may prove either a
    "precious" husband or a "costly"
    one.

disparaging / whatever tainting° his discipline, or from what° other course you
offer please which the time shall more favorably minister.°

Roderigo

Well.

Iago

anger / perhaps Sir, he's rash and very sudden in choler,° and haply°
may strike at you. Provoke him that he may, for even
i.e., the people / riot out of that will I cause these° of Cyprus to mutiny,°   270
whose qualification shall come into no true taste again
but by the displanting of Cassio.[1] So shall you have a
shorter journey to your desires by the means I shall
advance / i.e., Cassio then have to prefer° them, and the impediment° most   275
most profitably removed, without the which there
would be were° no expectation of our prosperity.

Roderigo

I will do this, if you can bring it to any opportunity.[2]

Iago

guarantee I warrant° thee. Meet me by and by at the citadel. I must
fetch his necessaries ashore. Farewell.   280

Roderigo

Adieu.   *He exits.*

Iago

That Cassio loves her, I do well believe 't.
likely / plausibility That she loves him, 'tis apt° and of great credit.°
in spite of the fact The Moor—howbeit° that I endure him not—
Is of a constant, loving, noble nature,   285
And I dare think he'll prove to Desdemona
A most dear husband.[3] Now, I do love her too,
mere / very likely Not out of absolute° lust—though peradventure°
answerable I stand accountant° for as great a sin—

1   *the lusty Moor*

Othello shows no sign of being
excessively *lusty* or *lascivious*
(1.1.127). In fact he describes
himself as one in whom the *young
affects* (i.e., youthful passions) are
defunct (1.3.262–63), but here Iago
draws upon the received wisdom
of the day, which described Moors
as lustful, intemperate, and easily
made jealous. (See LONGER NOTE on
page 365.)

2   *leaped into my seat*

I.e., cuckolded me (by sleeping
with Emilia)

3   *judgment cannot cure*

No amount of reason can remedy

4   *whom I trace / For his quick hunting*

Whose steps I closely follow to
keep him in lively pursuit (of
Desdemona)

5   *stand the putting on*

Do what I have urged him to do

6   *on the hip*

Ready to fall

7   *Abuse him to the Moor in the rank garb*

Slander him in front of Othello for
being lecherous (*rank*)

8   *I fear Cassio with my night-cap too*

I think that Cassio, too, has been
sleeping with my wife.

9   *to madness*

I.e., to the point of driving Othello
mad

10   *'Tis here, but yet confused*

The idea is in my head, but not yet
fully worked out.

feed	But partly led to diet° my revenge, 290
	For that I do suspect the lusty Moor [1]
of which	Hath leaped into my seat, [2] the thought whereof°
insides	Doth, like a poisonous mineral, gnaw my in'ards,°
	And nothing can or shall content my soul
	Till I am evened with him, wife for wife, 295
	Or, failing so, yet that I put the Moor
	At least into a jealousy so strong
	That judgment cannot cure. [3] Which thing to do,
i.e., Roderigo	If this poor trash° of Venice, whom I trace
	For his quick hunting, [4] stand the putting on, [5] 300
	I'll have our Michael Cassio on the hip, [6]
	Abuse him to the Moor in the rank garb [7]
	(For I fear Cassio with my night-cap too), [8]
	Make the Moor thank me, love me, and reward me
	For making him egregiously an ass 305
plotting	And practicing° upon his peace and quiet
	Even to madness. [9] 'Tis here, but yet confused; [10]
	Knavery's plain face is never seen till used. *He exits.*

He will have power over Othello
and Cassio and he feels
as if Cassio has seduced
his wife as well

1   *triumph*
    Public celebration

2   *So much was his pleasure should be*
    proclaimed.
    It was this that he wished to have
    announced.

3   *full liberty of feasting*
    Full freedom to feast

Act 2, Scene 2

*Enter **Othello**'s **Herald**, with a proclamation.*

Herald

wish   [*reads*] "It is Othello's pleasure,° our noble and valiant General,

on account of / relating to   that, upon° certain tidings now arrived importing°

total   the mere° perdition of the Turkish fleet, every man put

himself into triumph: [1] some to dance, some to make

rank   bonfires, each man to what sport and revels his addition°   5

leads him. For besides these beneficial news, it is the

Othello's   celebration of his° nuptial." So much was his pleasure

pantries and kitchens   should be proclaimed. [2] All offices° are open, and there is

full liberty of feasting [3] from this present hour of five till

struck   the bell have told° eleven. Heaven bless the isle of Cyprus   10

and our noble General Othello!   *He exits.*

1   *look you to*

    Keep an eye on

2   *outsport discretion*

    Revel and celebrate excessively

3   *she is sport for Jove*

    She is a sexual plaything worthy of Jove (king of the Roman gods and famous for his amorous dalliances with mortals)

Act 2, Scene 3

*Enter **Othello**, **Desdemona**, **Cassio**, and attendants.*

Othello

Good Michael, look you to[1] the guard tonight.

restraint   Let's teach ourselves that honorable stop°

Not to outsport discretion.[2]

Cassio

Iago hath direction what to do,

But, notwithstanding, with my personal eye

Will I look to 't.

Othello

             Iago is most honest.

earliest opportunity   Michael, good night. Tomorrow with your earliest°

Let me have speech with you.—Come, my dear love,

i.e., marriage / enjoyments   The purchase° made, the fruits° are to ensue;

That profit's yet to come 'tween me and you.   10

Good night.

         [**Othello**, **Desdemona**, *and attendants*] *exit.*

        *Enter **Iago**.*

Cassio

must go   Welcome, Iago. We must° to the watch.

Iago

Not this hour, lieutenant; 'tis not yet ten o' th' clock.

released   Our General cast° us thus early for the love of his Desde-

mona—who let us not therefore blame. He hath not   15

yet made wanton the night with her, and she is sport

for Jove.[3]

Cassio

She's a most exquisite lady.

[handwritten annotations:]

tells Cassio and Iago to keep watch   5

Cassio says that Desdemona is beautiful

139

1   *I'll warrant her, full of game*
    **I guarantee you that she has a
    strong sexual appetite.**

2   *alarum*
    **Incitement (literally "a call
    to arms")**

Iago

And, I'll warrant her, full of game. [1]

Cassio

young Indeed, she's a most fresh° and delicate creature.

Iago

invitation What an eye she has! Methinks it sounds a parley° to
lustful thoughts provocation.°

Cassio

altogether An inviting eye, and yet methinks right° modest

Iago

And when she speaks, is it not an alarum [2] to love?

Cassio

She is indeed perfection. 25

Iago

Well, happiness to their sheets! Come, lieutenant, I
jug/outside/pair have a stoup° of wine, and here without° are a brace°
gladly/drink of Cyprus gallants that would fain° have a measure°
to the health of black Othello.

Cassio

unfortunate Not tonight, good Iago. I have very poor and unhappy° 30
social convention brains for drinking. I could well wish courtesy° would
invent some other custom of entertainment.

Iago

Oh, they are our friends. But one cup. I'll drink for you.

Cassio

skillfully I have drunk but one cup tonight, and that was craftily°
diluted/transformation qualified° too, and behold what innovation° it makes 35
unlucky here. I am infortunate° in the infirmity and dare not
task my weakness with any more.

Iago

What, man, 'tis a night of revels! The gallants desire it.

Cassio

Where are they?

1   *caroused / Potations pottle-deep*

    I.e., downed many large drinks (in
    Desdemona's name). A pottle was
    a two-quart vessel, so *pottle-deep*
    means "to the bottom of a large
    jug."

2   *hold their honors in a wary distance*

    Jealously guard their honor

3   *If consequence do but approve my dream*

    If the outcome only matches my
    hopes

Iago

Here at the door. I pray you call them in.   40

Cassio

troubles   I'll do 't, but it dislikes° me.   *He exits.*

Iago Cassio still has doubts

If I can fasten but one cup upon him

With that which he hath drunk tonight already,

He'll be as full of quarrel and offense

As my young mistress' dog. Now my sick fool Roderigo,   45

Whom love hath turned almost the wrong side out,

To Desdemona hath tonight caroused   In this

i.e., for Cassio   Potations pottle-deep, [1] and he's to watch.°   his plan

others / proud   Three else° of Cyprus, noble, swelling° spirits   is to

That hold their honors in a wary distance, [2]   have Cassio

embodiments   The very elements° of this warlike isle,   drunk and

Have I tonight flustered with flowing cups,   fight

And they watch too. Now, 'mongst this flock of drunkards

Am I to put our Cassio in some action   Rodrigo

That may offend the isle. But here they come.   55

*Enter **Cassio**, **Montano**, and gentlemen, [followed by servants].*

If consequence do but approve my dream, [3]

the current   My boat sails freely, both with wind and stream.°

Cassio

large drink   'Fore God, they have given me a rouse° already.

Montano

Good faith, a little one, not past a pint,

As I am a soldier.   60

Iago

Some wine, ho!

small drinking can   [*sings*] And let me the cannikin° clink, clink,

And let me the cannikin clink.

1   *sweats not to overthrow*

Has no difficulty outdoing

2   *do you justice*

I.e., match you in drinking

3   *King Stephen was and-a worthy peer . . .*

Iago's song is a version of a ballad called either "Bell my Wife" or "Take Your Old Cloak About Thee." This song, which would have been well known when Shakespeare wrote, consists of a dialogue between a man named Bell and his wife. It is the middle of a harsh winter, and she wants him to put on his old cloak to go out and rescue their cow. He says he will give up the life of a poor farmer and seek preferment at court, but she counsels him against folly, pride, and ambition. The verse sung by Iago invokes a sentiment of scorn for social climbers and those who are not satisfied with their lot in life. At the same time, it expresses discontent with a social hierarchy that keeps some men down while others live in luxury and excess. The song, thus, glances at the class tensions that exist between the earthy Iago and the genteel Cassio.

A soldier's a man,

brief period Oh, man's life's but a span.° 65

Why then let a soldier drink.

Some wine, boys!

Cassio

'Fore God, an excellent song.

Iago *where Iago learned songs*

I learned it in England, where indeed they are most

drinking potent in potting.° Your Dane, your German, and your 70

swag-bellied Hollander—Drink, ho!—are nothing to

your English.

Cassio

Is your Englishman so exquisite in his drinking?

Iago

Why, he drinks you with facility your Dane dead drunk.

German He sweats not to overthrow[1] your Almain.° He gives 75

jug your Hollander a vomit ere the next pottle° can be filled.

Cassio *says Englishmen drink very heavy*

To the health of our General!

Montano

I am for it, lieutenant, and I'll do you justice.[2]

Iago

O sweet England!

[*sings*] King Stephen was and-a worthy peer;[3] 80

five-shilling coin His breeches cost him but a crown.°

expensive He held them sixpence all too dear,°

loon; worthless idiot With that he called the tailor lown.°

man He was a wight° of high renown,

And thou art but of low degree. 85

extravagance 'Tis pride° that pulls the country down,

old And take thine auld° cloak about thee.

Some wine, ho!

Iago sings

1   *and there be souls must not be saved*

    Cassio's platitudinous theology is
    an indication of his drunkenness,
    which grows more apparent even
    as he denies it (see lines 103 and
    106–107)

2   *platform*

    Elevated area for mounted guns or
    a cannon

Cassio

'Fore God, this is a more exquisite song than the other.

Iago

Will you hear 't again? 90

Cassio

rank No, for I hold him to be unworthy of his place° that does those things. Well, God's above all, and there be souls must be saved, and there be souls must not be saved. [1]

Iago

God determines where

It's true, good lieutenant. *people go*

Cassio

For mine own part, no offence to the General nor any 95

high status man of quality,° I hope to be saved. *Cassio wants*

Iago *to go to heaven*

And so do I too, lieutenant.

Cassio

Ay, but, by your leave, not before me. The lieutenant is to be saved before the ancient. Let's have no more of this; let's to our affairs. God forgive us our sins! 100 Gentlemen, let's look to our business. Do not think, gentlemen, I am drunk. This is my ancient, this is my right hand, and this is my left. I am not drunk now. I can stand well enough, and I speak well enough.

Gentlemen *Tells Iago not to die*

Excellent well! *and asks God for* 105

Cassio *forgiveness*

Why, very well then. You must not think then that I am drunk. *He exits.*

Montano

To th' platform, [2] masters. Come; let's set the watch.

[*The* **Gentlemen** *exit.*]

1   *just equinox*

    Exact counterbalance

2   *On some odd time of his infirmity*

    **During some moment when his
weakness has surfaced**

3   *watch the horologe a double set*

    Stay awake twice round the clock

4   *rock not his cradle*

    Does not put him to sleep

5   *put in mind*

    Warned

6   *Should hazard such a place as his own
second / With one of an ingraft infirmity*

    **Should risk so important a
position as second-in-command
on a man (like Cassio) with such an
ingrained weakness**

Iago

You see this fellow that is gone before?   *Iago says*
He is a soldier fit to stand by Caesar   *Cassio is*[110] *a*
And give direction. And do but see his vice;   *good*
'Tis to his virtue a just equinox,[1]   *soldier, but*
about   The one as long as th' other. 'Tis pity of° him.   *he has*
I fear the trust Othello puts him in   *a flaw which*
On some odd time of his infirmity[2]   *will be our*[115]
Will shake this island.   *downfall*

Montano

i.e., drunk   But is he often thus?°

Iago

'Tis evermore his prologue to his sleep.
He'll watch the horologe a double set[3]   *Iago says*
If drink rock not his cradle.[4]   *that Cassio*
Montano   *drinks*
                            It were well   *often*[120]
The General were put in mind[5] of it.
Perhaps he sees it not, or his good nature
Prizes the virtue that appears in Cassio
And looks not on his evils. Is not this true?

                    Enter **Roderigo**.

Iago

[*aside to* **Roderigo**] How now, Roderigo?
I pray you, after the lieutenant, go!   125

                                    [**Roderigo** *exits.*]

Montano

And 'tis great pity that the noble Moor
Should hazard such a place as his own second
With one of an ingraft infirmity.[6]
It were an honest action to say so

1 *Not I, for this fair island.*

I.e., I wouldn't do it, even in
exchange for the island of Cyprus
itself.

2 *into a twiggen bottle*

I.e., so the welts on his body
resemble the wicker-work
encasing a bottle

3 *mazzard*

Noggin (the word is slang
for "head")

4 *cry a mutiny*

Yell "Riot!"

To the Moor.

Iago

                    Not I, for this fair island. [1]   130

I do love Cassio well and would do much

To cure him of this evil—

                                                    [*Cry within*]

                    But, hark! What noise?

                    Enter **Cassio**, *pursuing* **Roderigo**.

Cassio

Zounds! You rogue! You rascal!

Montano

What's the matter, lieutenant?

Cassio

A knave teach me my duty? I'll beat the knave into a   135

twiggen bottle. [2]

Roderigo

Beat me?

Cassio

speak idly Dost thou prate,° rogue? [*strikes him*]

Montano

stop Nay, good lieutenant! I pray you, sir, hold° your hand.

Cassio

Let me go, sir, or I'll knock you o'er the mazzard. [3]   140

Montano

Come, come, you're drunk.

Cassio

Drunk?   [*They fight.*]

Iago

[*aside to* **Roderigo**] Away, I say; go out and cry a mutiny. [4]

                                           [**Roderigo** *exits.*]

1   *Here's a goodly watch indeed!*
    I.e., this is a fine way to stand
    guard!

2   *place of sense*
    Both Quarto and Folio have it this
    way, but "sense of place" may
    indeed be the correct reading here.

3   *Are we turned Turks and to ourselves do*
    that / Which Heaven hath forbid the
    Ottomites?
    During the early modern period,
    the word *Turk* meant not only a
    native of Turkey or a subject of the
    Ottoman Empire, but also it was
    the word used to describe a
    person who today would be called
    a Muslim. Literally, *to turn Turk*
    meant to convert, or "turn," from
    Christianity to Islam, something
    that was occurring frequently in
    the Mediterranean region. At the
    time that Shakespeare wrote
    Othello, there were many hundreds
    (and by the 1620s, thousands) of
    Europeans who had converted to
    Islam and joined the Muslim
    communities of North Africa,
    becoming what were known as
    renegadoes. Beyond its reference to
    religious conversion, however, *to*
    turn Turk had a range of figurative
    meanings, including "turning" as
    sexual transgression and also a

more general sense of betrayal
and treachery. Thus Othello's
questions have several
implications: first, that Heaven
has providentially intervened to
protect the Christian fleet while
destroying the Turkish navy;
second, that the Turk's religious
precepts prohibited drinking and
brawling (the Ottoman military
was envied throughout Europe for
its disciplined troops, who—
unlike European armies—
conducted their campaigns
without the accompaniment of
liquor and prostitutes); and third,
that Christian order has turned to
un-Christian, "barbarous"
violence.

4   *carve*
    Act (suggesting most immediately
    "draw his sword")

5   *Holds his soul light*
    Values his life cheaply

6   *upon his motion*
    The moment he moves

7   *propriety*
    Proper state (i.e., of peace)

Nay, good lieutenant! God's will, gentlemen—
Help, ho!—Lieutenant—sir—Montano—   145
Help, masters!—Here's a goodly watch indeed![1]

[bell rings]

alarm bell / The devil Who's that which rings the bell?°—Diablo,° ho!
awaken The town will rise.° —God's will, lieutenant,
You'll be ashamed forever.

Enter **Othello** *and attendants.*

Othello
What is the matter here?
Montano
                                          Zounds, I bleed still;   150
I am hurt to th' death. He dies!   [*attacks* **Cassio**]
Othello
Stop   Hold,° for your lives!
Iago
Hold, ho! Lieutenant—sir—Montano—gentlemen,
Have you forgot all place of sense[2] and duty?
Hold! The General speaks to you. Hold, for shame!
Othello
Why, how now, ho! From whence ariseth this?   155
Are we turned Turks and to ourselves do that
Which Heaven hath forbid the Ottomites?[3]
aside For Christian shame, put by° this barbarous brawl.
He that stirs next, to carve[4] for his own rage,
Holds his soul light;[5] he dies upon his motion.[6]   160
Silence that dreadful bell; it frights the isle
From her propriety.[7] What is the matter, masters?
Honest Iago, that looks dead with grieving,
command Speak: who began this? On thy love, I charge° thee.

1   *friends all*

I.e., they were all friends

2   *In quarter and in terms like bride and groom / Divesting them for bed*

In their relations with one another and in their language, which was as affectionate as a bride and groom getting ready for bed

3   *As if some planet had unwitted men*

According to Elizabethan scientific belief, the planets had the power to induce madness.

4   *peevish odds*

Senseless quarrel

5   *And would in action glorious I had lost / Those legs that brought me to a part of it*

And I wish that I'd lost in some honorable battle the legs that brought me to take part in this brawl.

6   *are thus forgot*

Have forgotten yourself in this fashion

7   *your name is great / In mouths of wisest censure*

Your name is highly praised by men of the most prudent judgment.

8   *hurt to danger*

Seriously wounded

9   *spare speech*

Refrain from trying to talk

10   *something now offends me*

Now causes me some pain

11   *Nor know I aught / By me that's said or done amiss this night*

Nor do I know that I have said or done anything wrong tonight

Iago

only   I do not know: friends all, [1] but° now, even now,   165

In quarter and in terms like bride and groom

Divesting them for bed. [2] And then, but now,

As if some planet had unwitted men, [3]

one another's   Swords out and tilting one at other's° breasts

combat / identify   In opposition° bloody. I cannot speak°   170

Any beginning to this peevish odds, [4]

wish that   And would° in action glorious I had lost

Those legs that brought me to a part of it. [5]

Othello

How comes it, Michael, you are thus forgot? [6]

Cassio

I pray you pardon me; I cannot speak.   175

Othello

accustomed to   Worthy Montano, you were wont° be civil.

self-restraint   The gravity and stillness° of your youth

The world hath noted, and your name is great

In mouths of wisest censure. [7] What's the matter

undo   That you unlace° your reputation thus   180

reputation   And spend your rich opinion° for the name

Of a night-brawler? Give me answer to it.

Montano

Worthy Othello, I am hurt to danger. [8]

Your officer Iago can inform you,

While I spare speech, [9] which something now offends

me, [10]   185

Of all that I do know. Nor know I aught

By me that's said or done amiss this night, [11]

care for one's self   Unless self-charity° be sometimes a vice,

And to defend ourselves it be a sin

When violence assails us.

1 *My blood begins my safer guides to rule, /*
   And passion, having my best judgment
   collied, / Assays to lead the way

   Shakespeare's contemporaries
   believed that human passions and
   emotions were produced by a
   balance or imbalance of
   substances in the body called
   humors. Blood, along with phlegm,
   yellow bile, and black bile, was one
   of the four basic components
   believed to make up this balance
   that produced an individual's
   temperament or emotional
   condition. Blood was associated
   with both lust and anger. In her
   book *Humoring the Body: Emotions
   and the Shakespearean Stage,* Gail
   Kern Paster points out that the
   collying of Othello's blood is not
   just a metaphor: Othello's "heart's
   blood is heating in anger, and the
   sooty excrements formed in the
   central bodily furnace ascend to
   the brain to darken the rational
   faculties situated there" (66).
   Later, when Othello is driven to cry
   out *Oh, blood, blood, blood!* (3.3.455),
   he refers both to his own wrath and
   to Cassio and Desdemona's
   supposed lustfulness.

2 *sink in*

   Be ruined by

3 *twinned with me, both at a birth*

   Been born my twin, both from a
   single delivery

4 *in a town of war*

   In a town full of billeted soldiers
   (or merely "a town ready for war")

5 *on the court and guard of safety*

   While on the watch that is
   supposed to keep the peace

6 *If partially affined or leagued in office*

   I.e., if because you are partial
   (toward Cassio) or feel some
   loyalty to him as a fellow officer

7 *Touch me not so near.*

   I.e., do not offend my honor.

8 *Shall nothing wrong him*

   Will do him no harm

9 *entreats his pause*

   Begs him to stop

Othello

Now, by Heaven,　　　　　190

anger / faculties　My blood° begins my safer guides° to rule,

obscured　And passion, having my best judgment collied,°

Attempts　Assays° to lead the way.¹ Zounds, if I stir,

Or do but lift this arm, the best of you

Shall sink in² my rebuke. Give me to know　　195

brawl　How this foul rout° began, who set it on,

proved guilty　And he that is approved° in this offence,

Though he had twinned with me, both at a birth,³

my favor　Shall lose me.° What, in a town of war⁴

Still　Yet° wild, the people's hearts brimful of fear,　200

carry on　To manage° private and domestic quarrel?

In night, and on the court and guard of safety?⁵

'Tis monstrous. Iago, who began 't?

Montano

If partially affined or leagued in office⁶

Thou dost deliver more or less than truth,　　205

Thou art no soldier.

Iago

Touch me not so near.⁷

I had rather have this tongue cut from my mouth

Than that　Than° it should do offence to Michael Cassio,

that to　Yet I persuade myself to° speak the truth

Shall nothing wrong him.⁸ This it is, General:　210

comversation　Montano and myself being in speech,°

There comes a fellow crying out for help

And Cassio following him with determined sword

use　To execute° upon him. Sir, this gentleman

Steps in to Cassio and entreats his pause.⁹　215

I myself　Myself° the crying fellow did pursue,

Lest by his clamor—as it so fell out—

into　The town might fall in° fright. He, swift of foot,

[Handwritten margin note: In this Montano says that Iago was talking bad about Cassio and Iago denies it]

1 *For that*
   Because

2 *high in oath*
   Cursing angrily

3 *raised up*
   Awakened

4 *be your surgeon*
   **See to it that you are looked after
   (or perhaps literally, "dress your
   wounds myself")**

quickly   Outran my purpose, and I returned then rather°

For that[1] I heard the clink and fall of swords

And Cassio high in oath,[2] which till tonight

I ne'er might say before. When I came back—

For this was brief—I found them close together

At blow and thrust, even as again they were

When you yourself did part them.

More of this matter cannot I report.

But men are men: the best sometimes forget.

i.e., Montano   Though Cassio did some little wrong to him,°

As men in rage strike those that wish them best,

Yet surely Cassio, I believe, received

insult   From him that fled some strange indignity°

Ignore   Which patience could not pass.°

Othello

                        I know, Iago,

minimize   Thy honesty and love doth mince° this matter,

Making it light to Cassio. Cassio, I love thee,

But never more be officer of mine.

          Enter **Desdemona**, *attended.*

Look if my gentle love be not raised up![3]

I'll make thee an example.

Desdemona

What is the matter, dear?

Othello

sweetheart   All's well, sweeting,°

Come away to bed.—[*to* **Montano**] Sir, for your hurts,

Myself will be your surgeon.[4] Lead him off.

                       [**Montano** *is taken away.*]

Iago, look with care about the town

And silence those whom this vile brawl distracted.

[Handwritten margin notes:]

He says his version of what had just happened and says that Cassio was going to kill (line 220, 225, 230)

Othello says that Cassio will not be an officer again (line 235)

Iago will calm down public

1   *recover the General*

    I.e., get back into Othello's favor

2   *cast in his mood*

    Dismissed in a fit of anger

3   *in policy*

    For political considerations

4   *beat his offenseless dog to affright an imperious lion*

    From the proverbial expression "Beat the dog in front of the lion," i.e., punish the weak to impress or intimidate the strong.

5   *discourse fustian*

    Talk nonsensically

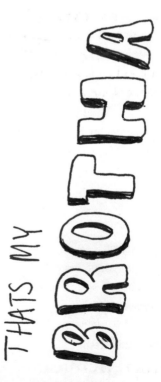

Come, Desdemona; 'tis the soldiers' life
To have their balmy slumbers waked with strife.

[*All except* **Iago** *and* **Cassio**] *exit.*

Iago

What, are you hurt, lieutenant?   245

Cassio

Ay, past all surgery.

[handwritten: Cassio is beyond healing and Iag is pretending to care]

Iago

Marry, God forbid!

Cassio

Reputation, reputation, reputation! Oh, I have lost
my reputation! I have lost the immortal part of
myself, and what remains is bestial. My reputation,   250
Iago, my reputation!

Iago

[handwritten left margin: Cassio is sad he lost his rep. which is his most ___ part of himself]

As I am an honest man, I had thought you had received
some bodily wound. There is more sense° in that than
in reputation. Reputation is an idle° and most false
imposition,° oft got without merit and lost without
deserving. You have lost no reputation at all unless you
repute yourself such a loser. What, man, there are
more ways to recover the General¹ again. You are but
now cast in his mood,² a punishment more in policy³
than in malice, even so as one would beat his offense-   260
less dog to affright an imperious lion.⁴ Sue° to him
again, and he's yours.

[margin glosses: feeling / useless / burden / appeal]

[handwritten right margin: Iago says that his rep. is not import.]

Cassio

I will rather sue to be despised than to deceive so good a
commander with so slight, so drunken, and so indiscreet
an officer. Drunk? And speak parrot?° And squabble?   265
Swagger? Swear? And discourse fustian⁵ with one's
own shadow? O thou invisible spirit of wine, if thou
hast no name to be known by, let us call thee devil!

[margin gloss: i.e., mindlessly]

[handwritten bottom: Cassio would rather Othello to ask him to be hated rather than ask for his job]

1 *Hydra*

In Greek mythology, a monster
with many heads (and therefore
many mouths), destroyed by
Hercules, despite the fact that it
could grow a new head when one
was cut off.

SO IF YOU CROSSIN HIM YOU

Iago

Who   What° was he that you followed with your sword? What
had he done to you?   270

Cassio

I know not.

Iago

Is't possible?

Cassio

> *cassio wonders wyhy men drink until they are like animals*

I remember a mass of things, but nothing distinctly—a

why   quarrel, but nothing wherefore.° O God, that men
should put an enemy in their mouths to steal away their   275

pleasure   brains! That we should, with joy, pleasance,° revel, and
applause, transform ourselves into beasts!

Iago

Why, but you are now well enough. How came you thus
recovered?

Cassio

It hath pleased the devil drunkenness to give place to   280

fault   the devil wrath. One unperfectness° shows me

thoroughly   another, to make me frankly° despise myself.

Iago

moralizer   Come; you are too severe a moraler.° As the time, the
place, and the condition of this country stands, I

happened   could heartily wish this had not befallen,° but since it is   285
as it is, mend it for your own good.

Cassio

> *Iago says why are u being so hard on yourself*

I will ask him for my place again; he shall tell me I am a
drunkard. Had I as many mouths as Hydra,[1] such an

close   answer would stop° them all. To be now a sensible

immediately after   man, by and by a fool, and presently° a beast! Oh,   290

immoderate   strange! Every inordinate° cup is unblessed, and the

content   ingredient° is a devil.

1   *I think you think I love you*

   I think you know I am your friend

2   *to the contemplation, mark, and*
   denotement of her parts and graces

   To the meditation upon,
   observation, and description of her
   qualities and accomplishments

3   *splinter*

   Apply a splint

4   *I am desperate of my fortunes if they*
   check me.

   My cause is lost if I am stopped now.

Iago

[handwritten: Iago says to Cassio that he is his friend]

congenial Come, come; good wine is a good, familiar° creature, if
it be well used. Exclaim no more against it. And, good
lieutenant, I think you think I love you. [1] 295

Cassio

proved I have well approved° it, sir. I, drunk!

Iago

some You or any man living may be drunk at a° time, man. I
tell you what you shall do. Our General's wife is now
the General. I may say so in this respect, for that he hath
devoted and given up himself to the contemplation, 300
mark, and denotement of her parts and graces. [2] Con-
unreservedly fess yourself freely° to her; importune her help to put
generous you in your place again. She is of so free,° so kind, so
eager apt,° so blessed a disposition, she holds it a vice in her
goodness not to do more than she is requested. This 305
broken joint between you and her husband entreat her
wager to splinter, [3] and, my fortunes against any lay° worth
fracture naming, this crack° of your love shall grow stronger
than it was before.

[handwritten: Iago tells Cassio that he needs to ask Desdemona for his position back]

Cassio

You advise me well.

[handwritten: Iago says that he trust him]

Iago

I protest, in the sincerity of love and honest kindness. 310

Cassio

early I think it freely, and betimes° in the morning I will
intervene beseech the virtuous Desdemona to undertake° for me
I am desperate of my fortunes if they check me. [4]

Iago

You are in the right. Good night, lieutenant; I must to 315
the watch.

Cassio

Good night, honest Iago. **Cassio** *exits.*

1 *She's framed as fruitful / As the free
  elements.*

  She was created to be as generous
  as the very substances from which
  the natural world is made.

2 *her appetite*

  Either (1) his desire for her; or (2)
  her desire to control him (as Iago
  imagines)

3 *put on*

  Encourage

4 *heavenly shows*

  The appearance of virtue

5 *repeals him*

  Pleads for his (Cassio's)
  reinstatement

6 *So will I turn her virtue into pitch*

  I.e., I will use Desdemona's
  goodness against her. *Pitch* is a
  foul, black, sticky substance
  like tar.

Iago

And what's he, then, that says I play the villain,

When this advice is free I give and honest,

Reasonable   Probal° to thinking, and indeed the course   320

To win the Moor again? For 'tis most easy

compliant / persuade   Th' inclining° Desdemona to subdue°

request   In any honest suit.° She's framed as fruitful

As the free elements. ¹ And then for her

To win the Moor, were 't to renounce his baptism,   325

signs   All seals° and symbols of redeemèd sin,

chained   His soul is so enfettered° to her love,

pleases   That she may make, unmake, do what she list,°

Even as her appetite² shall play the god

faculties   With his weak function.° How am I then a villain   330

To counsel Cassio to this parallel course,

Directly to his good? Divinity of Hell!

When devils will the blackest sins put on,³

They do suggest at first with heavenly shows,⁴

while / i.e., Cassio   As I do now. For whiles° this honest fool°   335

Urges   Plies° Desdemona to repair his fortune,

And she for him pleads strongly to the Moor,

I'll pour this pestilence into his ear,

That she repeals him⁵ for her body's lust;

And by how much she strives to do him good   340

She shall undo her credit with the Moor.

So will I turn her virtue into pitch⁶

And out of her own goodness make the net

That shall enmesh them all.

Enter **Roderigo**.

How now, Roderigo!

1   *I do follow here in the chase not like a
    hound that hunts, but one that fills up
    the cry.*

    **Roderigo compares himself to a
    dog that brings up the rear in a
    hunt, rather than one that
    aggressively tracks the quarry. (To
    fill up the cry means "to increase the
    volume of the dogs' baying," i.e.,
    to be merely one of the pack.)**

2   *I shall have so much experience for my
    pains*

    **I'll get nothing for my efforts but
    the experience itself**

3   *Though other things grow fair against
    the sun, / Yet fruits that blossom first will
    first be ripe.*

    **I.e., although our plans for
    winning Desdemona are growing
    slowly, our initial plan to get rid of
    Cassio has already borne fruit.**

4   *Content thyself*

    Be patient

5   *Dull not device by coldness and delay*

    **Do not let my plot lose its edge
    through lack of commitment or
    procrastination.**

NOW I BALL LIKE KOBE

Roderigo

I do follow here in the chase not like a hound that hunts,   345

but one that fills up the cry. [1] My money is almost

spent, I have been tonight exceedingly well cudgeled,

outcome   and I think the issue° will be I shall have so much

experience for my pains, [2] and so, with no money at all

and a little more wit, return again to Venice.   350

Iago

How poor are they that have not patience!

What wound did ever heal but by degrees?

Thou know'st we work by wit and not by witchcraft,

slowly moving   And wit depends on dilatory° time.

Does't not go well? Cassio hath beaten thee,   355

got rid of   And thou, by that small hurt, hath cashiered° Cassio.

exposed to   Though other things grow fair against° the sun,

Yet fruits that blossom first will first be ripe. [3]

Content thyself [4] awhile. By th' Mass, 'tis morning.

Pleasure and action make the hours seem short.   360

housed   Retire thee; go where thou art billeted.°

Away, I say; thou shalt know more hereafter.

Nay, get thee gone.   **Roderigo** *exits.*

Two things are to be done:

plead   My wife must move° for Cassio to her mistress.

on the job   I'll set her on.°   365

Myself, the while, to draw the Moor apart

at the exact moment   And bring him jump° when he may Cassio find

Soliciting his wife. Ay, that's the way;

Dull not device by coldness and delay. [5]   *He exits.*

1 Clown

A comic servant; it is possible, as the second Quarto (1630) has it, that the Clown enters separately after line 2, in response to the music rather than with the musicians.

2 *content your pains*

Make it worth your while. Cassio has hired musicians to serenade Othello and Desdemona the morning after their wedding, no doubt in the hope that his gesture will help regain Othello's favor.

3 *Why masters, have your instruments been in Naples, that they speak i' th' nose thus?*

Some of the musicians hired by Cassio are playing the bagpipes, an instrument that might be said to *speak i' th' nose*. There is also an allusion to what Shakespeare, in another play, calls the *Neapolitan bone-ache* (*Troilus* and *Cressida*, 2.3.18), otherwise known as syphilis, a disease that probably originated in the New World and arrived in Europe via Italy, where the first large scale outbreak occurred in Naples in 1494. Syphilis was known to eat away at the nose. The following passage continues the scatological wordplay. The Clown's obscene jokes, along with the rough music of the pipes, represent the tradition of bawdy festivity (or *charivari*) that took place on the wedding night and in the morning after. The presence of the musicians in this scene extends the musical theme found throughout the play, marking the descent of the play's harmonious tone into obscenity, violence, and discord (*Then murder's out of tune*, 5.2.114), thanks to the efforts of Iago (who predicts, *I'll set down the pegs that make this music* at 2.1.198).

4 *How, sir? How?*

What do you mean?

5 *thereby hangs a tale*

A proverbial phrase meaning "there's a story about that"

6 *Marry, sir, by many a wind instrument that I know.*

The Clown, punning on *tale* and "tail" (i.e., penis), jokes that a tail usually hangs near a *wind instrument* (i.e., an anus, which breaks wind).

7 *for love's sake*

(1) for the sake of good-fellowship; (2) so as not to disturb the newlyweds' lovemaking

8 *to 't again*

I.e., then you can play

Act 3, Scene 1

Enter **Cassio**, **Musicians**, *and* **Clown**. [1]

Cassio

Masters, play here; I will content your pains. [2]

morning Something that's brief, and bid "Good morrow,° General."

[*Musicians play.*]

Clown

Why masters, have your instruments been in Naples,
that they speak i' th' nose thus? [3]

Musician

How, sir? How? [4]   5

Clown

Are these, I pray you, wind instruments?

Musician

Ay, marry, are they, sir.

Clown

Oh, thereby hangs a tale. [5]

Musician

Whereby hangs a tale, sir?

Clown

Marry, sir, by many a wind instrument that I know. [6]   10
But, masters, here's money for you, and the General so
likes your music that he desires you, for love's sake, [7] to
make no more noise with it. *Othello*

Musician

Well, sir, we will not.

Clown

If you have any music that may not be heard, to 't again. [8] But   15
as they say, to hear music the General does not greatly care.

1   *keep up thy quillets*

    Stop with your puns.

2   *entreats her a little favor of speech*

    Who asks permission to speak
    briefly with her

3   *If she will stir hither, I shall seem to
    notify unto her.*

    The Clown mocks Cassio's stilted
    mode of speech.

4   *In happy time*

    At just the right moment
    (you've come)

5   *made bold*

    Gone so far

Musician

We have none such, sir.

Clown

away Then put up° your pipes in your bag, for I'll away. Go, vanish into air, away!

Musicians *exit.*

Cassio

Dost thou hear, mine honest friend? 20

Clown

No, I hear not your honest friend; I hear you.

Cassio *Cassio is questioning Clown*

Prithee, keep up thy quillets.[1] There's a poor piece of gold for thee. If the gentlewoman that attends the General's wife be stirring, tell her there's one Cassio entreats her a little favor of speech.[2] Wilt thou do this? 25

Clown

She is stirring, sir. If she will stir hither, I shall seem to notify unto her.[3]

Cassio

Do, good my friend. **Clown** *exits.*

Enter **Iago.**

In happy time,[4] Iago.

Iago

to bed You have not been abed,° then?

Cassio

Why, no. The day had broke
Before we parted. I have made bold,[5] Iago, 30
To send in to your wife. My suit to her
Is that she will to virtuous Desdemona
Procure me some access.

Cassio is asking Iago's wife to talk to desd.

1 *Florentine*

   Cassio is a Florentine (1.1.19) and
   claims that Iago is as amiable and
   honest as any of his own
   townsmen.

2 *great affinity*

   With powerful family connections

3 *in wholesome wisdom*

   Judicious caution

4 *He might not but refuse you*

   He had no choice but to cast
   you off.

5 *take the safest occasion by the front*

   Grab the first safe opportunity by
   the forelock (i.e., take advantage of
   the first good opportunity).
   Opportunity was often imagined as
   a woman with a single lock of hair
   in the front of her head, which was
   available to be seized.

Iago

I'll send her to you presently,

means And I'll devise a mean° to draw the Moor 35

so that Out of the way, that° your converse and business

May be more free.

[handwritten: Iago will distract Othello so Cassio can talk to Desdemona freely]

Cassio I humbly thank you for 't.

[**Iago**] *exits.*

I never knew a Florentine [1] more kind and honest.

Enter **Emilia**.

Emilia

Good morrow, good lieutenant. I am sorry

loss of favor For your displeasure,° but all will sure be well. 40

The General and his wife are talking of it,

boldly And she speaks for you stoutly.° The Moor replies

That he you hurt is of great fame in Cyprus

And great affinity, [2] and that in wholesome wisdom

incurs He might not but refuse you. [1] But he protests° he loves

you

own inclination And needs no other suitor but his liking°

To take the safest occasion by the front [5] 45

reinstate To bring° you in again.

[handwritten: Desdemona is trying to tell Othello to change his mind but Othello says that Cassio has hurt some1 very popular in Cyprus]

Cassio

Yet I beseech you,

If you think fit, or that it may be done,

the opportunity Give me advantage° of some brief discourse 50

With Desdemon alone.

1   *I am much bound to you*

**I am your servant (i.e., I am
very grateful).**

Emilia

                          Pray you come in.

place   I will bestow° you where you shall have time

feelings To speak your bosom° freely.

Cassio

                         I am much bound to you. [1]

                              [They exit.]

1 *do my duties*

Pay my respects

Act 3, Scene 2

Enter **Othello**, **Iago**, *and* **Gentlemen**.

Othello

ship's captain   These letters give, Iago, to the pilot,°

And by him do my duties ¹ to the Senate.

ramparts   That done, I will be walking on the works.°

Return   Repair° there to me.

Iago

                 Well, my good lord; I'll do 't.

Othello

This fortification, gentlemen, shall we see 't?   5

Gentlemen

attend   We'll wait° upon your lordship.   *They exit.*

1   *shall in strangeness stand no farther off /*
    Than in a politic distance
    Keep you at a distance no greater
    than is necessary for the sake of
    appearances

2   *such nice and waterish diet*
    So delicate and watery a diet.
    Cassio worries that with so little to
    sustain his relationship with
    Othello it will in time just fade
    away.

3   *Or breed itself so out of circumstances*
    I.e., or depend so much on luck

Act 3, Scene 3

Enter **Desdemona**, **Cassio**, *and* **Emilia**.

Desdemona

use Be thou assured, good Cassio, I will do°
All my abilities in thy behalf.

Emilia

promise Good madam, do. I warrant° it grieves my husband
As if the cause were his.

Desdemona

Oh, that's an honest fellow. Do not doubt, Cassio,   5
But I will have my lord and you again
As friendly as you were.

Cassio

Generous   Bounteous° madam,
Whatever shall become of Michael Cassio,
faithful He's never anything but your true° servant.

Desdemona

I know 't. I thank you. You do love my lord.   10
You have known him long, and be you well assured
He shall in strangeness stand no farther off
Than in a politic distance. **¹**

Cassio

                                        Ay, but, lady,
That policy may either last so long,
Or feed upon such nice and waterish diet, **²**   15
Or breed itself so out of circumstances, **³**
filled That, I being absent and my place supplied,°
My General will forget my love and service.

Desdemona

fear Do not doubt° that. Before Emilia here
assurance / yourself I give thee warrant° of thy place. Assure thee,° 20
If I do vow a friendship, I'll perform it

1 *watch him tame and talk him out of*
   patience
   **Keep him awake until he becomes
   less quarrelsome (a technique
   used to tame hawks) and talk to
   him past the limits of his patience**

2 *give thy cause away*
   Give up on your case

To the last article. My lord shall never rest:
I'll watch him tame and talk him out of patience;[1]

table / confessional His bed shall seem a school, his board° a shrift;°
I'll intermingle everything he does   25
With Cassio's suit. Therefore be merry, Cassio,

advocate For thy solicitor° shall rather die
Than give thy cause away.[2]

       Enter **Othello** *and* **Iago**.

Emilia
                 Madam, here comes my lord.

Cassio
Madam, I'll take my leave.

Desdemona
              Why, stay and hear me speak.

Cassio
Madam, not now; I am very ill at ease,   30
Unfit for mine own purposes.

Desdemona
use Well, do° your discretion.   **Cassio** *exits.*

Iago
Ha! I like not that.

Othello
What dost thou say?

Iago
Nothing, my lord, or if—I know not what.   35

Othello
Was not that Cassio parted from my wife?

Iago
Cassio, my lord? No, sure, I cannot think it

1   *His present reconciliation take*

   Restore him to your favor

2   *in ignorance and not in cunning*

   I.e., unintentionally rather than deliberately

That he would steal away so guilty-like
Seeing your coming.

Othello

I do believe 'twas he.

Desdemona

                                    How now, my lord?   40

petitioner I have been talking with a suitor° here,
A man that languishes in your displeasure.

Othello

Who is 't you mean?

Desdemona

Why, your lieutenant, Cassio. Good my lord,
pleasing quality If I have any grace° or power to move you,   45
His present reconciliation take, [1]
For if he be not one that truly loves you,
That errs in ignorance and not in cunning, [2]
of I have no judgment in° an honest face.
I prithee, call him back.

Othello

                                    Went he hence now?   50

Desdemona

Yes, faith, so humbled
That he hath left part of his grief with me
To suffer with him. Good love, call him back.

Othello

Not now, sweet Desdemon. Some other time.

Desdemona

But shall 't be shortly?

Othello

                                    The sooner, sweet, for you.   55

Desdemona

Shall 't be tonight at supper?

1   *in our common reason*

    By ordinary standards

2   *(Save that, they say, the wars must make*

    example / Out of her best)

    Except that, they say, in war time
    it's necessary to make an example
    of even our best men

3   *to have so much to do*

    I.e., why is it such a difficult job?

4   *sue you to do a peculiar profit*

    Beseech you to do something
    beneficial to you

Othello
                                    No, not tonight.
Desdemona
(the midday meal)   Tomorrow dinner,° then?
Othello
                                        I shall not dine at home.
I meet the captains at the citadel.
Desdemona
Why, then, tomorrow night, or Tuesday morn?
On Tuesday noon, or night, on Wednesday morn?   60
I prithee name the time, but let it not
Exceed three days. In faith, he's penitent,
offense   And yet his trespass,° in our common reason [1]
(Save that, they say, the wars must make example
really   Out of her best [2]), is not, almost,° a fault   65
reprimand   T' incur a private check.° When shall he come?
Tell me, Othello. I wonder in my soul
What you would ask me that I should deny
hesitating   Or stand so mamm'ring° on. What? Michael Cassio
That came a-wooing with you, and so many a time,   70
disparagingly When I have spoke of you dispraisingly,°
Hath ta'en your part—to have so much to do [3]
reinstate   To bring° him in? By'r Lady, I could do much—
Othello
Prithee, no more. Let him come when he will;
I will deny thee nothing.
Desdemona
favor   Why, this is not a boon.°   75
as if   'Tis as° I should entreat you wear your gloves,
Or feed on nourishing dishes, or keep you warm,
Or sue to you to do a peculiar profit [4]
To your own person. Nay, when I have a suit
test   Wherein I mean to touch° your love indeed,   80

1 *be full of poise and difficult weight*

   Be a serious matter and hard to decide

2 *Be as your fancies teach you*

   Act according to your inclinations.

3 *wretch*

   Here, a term of endearment

4 *But for a satisfaction of my thought*

   Just to satisfy my curiosity

Get Loose

It shall be full of poise and difficult weight [1]

terrible   And fearful° to be granted.

Othello

                                    I will deny thee nothing!

Therefore   Whereon° I do beseech thee, grant me this,

To leave me but a little to myself.

Desdemona

Shall I deny you? No. Farewell, my lord.   85

Othello

right away   Farewell, my Desdemona. I'll come to thee straight.°

Desdemona

Emilia, come. [*to* **Othello**] Be as your fancies teach you. [2]

Whate'er you be, I am obedient.

                         [**Desdemona** *and* **Emilia**] *exit.*

Othello

Damnation   Excellent wretch! [3] Perdition° catch my soul

Unless   But° I do love thee! And when I love thee not,   90

Chaos is come again.

Iago

My noble lord—

Othello

What dost thou say, Iago?

Iago

Did Michael Cassio, when you wooed my lady,

Know of your love?

Othello

                         He did, from first to last.   95

Why dost thou ask?

Iago

But for a satisfaction of my thought, [4]

No further harm.

Othello

                         Why of thy thought, Iago?

1   *went between us*

Acted as a go-between for us

Iago

I did not think he had been acquainted with her.

Othello

Oh, yes, and went between us¹ very oft. 100

Iago

Indeed?

Othello

anything "Indeed?" Ay, indeed! Discern'st thou aught° in that?

Is he not honest?

Iago

Honest, my lord?

Othello

Honest, ay, honest. 105

Iago

My lord, for aught I know.

Othello

What dost thou think?

Iago

Think, my lord?

Othello

"Think, my lord?" By Heaven, thou echo'st me

As if there were some monster in thy thought 110

Too hideous to be shown. Thou dost mean something.

I heard thee say even now thou lik'st not that

When Cassio left my wife. What didst not like?

confidence And when I told thee he was of my counsel°

During Of° my whole course of wooing, thou cried'st "Indeed?" 115

draw; contract And didst contract and purse° thy brow together

As if thou then hadst shut up in thy brain

idea Some horrible conceit.° If thou dost love me,

Show me thy thought.

Iago

My lord, you know I love you. 120

1   *tricks of custom*

    Characteristic ploys

2   *close dilations*

    Involuntary accusations

3   *would they might seem none*

    **I.e., I wish they did not seem to be
men at all.**

4   *As thou dost ruminate*

    As you go over things in your mind

5   *I am not bound to that all slaves are
free to*

    **I do not have to relinquish that
right which even slaves are granted
(i.e., the right to keep one's own
thoughts private).**

6   *As where's that palace whereinto foul
things / Sometimes intrude not*

    **And, after all, what palace has
never had foul things enter it?**

Othello

I think thou dost,

because And, for° I know thou'rt full of love and honesty

And, weigh'st thy words before thou giv'st them breath;

hesitations Therefore these stops° of thine fright me the more.

For such things in a false disloyal knave   125

Are tricks of custom,[1] but in a man that's just

They're close dilations,[2] working from the heart,

control That passion cannot rule.°

Iago

For Michael Cassio,

I dare be sworn, I think, that he is honest.

Othello

I think so too.

Iago

Men should be what they seem,   130

Or those that be not, would they might seem none![3]

Othello

Certainly Certain,° men should be what they seem.

Iago

Why, then I think Cassio's an honest man.

Othello

Nay, yet there's more in this.

I prithee speak to me as to thy thinkings,   135

As thou dost ruminate,[4] and give thy worst of thoughts

The worst of words.

Iago

Good my lord, pardon me,

Though I am bound to every act of duty,

what I am not bound to that° all slaves are free to.[5]

Utter my thoughts? Why, say they are vile and false,   140

As where's that palace whereinto foul things

Sometimes intrude not?[6] Who has that breast so pure

1 *Who has that breast so pure / Where no*
uncleanly apprehensions / Keep leets and
law-days and in sessions sit / With medi-
tations lawful?

This statement is one of many
examples of to legal discourse in
Othello, a tragedy that hinges upon
issues of crime, evidence, *ocular*
proof, and guilt. Iago draws an
analogy between the interior space
of a person's thoughts and a court
of law. In both cases, even if the
place is one where justice and
virtue prevail, it is a place where
lawful and unlawful thoughts (or
persons) come together to be
tried. The complex legal system of
early modern England included
leets, or special courts that were
convened once or twice a year by a
local manorial lord, and other
courts of law that met regularly but
only on *law-days* during certain
sessions when judges were sitting.

2 *Shapes faults that are not*
Invents nonexistent offenses

3 *that your wisdom, / From one that so*
imperfectly conceits, / Would take no
notice
That you, in your wisdom, take no
notice of the words of a man who
perceives things so unreliably

4 *nor build yourself a trouble / Out of his*
scattering and unsure observance
Nor take the disordered and
uncertain observations of *one that*
so imperfectly conceits as evidence
that a legitimate problem exists

5 *It were not for your quiet nor your good*
It would not be good for your
peace of mind or your well-being

6 *not enriches him*
Does not enrich him

impure   Where no uncleanly° apprehensions
             Keep leets and law-days and in sessions sit
             With meditations lawful?[1]   145

Othello

             Thou dost conspire against thy friend, Iago,
only   If thou but° think'st him wronged and mak'st his ear
             A stranger to thy thoughts.

Iago

                                  I do beseech you,
mistaken; wicked   Though I perchance am vicious° in my guess,
             As, I confess, it is my nature's plague   150
             To spy into abuses, and oft my jealousy
             Shapes faults that are not,[2] that your wisdom,
imagines   From one that so imperfectly conceits,°
             Would take no notice,[3] nor build yourself a trouble
             Out of his scattering and unsure observance.[4]   155
good for   It were not for° your quiet nor your good,[5]
             Nor for my manhood, honesty, and wisdom,
             To let you know my thoughts.

Othello

                                  Zounds! What dost thou mean?

Iago

             Good name in man and woman, dear my lord,
i.e., most cherished   Is the immediate° jewel of their souls.   160
             Who steals my purse steals trash. 'Tis something,
                 nothing:
             'Twas mine, 'tis his, and has been slave to thousands.
             But he that filches from me my good name
             Robs me of that which not enriches him[6]
             And makes me poor indeed.   165

Othello

             By Heaven, I'll know thy thoughts.

1   *Oh, beware, my lord, of jealousy! / It is
    the green-eyed monster which doth
    mock / The meat it feeds on.*

    See LONGER NOTE, page 366.

2   *That cuckold lives in bliss / Who, certain
    of his fate, loves not his wronger*

    **The cuckold lives happily who
    knows he has been wronged and
    therefore does not love his
    faithless wife.**

3   *what damnèd minutes tells he o'er*

    **How many tormented minutes
    must he count**

4   *Poor and content is rich*

    **I.e., the man who is poor but
    contented is rich.**

5   *To follow still the changes of the moon /
    With fresh suspicions*

    **Continuously to come up with new
    suspicions at each phase of the
    ever-changing moon**

Iago

even if   You cannot, if° my heart were in your hand,

Nor shall not, whilst 'tis in my custody.

Othello

Ha!

Iago

metaphor

Oh, beware, my lord, of jealousy!

It is the green-eyed monster which doth mock   170

The meat it feeds on.[1] That cuckold lives in bliss

Who, certain of his fate, loves not his wronger,[2]

But, oh, what damnèd minutes tells he o'er[3]

fully   Who dotes yet doubts, suspects yet soundly° loves![3]

Othello

O misery!   175

Iago

Poor and content is rich,[4] and rich enough,

boundless   But riches fineless° is as poor as winter

always   To him that ever° fears he shall be poor.

family   Good God the souls of all my tribe° defend

From jealousy!

Othello

Why? Why is this?   180

Think'st thou I'd make a life of jealousy,

continuously   To follow still° the changes of the moon

With fresh suspicions?[5] No! To be once in doubt

decided   Is to be resolved.° Exchange me for a goat

When I shall turn the business of my soul   185

improbable / rumored   To such exsufflicate° and blowed° surmises,

Matching thy inference. 'Tis not to make me jealous

To say my wife is fair, feeds well, loves company,

liberal   Is free° of speech, sings, plays, and dances.

Where virtue is, these are more virtuous.   190

deduce   Nor from mine own weak merits will I draw°

1   *love or jealousy*

    I.e., either love (if the doubt is
    confirmed) or jealousy (if the
    doubt is removed)

2   *Wear your eyes thus*

    Observe her in this way

3   *self-bounty*

    Innate generosity

4   *Their best conscience*

    I.e., their most serious moral
    commitment

5   *go to*

    I.e., there you are

6   *close as oak*

    I.e., tight (referring to the fine
    grain of the *oak*, a particularly
    dense wood)

betrayal The smallest fear or doubt of her revolt,°
For she had eyes and chose me. No, Iago,
test I'll see before I doubt; when I doubt, prove,°
having And on° the proof there is no more but this: 195
Away at once with love or jealousy![1]

Iago

I am glad of this, for now I shall have reason
To show the love and duty that I bear you
more open With franker° spirit. Therefore, as I am bound,
Receive it from me. I speak not yet of proof.   200
Look to your wife; observe her well with Cassio.
neither Wear your eyes thus,[2] not° jealous nor secure.
I would not have your free and noble nature
deceived Out of self-bounty[3] be abused.° Look to 't.
i.e., Venetian I know our country° disposition well.   205
In Venice they do let God see the pranks
They dare not show their husbands. Their best conscience[4]
Is not to leave 't undone, but keep 't unknown.

Othello

Dost thou say so?

Iago

She did deceive her father, marrying you,   210
And when she seemed to shake and fear your looks,
She loved them most.

Othello

                              And so she did.

Iago

                                          Why, go to,[5] then.
She that, so young, could give out such a seeming,
sew To seel° her father's eyes up close as oak[6]—
He thought 'twas witchcraft. But I am much to blame;   215
I humbly do beseech you of your pardon
For too much loving you.

1   *your love*

   I.e., my love of you

2   *I am to pray you not to strain my speech /*
   To grosser issues nor to larger reach /
   Than to suspicion.

   **I must ask you not to interpret
   what I have said as suggesting
   anything greater or of any more
   consequence than merely my
   suspicion (*grosser* means "larger,"
   but the meaning "indecent" is, of
   course, deliberately present).**

3   *My speech should fall into such vile*
   success / Which my thoughts aimed not

   **My words would have a terrible
   effect I hadn't intended.**

4   *honest*

   **Both "truthful" and "chaste" (but
   note the double negative with
   which Othello must assert it)**

5   *complexion*

   **The word means both "skin
   coloring" and "temperament."**

Othello

I am bound to thee forever.

Iago

I see this hath a little dashed your spirits.

Othello

Not a jot, not a jot.

Iago

                 I' faith, I fear it has.   220

I hope you will consider° what is spoke

Comes from your love. [1] But I do see you're moved.°

I am° to pray you not to strain my speech

To grosser issues nor to larger reach

Than to suspicion. [2]   225

Othello

I will not.

Iago

Should you do so, my lord,

My speech should fall into such vile success

Which my thoughts aimed not. [3] Cassio's my worthy

    friend—

My lord, I see you're moved.

Othello

                     No, not much moved.   230

I do not think but° Desdemona's honest. [4]

Iago

Long live she so, and long live you to think so.

Othello

And yet how nature, erring° from itself—

Iago

Ay, there's the point—as, to be bold with you,

Not to affect° many proposèd matches   235

Of her own clime,° complexion, [5] and degree,°

Whereto° we see in all things nature tends.

Marginal glosses (left column):

- *consider that* — consider°
- *distressed* — moved.°
- *have* — I am°
- *but that* — but°
- *deviating* — erring°
- *favor* — affect°
- *country / social rank* — clime,° ... degree,°
- *Toward which* — Whereto°

1 *a will most rank*

Sexual desire most corrupt

2 *Foul disproportions*

Vile imbalance (of the fluids, or humors, that determined human nature; see 2.3.191–192 and note)

3 *I do not in position / Distinctly speak of her*

Though I am setting forth this general line of thought, I am not in this assertion (*position*) speaking specifically about her

4 *her country forms*

I.e., Venetian standards of beauty

5 *Set on*

Order

6 *As worthy cause I have to fear I am*

As I have good reason to think I am

7 *hold her free*

Regard her as innocent (though *free* also could mean "promiscuous," a sense Iago knows Othello will hear)

such a woman   Foh! One may smell in such° a will most rank, [1]

Foul disproportions, [2] thoughts unnatural.

But pardon me; I do not in position   240

Distinctly speak of her, [3] though I may fear

deferring   Her will, recoiling° to her better judgment,

begin / compare   May fall° to match° you with her country forms, [4]

perhaps   And happily° repent.

Othello

                Farewell, farewell.

If more thou dost perceive, let me know more.   245

Set on [5] thy wife to observe. Leave me, Iago.

Iago

My lord, I take my leave.

Othello

[*aside*] Why did I marry? This honest creature doubtless

reveals   Sees and knows more, much more, than he unfolds.°

Iago

wish   My lord, I would° I might entreat your honor   250

examine   To scan° this thing no farther. Leave it to time.

Although 'tis fit that Cassio have his place—

For sure, he fills it up with great ability—

Yet, if you please to hold him off awhile,

see into   You shall by that perceive° him and his means.   255

urge / favorable reception   Note if your lady strain° his entertainment°

persistence   With any strong or vehement importunity.°

Much will be seen in that. In the meantime,

meddling   Let me be thought too busy° in my fears—

As worthy cause I have to fear I am [6]—   260

And hold her free, [7] I do beseech your honor.

Othello

self-control   Fear not my government.°

1 *with a learned spirit / Of human dealings*

With an insight born of the experience of human behavior

2 *If I do prove her haggard, / Though that her jesses were my dear heartstrings, / I'd whistle her off and let her down the wind / To prey at fortune.*

The use of trained hawks for hunting was an aristocratic pastime in Shakespeare's England. Othello compares himself to a falconer and Desdemona to a bird of prey whose legs are tied to the falconer's wrist by strips of leather called *jesses.* But Othello believes that Desdemona is a *haggard,* a hawk that resists training and remains wild and untamable. (Compare *Twelfth Night,* 3.1.60–61: *like the haggard, check at every feather / That comes before his eye.*) To *whistle her off and let her down the wind* is to let loose the untrainable hawk in flight.

3 *delicate*

The word has a range of possible meanings, including "exquisite," "finely made," "delightful," "wanton," and "cunning."

4 *Yet 'tis the plague to great ones: / Prerogatived are they less than the base.*

But this is the affliction of great men: they have fewer privileges than those who are humbly born.

5 *forkèd plague*

I.e., the cuckold's horns that come with a wife's infidelity

6 *do quicken*

Are born

Iago

                                        I once more take my leave.

                                                        He exits.

Othello

surpassing   This fellow's of exceeding° honesty

natures   And knows all qualities,° with a learned spirit

                 Of human dealings.[1] If I do prove her haggard,   265

                 Though that her jesses were my dear heartstrings,

                 I'd whistle her off and let her down the wind

Perhaps / because To prey at fortune.[2] Haply° for° I am black

                 And have not those soft parts of conversation

gallants   That chamberers° have, or for I am declined   270

                 Into the vale of years—yet that's not much—

                 She's gone, I am abused, and my relief

                 Must be to loathe her. O curse of marriage,

                 That we can call these delicate[3] creatures ours

would   And not their appetites! I had° rather be a toad   275

                 And live upon the vapor of a dungeon

small part   Than keep a corner° in the thing I love

                 For others' uses. Yet 'tis the plague to great ones:

                 Prerogatived are they less than the base.[4]

                 'Tis destiny unshunnable, like death;   280

                 Even then this forkèd plague[5] is fated to us

                 When we do quicken.[6] Look where she comes.

                 Enter **Desdemona** *and* **Emilia**.

                 If she be false, Heaven mocked itself.

                 I'll not believe 't.

Desdemona

                                 How now, my dear Othello?

                 Your dinner, and the generous islanders   285

await   By you invited, do attend° your presence.

1   *work ta'en out*

Embroidery copied (Emilia's first
thought seems to be to give a copy
of the handkerchief to Iago,
knowing how much Desdemona
values the original.)

2   *nothing but*

Am nothing but a creature
designed

Othello

I am to blame.

Desdemona

                  Why do you speak so faintly?

Are you not well?

Othello

I have a pain upon my forehead, here.

Desdemona

lack of sleep   Faith, that's with watching;° 'twill away again.   290

Let me but bind it hard; within this hour

It will be well.   *[pulls out a handkerchief]*

Othello

handkerchief   Your napkin° is too little,

Let it alone.   *[Her handkerchief drops.]*

        Come, I'll go in with you.

Desdemona

I am very sorry that you are not well.

         *[***Othello*** *and* ***Desdemona****] exit.*

Emilia

[picks up the handkerchief] I am glad I have found this napkin.   295

keepsake   This was her first remembrance° from the Moor.

willful   My wayward° husband hath a hundred times

Urged   Wooed° me to steal it, but she so loves the token

solemnly entreated   (For he conjured° her she should ever keep it)

keeps   That she reserves° it evermore about her   300

To kiss and talk to. I'll have the work ta'en out [1]

And give 't Iago. What he will do with it

Heaven knows, not I;

whim   I nothing but [2] to please his fantasy.°

Enter **Iago**.

1   *What do you*

    What are you doing

2   *You have a thing for me? It is a common*

    thing——

    Punning on *thing* **as slang for "vagina"**
    and implying that Emilia is enjoyed
    by many men (*common* = **both**
    "ordinary" and "free to everyone")

Iago

How now! What do you ¹ here alone?   *305*

Emilia

Do not you chide. I have a thing for you.

Iago

You have a thing for me? It is a common thing ²—

Emilia

Ha?

Iago

To have a foolish wife.

Emilia

Oh, is that all? What will you give me now   *310*

For the same handkerchief?

Iago

                              What handkerchief?

Emilia

What handkerchief?

Why, that the Moor first gave to Desdemona,

That which so often you did bid me steal.

Iago

Hast stol'n it from her?   *315*

Emilia

No, faith, she let it drop by negligence,

seizing   And, to° th' advantage, I, being here, took 't up.

Look, here 'tis.

Iago

                    A good wench! Give it me.

Emilia

eager   What will you do with 't, that you have been so earnest°

To have me filch it?   [**Iago** *grabs the hankerchief*]

Iago

                    Why, what is that to you?   *320*

1   *Be not acknown on 't.*

An unusual phrase that must mean
something like "do not
acknowledge that you know about
this" or perhaps merely means
"mind your own business."

2   *lose*

The Folio spells this "loose," and,
although early modern spelling
did not distinguish between the
two words, it is possible Iago does
mean "let loose" rather than *lose*
(i.e., leave behind).

3   *proofs of holy writ*

Evidence from the Bible

4   *act upon the blood*

Stimulation of Othello's emotions
(*blood*)

5   *Not poppy nor mandragora*

Neither opium nor the mandrake
root (thought to be a soporific)

6   *med'cine thee to*

I.e., serve as medicine to help you
recover

7   *the rack*

A medieval instrument of torture
that pulled and twisted the victim's
limbs

8   *Than but to know 't a little*

Than only to know a little (of what
is going on)

Emilia

importance If it be not for some purpose of import,°

Give 't me again. Poor lady, she'll run mad

miss When she shall lack° it.

Iago

Be not acknown on 't. [1]

I have use for it. Go, leave me.   **Emilia** *exits.*

I will in Cassio's lodging lose [2] this napkin   325

And let him find it. Trifles light as air

Are to the jealous confirmations strong

As proofs of holy writ. [3] This may do something;

The Moor already changes with my poison.

imaginings Dangerous conceits° are in their natures poisons,   330

he distasteful Which at the first are scarce found to distaste,°

But, with a little act upon the blood, [4]

Burn like the mines of sulfur.

Enter **Othello**.

I did say so.

Look where he comes. Not poppy nor mandragora [5]

sleep-inducing Nor all the drowsy° syrups of the world   335

Shall ever med'cine thee to [6] that sweet sleep

did possess Which thou owed'st° yesterday.

Othello

Ha! Ha! False to me?

Iago

Why, how now, General? No more of that.

Othello

Get away Avaunt!° Be gone! Thou hast set me on the rack. [7]

wronged I swear 'tis better to be much abused°   340

Than but to know 't a little. [8]

1 *Let him not know 't and he's not robbed*
   at all

   So long as he remains unaware of the theft, he hasn't been robbed at all.

2 *general camp*

   Whole army

3 *Pioneers*

   Trench and tunnel digging soldiers, i.e., those who performed the lowest and dirtiest forms of military service

4 *mortal engines*

   Deadly machinery of war (i.e., cannon)

5 *Th' immortal Jove's dread clamors*
   counterfeit

   I.e. imitate the terrifying thunder. In Roman mythology, Jove used thunder and lighting bolts as weapons.

6 *Thou hadst been better*

   I.e., it would be better for you to

Iago

                     How now, my lord?

Othello

knowledge   What sense° had I of her stol'n hours of lust?

I saw 't not, thought it not; it harmed not me.

carefree   I slept the next night well, fed well, was free° and merry.

I found not Cassio's kisses on her lips.   345

missing   He that is robbed, not wanting° what is stol'n,

Let him not know 't and he's not robbed at all. [1]

Iago

I am sorry to hear this.

Othello

would have   I had° been happy if the general camp, [2]

As long as   Pioneers [3] and all, had tasted her sweet body,   350

So° I had nothing known. Oh, now forever

Farewell the tranquil mind. Farewell content.

Farewell the plumèd troops and the big wars

That makes ambition virtue. Oh, farewell.

trumpet   Farewell the neighing steed and the shrill trump,°   355

The spirit-stirring drum, th' ear-piercing fife,

excellence   The royal banner, and all quality,°

pageantry   Pride, pomp, and circumstance° of glorious war.

harsh; discordant   And O you mortal engines, [4] whose rude° throats

Th' immortal Jove's dread clamors counterfeit, [5]   360

Farewell. Othello's occupation's gone.

Iago

Is 't possible, my lord?

Othello

Villain, be sure thou prove my love a whore;

visible   Be sure of it. Give me the ocular° proof,

Or, by the worth of mine eternal soul   365

Thou hadst been better [6] have been born a dog

Than answer my waked wrath!

1   *God by you*

    God be with you (i.e., do what you
    want)

2   *breeds such offense*

    Results in so much pain. (Iago is
    seemingly talking about "the pain
    his *love* has inadvertantly caused
    Othello, but the language must
    remind Othello of how his own
    love for Desdemona—and
    Desdemona's supposed love for
    Cassio—has also bred *such offense*.)

Iago

                              Is 't come to this?

Othello

Make me to see 't, or at the least so prove it

proof / hook That the probation° bear no hinge° nor loop

To hang a doubt on, or woe upon thy life!   *370*

Iago

My noble lord—

Othello

If thou dost slander her and torture me,

Never pray more. Abandon all remorse.

let horrors On horror's head horrors° accumulate,

Do deeds to make Heaven weep, all Earth amazed,   *375*

For nothing canst thou to damnation add

Greater than that.

Iago

                 O grace! O Heaven forgive me!

Are you a man? Have you a soul or sense?

dismiss me from God by you,[1] take° mine office. O wretched fool

That lov'st to make thine honesty a vice!   *380*

O monstrous world! Take note, take note, O world:

To be direct and honest is not safe.

lesson I thank you for this profit,° and from hence

since I'll love no friend, sith° love breeds such offense.[2]

Othello

Nay, stay. Thou shouldst be honest.   *385*

Iago

I should be wise, for honesty's a fool

what And loses that° it works for.

Othello

                By the world,

I think my wife be honest and think she is not.

I think that thou art just and think thou art not.

1 *Her*

The Folio prints "My,"which is not impossible, Othello thinking of his devastated reputation, but the comparison with Diana (line 391) suggests the focus is a woman.

2 *Dian's visage*

The face of Diana (Roman goddess of the moon and patron deity of chastity)

3 *If there be cords or knives, / Poison or fire, or suffocating streams, / I'll not endure it. Would I were satisfied!*

Ambiguous lines, perhaps reflecting Othello's own disordered mental state. It is clear that Othello wants to do violence to someone, but it is unclear whom the object of that violence might be; Othello may want to harm Iago, Cassio, Desdemona, or even himself. Similarly, it is unclear whether Othello wants to be *satisfied* (convinced) of Desdemona's constancy or of her infidelity.

4 *put it to you*

Suggested it (i.e., the question of Desdemona's fidelity) to you

5 *topped*

I.e., with Cassio on top of her in the act of sex; *topped* perhaps should be "tupped" (see *tupping*, 1.1.89), and *top* (5.2.134) similarly changed to "tup."

6 *that prospect*

I.e., a situation in which they could be observed committing adultery

7 *bolster / More than their own*

An obscure phrase, probably meaning: "share a pillow (*bolster*) with anyone other than their partners"

8 *circumstances*

Circumstantial evidence

I'll have some proof. Her¹ name, that was as fresh   390
covered with soot As Dian's visage,² is now begrimed° and black
hangmen's ropes As mine own face. If there be cords° or knives,
Poison or fire, or suffocating streams,
I'll not endure it. Would I were satisfied!³

Iago

I see you are eaten up with passion.   395
I do repent me that I put it to you.⁴
You would be satisfied?

Othello

                    Would? Nay, and I will.

Iago

And may—but how? How satisfied, my lord?
onlooker Would you, the supervisor,° grossly gape on?
Behold her topped?⁵

Othello

                    Death and damnation! Oh!   400

Iago

would be It were° a tedious difficulty, I think,
To bring them to that prospect.⁶ Damn them, then,
If ever mortal eyes do see them bolster
More than their own!⁷ What then? How then?
What shall I say? Where's satisfaction?   405
It is impossible you should see this,
lecherous / lascivious Were they as prime° as goats, as hot° as monkeys,
lustful / heat As salt° as wolves in pride,° and fools as gross
As ignorance made drunk. But yet, I say,
accusation If imputation° and strong circumstances,⁸   410
Which lead directly to the door of truth,
Will give you satisfaction, you might have 't.

Othello

compelling Give me a living° reason she's disloyal.

1　*loose of soul*

　Indiscreet

2　*a foregone conclusion*

　I.e., something that has already
　happened

3　*shrewd doubt*

　Telling clue

4　*yet . . . yet . . . yet*

　Various meanings of the word are
　in play: "still," "as yet," and
　"nevertheless" or "in spite of
　everything," but the final *yet* may
　well be spoken to mean "up to
　now" and thus be part of Iago's
　subtle assault on Othello's
　confidence.

Iago

task   I do not like the office,°

But, sith I am entered in this cause so far,   415

Urged on   Pricked° to 't by foolish honesty and love,

shared a bed I will go on. I lay° with Cassio lately,

painful   And, being troubled with a raging° tooth,

I could not sleep. There are a kind of men

So loose of soul [1] that in their sleeps will mutter   420

Their affairs. One of this kind is Cassio.

In sleep I heard him say "Sweet Desdemona,

Let us be wary; let us hide our loves."

clutch   And then, sir, would he gripe° and wring my hand,

Cry "O sweet creature," then kiss me hard,   425

As if he plucked up kisses by the roots

That grew upon my lips, lay his leg o'er my thigh,

And sigh, and kiss, and then cry, "Cursèd fate

That gave thee to the Moor!"

Othello

                                   Oh, monstrous! Monstrous!

Iago

only   Nay, this was but° his dream.   430

Othello

But this denoted a foregone conclusion. [2]

'Tis a shrewd doubt, [3] though it be but a dream.

Iago

strengthen   And this may help to thicken° other proofs

That do demonstrate thinly.

Othello

I'll tear her all to pieces!   435

Iago

Nay, yet be wise; yet we see nothing done;

She may be honest yet. [4] Tell me but this:

Have you not sometimes seen a handkerchief

1   *a handkerchief / Spotted with*
    strawberries
    In Cinthio, Shakespeare's Italian
    source, the handkerchief is
    decorated "in the Moorish
    manner," but Shakespeare
    introduced the image of the blood-
    red strawberries on the white cloth
    to provide an important visual
    symbol. In the emblem tradition
    that was well known to early
    modern audiences, the strawberry
    pattern embroidered onto the
    handkerchief would have been
    associated with the Virgin Mary
    and thus with virginity. Building on
    this signification, the red spots on
    the white *napkin* constitute a
    version of the wedding-bed sheets
    that were customarily displayed on
    the morning after the wedding as
    the sign of sexual consummation.
    The handkerchief also functions as
    a traditional love token or favor,
    and, for Othello, its possession by
    Cassio is an indication that Cassio
    has possessed, and perhaps
    deflowered, Desdemona. *Spotted*
    means "decorated," but it also
    suggests "stained," possibly with
    strawberry-red blood, and the
    word is echoed later when Othello
    tells Desdemona, *Thy bed, lust-*
    stained, shall with lust's blood be
    spotted (5.1.37).

2   *the slave*
    An epithet of contempt; it is
    unclear whether Othello means
    Cassio or Desdemona here.

3   *For 'tis of aspics' tongues*
    For it (love) is poisonous, (i.e.,
    from the tongues of asps; small,
    venomous snakes found in
    Africa)

4   *Ne'er keeps retiring ebb*
    Never reverses the current

5   *To the Propontic and the Hellespont*
    Through the Sea of Marmora and into
    the Dardanelles (and, eventually, into
    the Mediterranean Sea)

Spotted with strawberries[1] in your wife's hand?

Othello

I gave her such a one; 'twas my first gift.   *440*

Iago

I know not that, but such a handkerchief—
I am sure it was your wife's—did I today
See Cassio wipe his beard with.

Othello

                    If it be that—

Iago

If it be that, or any that was hers,
It speaks against her with the other proofs.   *445*

Othello

Oh, that the slave[2] had forty thousand lives.
One is too poor, too weak for my revenge.
Now do I see 'tis true. Look here, Iago,

foolish   All my fond° love thus do I blow to Heaven.
'Tis gone.   *450*
Arise, black vengeance, from the hollow Hell!

lodged in the heart   Yield up, O love, thy crown and hearted° throne
burden   To tyrannous hate! Swell, bosom, with thy fraught,°
For 'tis of aspics' tongues![3]

Iago

calm   Yet be content.°

Othello

Oh, blood, blood, blood!

Iago

              Patience, I say. Your mind may change.   *455*

Othello

Black   Never, Iago. Like to the Pontic° Sea,
forward driving   Whose icy current and compulsive° course
straight   Ne'er keeps retiring ebb[4] but keeps due° on
To the Propontic and the Hellespont,[5]

1 *give up*

Commit; pledge

2 *What bloody business ever*

I.e., however bloody the business

3 *put thee to 't*

Test that pledge

4 *lieutenant*

Iago has now succeeded in
replacing Cassio as Othello's
lieutenant; see 1.1.7–32.

Even so my bloody thoughts with violent pace   460
Shall ne'er look back, ne'er ebb to humble love,

comprehensive   Till that a capable° and wide revenge
Swallow them up. [*He kneels.*] Now, by yond marble Heaven,
In the due reverence of a sacred vow

pledge   I here engage° my words.

Iago

                      Do not rise yet. [**Iago** *kneels.*]   465
Witness, you ever-burning lights above,

encompass   You elements that clip° us round about,
Witness that here Iago doth give up [1]

performance   The execution° of his wit, hands, heart,
To wronged Othello's service. Let him command,   470

an act of pity   And to obey shall be in me remorse,°
What bloody business ever. [2]

Othello

                    I greet thy love

lavish   Not with vain thanks but with acceptance bounteous,°
And will upon the instant put thee to 't. [3]   [*They rise.*]
Within these three days let me hear thee say   475
That Cassio's not alive.

Iago

                My friend is dead.
'Tis done at your request, but let her live.

Othello

i.e., harlot   Damn her, lewd minx!° Oh, damn her, damn her!

away from here   Come; go with me apart.° I will withdraw
To furnish me with some swift means of death   480
For the fair devil. Now art thou my lieutenant. [4]

Iago

I am your own forever.   *They exit.*

1   *sirrah*

    A form of address generally used
    with social inferiors

2   *I dare not say he lies*

    With a pun on *lies* (i.e., tells lies)

3   *'tis stabbing*

    I.e., a statement that could lead to
    one's getting stabbed. (Accusing a
    soldier of telling a lie was an
    assault on his honor, which might
    easily provoke a challenge to a
    duel.)

4   *Go to.*

    An expression of impatience

5   *lie in mine own throat*

    I.e., tell an out-and-out falsehood.

6   *inquire him out and be edified by report*

    I.e., ask around (about Cassio) and
    find out from someone

Act 3, Scene 4

Enter **Desdemona**, **Emilia**, *and* **Clown**.

Desdemona

is staying   Do you know, sirrah, [1] where Lieutenant Cassio lies?°

Clown

I dare not say he lies [2] anywhere.

Desdemona

Why, man?

Clown

He's a soldier, and for me to say a soldier lies, 'tis stabbing. [3]

Desdemona

Go to. [4] Where lodges he?   5

Clown

To tell you where he lodges is to tell you where I lie.

Desdemona

i.e., this foolishness   Can anything be made of this?°

Clown

invent   I know not where he lodges, and for me to devise° a
lodging and say he lies here or he lies there, were to lie
in mine own throat. [5]   10

Desdemona

Can you inquire him out and be edified by report? [6]

Clown

interrogate   I will catechize° the world for him: that is, make
questions and by them answer.

Desdemona

entreated   Seek him; bid him come hither. Tell him I have moved°
my lord on his behalf and hope all will be well.   15

Clown

scope   To do this is within the compass° of man's wit, and
therefore I will attempt the doing it.   **Clown** *exits.*

1 *should I lose*

Could I have lost

2 *crusadoes*

Portuguese coins made of gold and stamped with a cross

3 *Is he not jealous?*

Desdemona's denial of Emilia's accusation is based on her faith in the *noble Moor* (line 21) she loves, but Iago's words have transformed him into a different man. The new Othello fits the stereotype of the jealous man, a figure described by Robert Burton's 1621 book, *The Anatomy of Melancholy*: "Besides those strange gestures of staring, frowning, grinning, rolling of eyes, menacing ghastly looks, broken pace, interrupt, precipitate, half-turns. He will sometimes sigh, weep, sob for anger . . . curse, threaten, brawl, scold, fight, and sometimes again flatter and speak fair . . . and then eftsoons, impatient as he is, rave, roar, and lay about him like a madman, thump her sides, drag her about perchance . . . accurately observing on whom she looks, who looks at her, what she saith, doth, at dinner, at supper, sitting, walking . . . he is the same . . . maundering [i.e., muttering], gazing, listening, affrighted with every small object; why did she smile, why did she pity him, commend him? Why did she drink twice to such a man? Why

did she offer to kiss, to dance? Etc. a whore, a whore, an arrant whore" (3.3.2).

4 *humors*

I.e., dispositions; see 2.3.191–193, 3.3.239, and notes.

5 *Oh, hardness to dissemble!*

(1) how difficult it is to pretend; (2) how hard of heart (Desdemona must be) to pretend like this

6 *This hand is moist, my lady.*

Constitution and temperament, including sexuality, were believed to be determined by a mixture of the hot, cold, moist, and dry *humors* in the body (see note 4 above). In particular, a sweaty palm was thought to be a sign of youthful energy and sexual vigor. "A moist palm argues an amorous nature" was proverbial. Nonetheless, Othello may be mistaking what is merely a nervous sweat for the sign of lasciviousness.

Desdemona

Where should I lose[1] the handkerchief, Emilia?

Emilia

I know not, madam.

[handwritten: Desdemona asks Emilia if she knows where her handkercheif is]

Desdemona

would Believe me, I had° rather have lost my purse 20
were it not that Full of crusadoes.[2] And but° my noble Moor

Is true of mind and made of no such baseness

would be As jealous creatures are, it were° enough

To put him to ill thinking.

[handwritten: and Emilia lises about not knowing]

Emilia

[handwritten: Desdemona doesn't want Othello to know that she lost it] Is he not jealous?[3]

Desdemona

Who? He? I think the sun where he was born 25
Emptied Drew° all such humors[4] from him.

Emilia

Look where he comes.

Enter **Othello**.

Desdemona

[handwritten: Desdemona wants Cassio to have his job back]

I will not leave him now till Cassio
recalled; reconciled Be called° to him.—How is 't with you, my lord?

Othello

Well, my good lady.—[*aside*] Oh, hardness to dissemble![5]
—How do you, Desdemona?

Desdemona

Well, my good lord. 30

Othello

Give me your hand. This hand is moist, my lady.[6]

Desdemona

It hath felt no age nor known no sorrow.

[handwritten: moist hands]

1   *fruitfulness and liberal heart*

    **Can mean either a "productive and
    generous heart" or, equally, refer
    to her fertility and her promiscuity.
    Othello lets her hear one thing
    while he suspects the other.**

2   *castigation, exercise devout*

    Penitence, religious devotion

3   *commonly*

    **Often (but with a bitter play on the
    meaning "promiscuously")**

4   *The hearts of old gave hands, / But our
    new heraldry is hands, not hearts.*

    **I.e., in former times people
    married for love, giving their
    hearts and hands together, but
    now it's the fashion to give one's
    hand (in marriage) without giving
    one's heart.**

5   *chuck*

    A term of endearment

6   *a salt and sorry rheum offends me*

    **A heavy and painful cold (that)
    distresses me**

Othello

indicates   This argues° fruitfulness and liberal heart: [1]

    Hot, hot and moist. This hand of yours requires

removal   A sequester° from liberty, fasting and prayer,   35

    Much castigation, exercise devout, [2]

i.e., the hand   For here's° a young and sweating devil here

    That commonly[3] rebels. 'Tis a good hand,

    A frank one.

Desdemona

           You may indeed say so,

    For 'twas that hand that gave away my heart.   40

Othello

    A liberal hand. The hearts of old gave hands,

    But our new heraldry is hands, not hearts. [4]

Desdemona

    I cannot speak of this. Come now, your promise.

Othello

    What promise, chuck? [5]

Desdemona

    I have sent to bid Cassio come speak with you.   45

Othello

    I have a salt and sorry rheum offends me; [6]

    Lend me thy handkerchief.

Desdemona

           Here, my lord.

Othello

    That which I gave you.

Desdemona

with   I have it not about° me.

Othello

    Not?

Desdemona

    No, faith, my lord.

1   *numbered in the world / The sun to*
    course two hundred compasses
    I.e., lived two hundred years
    (literally, "numbered her years in
    the world according to the sun,
    which had in her lifetime
    completed two hundred
    revolutions")

2   *mummy*
    A medicinal preparation made
    from mummified flesh

3   *Conserved of*
    Prepared from

4   *look to 't*
    Care for it

Othello

[handwritten: thinks that handkerchief is]

That's a fault. That handkerchief 50

Did an Egyptian to my mother give.

enchantress She was a charmer° and could almost read *[handwritten: and is mad]*

i.e., Othello's mother The thoughts of people. She told her° while she kept it *[handwritten: special]*

lovable 'Twould make her amiable° and subdue my father *[handwritten: at desdemona]*

Entirely to her love, but if she lost it, 55

Or made gift of it, my father's eye

find / repulsive Should hold° her loathèd° and his spirits should hunt

lovers After new fancies.° She, dying, gave it me

married And bid me, when my fate would have me wived,°

i.e., to my wife To give it her.° I did so, and, take heed on 't, *[handwritten: foreshadow ing]* 60

thing to cherish Make it a darling° like your precious eye;

ruin To lose 't or give 't away were such perdition°

equal As nothing else could match.°

Desdemona

Is 't possible?

Othello

woven fabric 'Tis true. There's magic in the web° of it. *[handwritten: Its true]*

seer A sibyl,° that had numbered in the world 65

The sun to course two hundred compasses,[1]

frenzy In her prophetic fury° sewed the work.

holy; sanctified The worms were hallowed° that did breed the silk,

i.e., the sibyl And it was dyed in mummy,[2] which the skillful°

Conserved of[3] maidens' hearts.

Desdemona

I' faith? Is 't true? 70

Othello

true Most veritable,° therefore look to 't[4] well.

Desdemona

Then would to God that I had never seen 't!

Othello

Why Ha! Wherefore?° *[handwritten: Desdemona wishes she would've never seen it]*

1 *out o' th' way*

   Lost

2 *an if*

   If

3 *My mind misgives.*

   I have a bad feeling.

Brotha

Desdemona

haltingly / passionately Why do you speak so startingly° and rash?°

Othello

Is 't lost? Is 't gone? Speak! Is 't out o' th' way?[1]   75

Desdemona

Heaven bless us!

Othello

Say you?

Desdemona

It is not lost, but what an if[2] it were?

Othello

How!

Desdemona

I say it is not lost.

Othello

                    Fetch 't; let me see 't.   80

Desdemona

Why, so I can, but I will not now.

distract / request This is a trick to put° me from my suit.°

Pray you, let Cassio be received again.

Othello

Fetch me the handkerchief. [*aside*] My mind misgives.[3]

Desdemona

capable Come, come; you'll never meet a more sufficient° man. 85

Othello

The handkerchief!

Desdemona

lifetime   A man that all his time°

set Hath founded° his good fortunes on your love,

Shared dangers with you—

Othello

The handkerchief!

1   *all the office of my heart*
    My fully devoted service

2   *purposed merit in futurity*
    The merit I intend to show in the
    future

Desdemona

I' faith, you are to blame.   90

Othello

Zounds!   **Othello** *exits.*

Emilia

Is not this man jealous?

Desdemona

I ne'er saw this before;

Sure there's some wonder in this handkerchief.

unfortunate, miserable I am most unhappy° in the loss of it.   95

Emilia

'Tis not a year or two shows us a man.

merely They are all but° stomachs, and we all but food;

eagerly They eat us hungerly,° and, when they are full,

They belch us. Look you, Cassio and my husband!

*Enter **Iago** and **Cassio**.*

Iago

[*to **Cassio***]There is no other way. 'Tis she must do 't,   100

urge And, lo, the happiness! Go and importune° her.

Desdemona

How now, good Cassio, what's the news with you?

Cassio

Madam, my former suit. I do beseech you

That by your virtuous means I may again

Exist and be a member of his love,   105

Whom I, with all the office of my heart, [1]

Entirely honor. I would not be delayed.

unpardonable If my offense be of such mortal° kind

neither / regrets That nor° my service past, nor present sorrows,°

Nor purposed merit in futurity, [2]   110

restore Can ransom° me into his love again,

1   *So shall I clothe me in a forced content, /
    And shut myself up in some other course /
    To fortune's alms.*

    **If it is so (that Othello will not
    forgive me), I will pretend to be
    contented and resign myself to
    whatever path fortune's charity
    provides me. (*Alms* are charitable
    offerings given to beggars.)**

2   *within the blank*

    **I.e., in the line of fire (the *blank* was
    the white center of an archery target)
    though it could, alternatively, here
    suggest "point- blank" range; the
    effect would not be very different.**

3   *and is he angry*

    **And now is he angry at this (little
    thing)?**

4   *Something of the moment then.*

    **It must, then, be something of
    great importance.**

5   *Something, sure, of state*

    **Something, no doubt, related to
    matters of state**

6   *unhatched practice*

    I.e., some plot not yet carried out

7   *Made demonstrable*

    Revealed

Merely   But° to know so must be my benefit.

So shall I clothe me in a forced content,

And shut myself up in some other course

To fortune's alms. [1]

Desdemona

                              Alas, thrice-gentle Cassio,   115

advocacy   My advocation° is not now in tune.

My lord is not my lord, nor should I know him

appearance Were he in favor° as in humor altered.

So help me every spirit sanctified

As I have spoken for you all my best   120

And stood within the blank [2] of his displeasure

unrestrained For my free° speech. You must awhile be patient.

What I can do I will, and more I will

Than for myself I dare. Let that suffice you.

Iago

Is my lord angry?

Emilia

just   He went hence but° now,   125

agitation   And certainly in strange unquietness.°

Iago

Can he be angry? I have seen the cannon

When it hath blown his ranks into the air

And, like the devil, from his very arm

Blew up   Puffed° his own brother—and is he angry? [3]   130

Something of moment then. [4] I will go meet him.

something consequential There's matter° in 't indeed, if he be angry.

Desdemona

I prithee, do so.   [**Iago**] *exits.*

                      Something, sure, of state, [5]

Either from Venice or some unhatched practice [6]

Made demonstrable [7] here in Cyprus to him,   135

1   *Though great ones are their object*

Even though important issues are the real object of their concern

2   *we must think men are not gods, / Nor of them look for such observancy / As fit the bridal*

I.e., we must acknowledge that men are only imperfect men, and also not continue to expect from them the attentiveness of bridegrooms on their wedding day.

3   *Beshrew me much*

Let evil befall me (a mild oath, like the modern "I'll be damned")

4   *Arraigning his unkindness*

Indicating his unnatural cruelty

5   *the cause*

The stated reason

6   *fit*

I.e, in a suitable mood to hear my request

muddied   Hath puddled° his clear spirit, and in such cases

Men's natures wrangle with inferior things,

Though great ones are their object. [1] 'Tis even so;

brings   For let our finger ache, and it endues°

limbs   Our other healthful members° even to a sense   140

Of pain. Nay, we must think men are not gods,

Nor of them look for such observancy

As fits the bridal. [2] Beshrew me much, [3] Emilia,

unskillful   I was, unhandsome° warrior as I am,

Arraigning his unkindness [4] with my soul,   145

But now I find I had suborned the witness,

And he's indicted falsely.

Emilia

                        Pray Heaven it be

notion   State matters, as you think, and no conception°

whim   Nor no jealous toy° concerning you.

Desdemona

Alas the day! I never gave him cause.   150

Emilia

But jealous souls will not be answered so.

on account of   They are not ever jealous for° the cause, [5]

because   But jealous for° they're jealous. It is a monster

Begot upon itself, born on itself.

Desdemona

Heaven keep the monster from Othello's mind!   155

Emilia

Lady, amen.

Desdemona

I will go seek him.—Cassio, walk hereabout.

If I do find him fit, [6] I'll move your suit

And seek to effect it to my uttermost.

Cassio

I humbly thank your Ladyship.   160

1 *Save you*

   God save (i.e., protect) you.

2 *this while with leaden thoughts been*
   pressed

   For a while been oppressed with
   burdensome issues

3 *Strike off this score*

   Settle this debt

4 *Take me this work out.*

   Copy this embroidery for me.

5 *To the felt absence now I feel a cause.*

   I now perceive the reason for the
   absence I noticed.

[**Desdemona** *and* **Emilia**] *exit.*

Enter **Bianca**.

Bianca

Save you, [1] friend Cassio!

Cassio

i.e., brings   What make° you from home?

How is 't with you, my most fair Bianca?

I' faith, sweet love, I was coming to your house.

Bianca

And I was going to your lodging, Cassio.

stay   What, keep° a week away? Seven days and nights?   165

i.e., 168   Eight-score-eight° hours? And lovers' absent hours

clock   More tedious than the dial° eightscore times!

calculation   Oh weary reck'ning!°

Cassio

              Pardon me, Bianca.

I have this while with leaden thoughts been pressed, [2]

uninterrupted   But I shall, in a more continuate° time,   170

Strike off this score [3] of absence. Sweet Bianca,

          [*giving her* **Desdemona**'s *handkerchief*]

Take me this work out. [4]

Bianca

            O Cassio, whence came this?

lover   This is some token from a newer friend!°

To the felt absence now I feel a cause. [5]

Is 't come to this? Well, well.

Cassio

            Go to, woman!   175

Throw your vile guesses in the devil's teeth

From whence you have them. You are jealous now

That this is from some mistress, some remembrance.

1 *Ere it be demanded*

   Before someone claims it

2 *like enough*

   Probably

3 *attend here on*

   Wait here for

4 *soon at night*

   I.e., tonight

5 *be circumstanced*

   Accept the situation

No, by my faith, Bianca.

Bianca

                                        Why, whose is it?

Cassio

I know not neither; I found it in my chamber.   180

I like the work well. Ere it be demanded,[1]

want to As like enough[2] it will, I would° have it copied.

Take it and do 't, and leave me for this time.

Bianca

Leave you? Wherefore?

Cassio

I do attend here on[3] the General   185

advantage And think it no addition,° nor my wish,

with a woman To have him see me womaned.°

Bianca

                                        Why, I pray you?

Cassio

Not that I love you not.

Bianca

                                        But that you do not love me.

accompany I pray you bring° me on the way a little

And say if I shall see you soon at night.[4]   190

Cassio

'Tis but a little way that I can bring you,

For I attend here. But I'll see you soon.

Bianca

'Tis very good. I must be circumstanced.[5]   *They exit.*

1 *It is hypocrisy against the devil.*

I.e., if they were naked in bed together but did not intend to commit adultery, they behaved hypocritically toward the devil, because their behavior seemed to promise that they would sin.

2 *do so*

I.e., be naked with her friend in bed

Act 4, Scene 1

*Enter **Othello** and **Iago**.*

Iago

Will you think so?

Othello

              Think so, Iago?

Iago

                          What,

To kiss in private?

Othello

unlawful   An unauthorized° kiss!

Iago

Or to be naked with her friend in bed

An hour or more, not meaning any harm?

Othello

Naked in bed, Iago, and not mean harm?   5

It is hypocrisy against the devil. ¹

They that mean virtuously and yet do so, ²

tests   The devil their virtue tempts,° and they tempt Heaven.

Iago

pardonable   If they do nothing, 'tis a venial° slip.

But if I give my wife a handkerchief—   10

Othello

What then?

Iago

Why then 'tis hers, my lord, and, being hers,

She may, I think, bestow 't on any man.

Othello

She is protectress of her honor too.

May she give that?   15

Handwritten annotations:

Talking ab Cassio and Desdemona

were they in bed

If they didn't do anything then its ok

can she give away her reputation

1 *They have it very oft that have it not*

   I.e., those who reputedly possess
   the *quality* of honor very often
   lack that essence in reality.

2 *the raven o'er the infectious house*

   Ravens were believed to be omens
   of misfortune (*infectious* = plague-
   infected).

3 *as knaves be such abroad*

   Since such villains do exist in the
   world

4 *Convincèd or supplied*

   I.e., seduced or (sexually) gratified

Iago

Her honor is an essence that's not seen;
They have it very oft that have it not. [1]
But for the handkerchief—

[you can't see a reputatio but a handkercheif]

Othello

By Heaven, I would most gladly have forgot it.
Thou said'st—Oh, it comes o'er my memory,
As doth the raven o'er the infectious house, [2]

Ominous   Boding° to all—he had my handkerchief.

20

Iago

Ay, what of that?

[I wish I could forget the handkercheif]

Othello

That's not so good now.

Iago

What

If I had said I had seen him do you wrong?
Or heard him say—as knaves be such abroad, [3]

strongly urged   Who having, by their own importunate° suit,
infatuation   Or voluntary dotage° of some mistress,
Convincèd or supplied [4] them, cannot choose
But they must blab—

[what if Cassio said som. to hurt Othello]

25

Othello

Hath he said anything?

Iago

He hath, my lord, but be you well assured
No more than he'll unswear.

[Lies]

30

Othello

What hath he said?

Iago

Faith, that he did—I know not what he did.

Othello

What? What?

1   *We say "lie on her" when they belie her!*

To *lie on* or *belie* someone means to "tell lies about" that person; if Cassio lies *on* Desdemona, Othello reasons, he slanders her, but he cannot avoid the sexual implication of "lie with her."

2   *Nature would not invest herself in such shadowing passion without instruction.*

I.e., I couldn't be this disturbed if there were no real cause for it.

3   *It is not words that shakes me thus.*

I.e., it would take more than words to have this effect on me. In fact, it is the mental image of Desdemona as an adulteress that brings upon the fit, an image that Iago's *words* have generated.

4   *Noses, ears, and lips. Is 't possible? Confess!—Handkerchief!—Oh, devil!*

Othello's disordered and increasingly fragmented prose is the verbal prelude to his physical collapse. *Noses, ears,* and *lips* stem from Othello's imagining the intimacies that Desdemona and Cassio share.

5   *My med'cine*

I.e., the suspicions I have set into motion

6   *My lord is fall'n into an epilepsy.*

Epilepsy was known as "the falling sickness." It was associated with both divine and demonic possession, and was said to have afflicted Julius Caesar and the prophet Muhammad. According to Leo Africanus, one of Shakespeare's sources for *Othello*, Muhammad falsely claimed that he had "conversed with the angel Gabriel, unto whose brightness he ascribed the falling sickness, which many times prostrated himself upon the earth: dilating and amplifying the same in like sort, by permitting all that was plausible to sense and the flesh."

Iago

Lie—

Iago says Cassio said he was in bed with Desdemona

Othello

With her?

Iago

whatever   With her, on her—what° you will.

Othello

Lie with her? Lie on her? We say "lie on her" when they
nauseating   belie her! [1] Lie with her! Zounds, that's fulsome.°   35
Handkerchief—confessions—handkerchief! To con-
fess, and be hanged for his labor? First to be hanged,
and then to confess—I tremble at it. Nature would not
invest herself in such shadowing passion without some
(A disgusted exclamation) instruction. [2] It is not words that shakes me thus. [3] Pish!° 40
Noses, ears, and lips. Is 't possible? Confess!—Hand-
kerchief!—Oh, devil! [4]

(falls in a trance)

Iago

Othello is in rage

In this manner Work on! My med'cine [5] works! Thus° credulous fools
    are caught,
this way And many worthy and chaste dames even thus,°
disgrace All guiltless, meet reproach.°—What, ho! My lord!   45
My lord, I say! Othello!

Iago is happy how gullible Othello is

Enter **Cassio**.

(A greeting)   How now,° Cassio!

Cassio

What's the matter?

Iago

My lord is fall'n into an epilepsy. [6]
This is his second fit. He had one yesterday.

Othello having a seizure

Cassio

Rub him about the temples.

1   *lethargy*

I.e., state of unconsciousness

2   *have his quiet course*

Run its *quiet* (since Othello cannot speak) *course*

3   *on great occasion*

About an important matter

4   *Dost thou mock me?*

Othello takes Iago's question in the previous line as a reference to the cuckold's horns.

5   *A hornèd man's a monster and a beast.*

Continuing the play's pattern of animal-monster imagery, Othello links the figure of the *cuckold*, a man with the horns of a beast, to the degraded, bestial sexuality emphasized by Iago. The cuckold was frequently the butt of humor in the comic drama of the day, but as many critics have pointed out, *Othello* is a tragedy that contains many of the generic features of comedy: jealous husbands, a parental blocking figure, marriage, eavesdropping, mistaken identity, et cetera.

6   *Think every bearded fellow that's but yoked / May draw with you*

Consider that every married man is yoked to the same plow (i.e., also wears the cuckold's horns)

7   *That nightly lie in those unproper beds / Which they dare swear peculiar*

I.e., that lie every night in beds that they believe to be theirs alone, but which in fact have been contaminated by their wives' lovers.

8   *Your case is better*

I.e., because you know your situation

9   *To lip a wanton in a secure couch*

I.e., for a man to kiss a woman believing in her fidelity

Iago

refrain
                                        No, forbear.°   50
its   The lethargy[1] must have his° quiet course.[2]

Iago says to leave him alone or he will foam

        If not, he foams at mouth and, by and by,
        Breaks out to savage madness. Look; he stirs.
        Do you withdraw yourself a little while.
straightaway   He will recover straight.° When he is gone,   55
        I would on great occasion[3] speak with you.

                                        [**Cassio** *exits.*]

        How is it, General? Have you not hurt your head?

Othello

and tells Cassio to leave

        Dost thou mock me?[4]

Iago

                                        I mock you not, by Heaven.
I wish   Would° you would bear your fortune like a man!

Othello

        A hornèd man's a monster and a beast.[5]   60

Iago

        There's many a beast then in a populous city,
civilized   And many a civil° monster.

Othello

        Did he confess it?

Iago

                                        Good sir, be a man;

Iago says every rich man has been cheated on

        Think every bearded fellow that's but yoked
pull   May draw° with you.[6] There's millions now alive   65
        That nightly lie in those unproper beds
situation   Which they dare swear peculiar.[7] Your case° is better.[8]
devil's / worst trick   Oh, 'tis the spite of Hell, the fiend's° arch-mock,°
        To lip a wanton in a secure couch[9]
        And to suppose her chaste. No, let me know,   70
i.e., a man betrayed   And knowing what I am,° I know what she shall be.

1   *'Tis certain.*

It is unclear whether Othello refers here to Iago's wisdom or Desdemona's infidelity.

2   *Confine yourself but in a patient list*

Stay within the bounds of patience (but *list* also means "listening," and so prepares for what follows)

3   *laid good 'scuses upon your ecstasy*

I.e., gave a plausible explanation for your fit

4   *the fleers, the gibes, and notable scorns*

The sneers, the mocks, and the discernible scorn

5   *cope*

Encounter; a secondary meaning is "cover," and both combine to give the verb a strong sexual sense.

6   *all in all in spleen*

I.e., completely transformed by anger (the *spleen* was thought to be the seat of choler, or rage)

7   *keep time in all*

Control yourself; hold off until later.

8   *huswife*

hussy (pronounced "hussif")

9   *'tis the strumpet's plague / To beguile many and be beguiled by one*

It is the prostitute's bad fortune to *beguile* (charm; deceive) many men and then be beguiled, in turn, *by one* man.

Othello

Oh, thou art wise! 'Tis certain. ¹

Iago

Stand you awhile apart;

Confine yourself but in a patient list. ²

Whilst you were here o'erwhelmèd with your grief—   75

A passion most unsuiting such a man—

Cassio came hither. I shifted him away

And laid good 'scuses upon your ecstasy, ²

presently   Bade him anon° return and here speak with me,

conceal   The which he promised. Do but encave° yourself   80

take note of   And mark° the fleers, the gibes, and notable scorns ⁴

That dwell in every region of his face,

For I will make him tell the tale anew:

Where, how, how oft, how long ago, and when

He hath, and is again to cope ⁵ your wife.   85

demeanor   I say but mark his gesture.° Marry, patience,

Or I shall say you're all in all in spleen, ⁶

And nothing of a man.

Othello

Dost thou hear, Iago?

skillful   I will be found most cunning° in my patience,

violent   But—dost thou hear?—most bloody.°   90

Iago

inappropriate That's not amiss,°

But yet keep time in all. ⁷ Will you withdraw?

[**Othello** *hides.*]

about   Now will I question Cassio of° Bianca,

A huswife ⁸ that by selling her desires

She   Buys herself bread and clothes. It° is a creature   95

That dotes on Cassio, as 'tis the strumpet's plague

To beguile many and be beguiled by one. ⁹

He, when he hears of her, cannot restrain

1 *Quite in the wrong*
  Completely erroneously

2 *The worser that you give me the addition /*
  Whose want even kills me.
  **Worse, now that you name the title
  (i.e., of lieutenant), the lack of
  which almost destroys me**

3 *sure on 't*
  I.e., certain to be reinstated

4 *gives it out*
  Reports; let's it be known

From the excess of laughter. Here he comes.

Enter **Cassio**.

| | As he shall smile, Othello shall go mad, | 100 |
ignorant / interpret And his unbookish° jealousy must construe°
frivolous Poor Cassio's smiles, gestures, and light° behaviors
Quite in the wrong. ¹— How do you, lieutenant?

Cassio

title The worser that you give me the addition° *Cassio wants*
Whose want even kills me. ² *his position back* 105

Iago

Implore Ply° Desdemona well, and you are sure on 't. ³ *Iago tells*
Now if this suit lay in Bianca's power, *Cassio to keep*
meet with success How quickly should you speed!° *trying*

Cassio

wretch   Alas, poor caitiff!°

Othello

[*aside*] Look how he laughs already!

Iago

I never knew woman love man so. 110

Cassio

Alas, poor rogue, I think i' faith she loves me. *talking about*

Othello

half-heartedly / off [*aside*] Now he denies it faintly° and laughs it out.° *Bianca*

Iago *Loving Cassio*

Do you hear, Cassio?

Othello

urges   [*aside*] Now he importunes° him
again To tell it o'er.° Go to, well said, well said.

Iago

She gives it out ⁴ that you shall marry her. 115
Do you intend it?

1   *Do ye triumph, Roman?*

The *triumph* was the public
ceremony with which a Roman
general was greeted upon his
return from a conquest; Othello
calls Cassio *Roman* in reference to
his exultation over his sexual
conquest.

2   *bear some charity to my wit; do not think
it so unwholesome*

Give me credit for some judgment;
don't think it (my judgment) is
that impaired.

3   *say true*

I.e., be serious; don't lie.

4   *I am a very villain else*

Otherwise (i.e., if this isn't so) I
am a complete scoundrel

5   *the monkey's own giving out*

The monkey's (i.e., Bianca's) own
report (*monkey* being a half-
dismissive term of endearment,
generally used of children)

6   *bauble*

Fool (the word *bauble* literally
means "plaything")

7   *falls me thus*

Drapes herself over me in this way
(Cassio demonstrates on Iago)

Cassio

Ha, ha, ha!

Othello

[*aside*] Do ye triumph, Roman?[1] Do you triumph?

Cassio

prostitute / Please I marry? What? A customer?° Prithee° bear some

charity to my wit; do not think it so unwholesome.[2] 120

Ha, ha, ha!

Othello

[*aside*] So, so, so, so! They laugh that wins!

Iago

rumor Faith, the cry° goes that you marry her.

Cassio

Prithee say true![3]

Iago

I am a very villain else.[4]

Othello

wounded [*aside*] Have you scored° me? Well.

Cassio

This is the monkey's own giving out.[5] She is persuaded

self-flattery I will marry her, out of her own love and flattery,° not

out of my promise.

Othello

[*aside*] Iago beckons me. Now he begins the story. 130

Cassio

She was here even now. She haunts me in every place. I

was the other day talking on the sea-bank with certain

Venetians, and thither comes the bauble[6] and

falls me thus[7] about my neck—

Othello

[*aside*] Crying "O dear Cassio!" as it were. His gesture 135

suggests imports° it.

1   *plucked*

    Pulled him by the coat or sleeve

2   *Oh, I see that nose of yours, but not*
    that dog I shall throw it to.

    The practice of cutting off a man's
    nose to redress a wrong was not
    outlawed in England until 1670.

3   *Before me!*

    A mild oath

4   *fitchew*

    Prostitute (literally "polecat")

5   *a perfumed one*

    Like skunks, fitchews emit a foul
    odor when frightened or
    disturbed.

6   *take out the work*

    Copy the embroidery

7   *piece of work*

    Story

8   *are next prepared for*

    Are next invited (i.e., never)

Cassio

drapes herself So hangs and lolls° and weeps upon me, so shakes and
pulls me! Ha, ha, ha!

Othello

[*aside*] Now he tells how she plucked[1] him to my chamber.
Oh, I see that nose of yours, but not that dog I shall   140
throw it to.[2]

Cassio

Well, I must leave her company.

Iago

Before me![3] Look where she comes.

Enter **Bianca**.

Cassio

'Tis such another fitchew,[4] marry, a perfumed one.[5]
[*to* **Bianca**] What do you mean by this haunting of me?   145

Bianca

mother Let the devil and his dam° haunt you! What did you mean
just by that same handkerchief you gave me even° now?
I was a fine fool to take it. I must take out the work?[6] A
likely piece of work,[7] that you should find it in your
chamber and not know who left it there! This is some   150
minx's token, and I must take out the work? There; give
whore it your hobby-horse.° Wheresoever you had it, I'll take
from out no work on° 't.

Cassio

How now, my sweet Bianca! How now? How now?

Othello

must [*aside*] By Heaven, that should° be my handkerchief!   155

Bianca

If you'll come to supper tonight, you may. If you will
not, come when you are next prepared for.[8]   *She exits.*

1 *fain*
   Much like to

2 *prizes*
   Esteems (i.e., not at all)

3 *I would have him nine years a-killing.*
   I'd like to kill him slowly, over nine
   years.

Iago

After her, after her.

Cassio

Faith, I must; she'll rail in the streets else.

Iago

Will you sup there? 160

Cassio

Faith, I intend so.

Iago

Well, I may chance to see you, for I would very fain [1]
speak with you.

Cassio

Prithee come, will you?

Iago

Go to! Say no more. [**Cassio** exits.] 165

Othello

[advancing] How shall I murder him, Iago?

Iago

Did you perceive how he laughed at his vice?

Othello wants to kill Cassio

Othello

O Iago!

Iago

And did you see the handkerchief?

Othello

Was that mine? 170

Iago

Yours, by this hand. And to see how he prizes [2] the
foolish woman your wife! She gave it him, and he
hath giv'n it his whore.

Othello

I would have him nine years a-killing. [3] A fine woman! A
fair woman! A sweet woman! 175

1   *not your way*

    No way for you to think

2   *so gentle a condition*

    The phrase could mean either
    "such noble birth" or "such a
    pliant disposition." Iago chooses
    to pick up on the second meaning.

3   *fond over*

    Indulgent of

4   *comes near*

    Bothers

Iago

Nay, you must forget that.

Othello

Ay, let her rot and perish and be damned tonight, for
she shall not live. No, my heart is turned to stone: I

i.e., my heart strike it,° and it hurts my hand. Oh, the world hath not
a sweeter creature. She might lie by an emperor's side 180
and command him tasks.

Iago

Nay, that's not your way. [1]

Othello

skilled Hang her! I do but say what she is: so delicate° with her
needle, an admirable musician—oh, she will sing the
savageness out of a bear—of so high and plenteous wit 185

imagination and invention!°

Iago

She's the worse for all this.

Othello

Oh, a thousand, a thousand times!—and then of so
gentle a condition! [2]

Iago

Ay, too gentle. 190

Othello

Nay, that's certain. But yet the pity of it, Iago! O Iago,
the pity of it, Iago!

Iago

license If you are so fond over[3] her iniquity, give her patent° to
affects offend, for if it touch° not you it comes near[4] nobody.

Othello

little bits I will chop her into messes!° Cuckold me? 195

Iago

Oh, 'tis foul in her.

[Handwritten margin notes: "her wants to let Desd. die and rot" / "Iago says that Othello should give Desd. the ability to cheat" / "Othello will chop her into pieces"]

1   *unprovide my mind*

    Weaken my resolve

2   *let me be his undertaker*

    I.e., let him be my responsibility (the
    modern sense of "undertaker" as
    "one who prepares funerals" did not
    come into use until the very end of
    the 17th century)

3   *With*

    Short for some such phrase as "I
    thank you with all my heart"

Othello

With mine officer?

Iago

That's fouler.

Othello

Get me some poison, Iago, this night. I'll not

debate expostulate° with her, lest her body and beauty
unprovide my mind¹ again. This night, Iago!

Iago

Do it not with poison. Strangle her in her bed, even the
bed she hath contaminated.

Othello

Good, good, the justice of it pleases! Very good!

Iago

And for Cassio, let me be his undertaker.² You shall   205
hear more by midnight.

Othello

Excellent good. [*trumpet within*]

What trumpet is that same?

Iago

am certain I warrant° something from Venice.

Enter **Lodovico**, **Desdemona**, *and attendants.*

i.e., this embassy 'Tis Lodovico. This° comes from the Duke.
See, your wife's with him.   210

Lodovico

God save you, worthy General!

Othello

With³ all my heart, sir.

Handwritten margin notes: "Othello wants poison for Desd." and "Iago says he should strangle he will" (line 200 marked)

1 *instrument of their pleasures*

   I.e., the document that conveys
   their wishes

2 *He did not call; he's busy in the paper.*

   He wasn't speaking to you; he's
   busy reading the letter.

3 *Fire and brimstone!*

   A strong oath (referring to the
   torments of Hell)

Lodovico *someone from venice*

The Duke and the senators of Venice greet you.

[*gives him a letter*]

Othello *and he brings orders from the Duke*

I kiss the instrument of their pleasures. ¹

Desdemona

And what's the news, good cousin Lodovico?

Iago

I am very glad to see you, signior. Welcome to Cyprus.   ²¹⁵

Lodovico

I thank you. How does lieutenant Cassio?

Iago

Lives, sir.

Desdemona

Cousin, there's fall'n between him and my lord

unnatural An unkind° breach, but you shall make all well.

Othello

Are you sure of that?   220

Desdemona

My lord?

Othello

[*reads*] "This fail you not to do, as you will—"

Lodovico

He did not call; he's busy in the paper. ²

discord Is there division° 'twixt my lord and Cassio?

Desdemona

unfortunate A most unhappy° one. I would do much   225

reconcile T' atone° them, for the love I bear to Cassio.

Othello

Fire and brimstone! ³ *He's mad*

Desdemona

My lord?

1   *Deputing Cassio in his government*

Appointing Cassio as governor

2   *I am glad to see you mad.*

An obscure line that has never
been satisfactorily explained;
perhaps "I am glad that you are so
mad (foolish) as to demonstrate
your love for Cassio so blatantly,"
although *mad* may in fact have
been an abbreviation in the
manuscript for "madam," a mark
of chilling politeness.

3   *'Tis very much.*

This is too much.

4   *Each drop she falls would prove a
crocodile*

Each tear she lets fall would give
birth to a *crocodile*; "crocodile
tears" are proverbially false,
hypocritical expressions of sorrow.

Othello

i.e., sane Are you wise?°

Desdemona

What, is he angry?

Lodovico

                         Maybe the letter moved him,   230

For, as I think, they do command him home,

Deputing Cassio in his government. [1]

Desdemona

of By my troth, I am glad on° 't.

Othello

Indeed?

Desdemona

My lord?   235

Othello

I am glad to see you mad. [2]   *Othello is mad*

Desdemona

Why, sweet Othello—

Othello

[*striking her*] Devil!   *he hits Desdemona*

Desdemona

I have not deserved this.

Lodovico

My lord, this would not be believed in Venice,   240

Even if Though° I should swear I saw 't. 'Tis very much. [3]

Make her amends; she weeps.

Othello

                            Oh, devil, devil!

be impregnated If that the earth could teem° with woman's tears,

Each drop she falls would prove a crocodile. [4]

Out of my sight!

Desdemona

                   [*going*] I will not stay to offend you.   245

1   *turn, and turn*

I.e., return but also rebel and
change (sexual) partners; as
Othello is a Moor "turned"
Christian and one who condemns
Christians *turned Turks* (2.3.156), a
further complexity is introduced.

2   *obedient*

(1) dutiful; (2) sexually available

3   *well-painted passion*

Cleverly feigned emotion

4   *Goats and monkeys!*

Proverbially promiscuous animals
(the line echoes Iago's similes at
3.3.407 *as prime as goats, as hot as
monkeys*)

5   *all in all sufficient*

Competent in everything

6   *shot of accident nor dart of chance*

I.e., unexpected strokes of
misfortune

Lodovico

Truly, an obedient lady.

I do beseech your lordship call her back.

Othello

Mistress!

Desdemona

[*turns back*] My lord?

Othello

wish [*to* **Lodovico**] What would° you with her, sir? 250

Lodovico

Who, I, my lord?

Othello

Ay, you did wish that I would make her turn.

Sir, she can turn, and turn,[1] and yet go on

And turn again. And she can weep, sir, weep.

And she's obedient,[2] as you say, obedient, 255

Very obedient. [*to* **Desdemona**] Proceed you in your

tears?

i.e., the letter —Concerning this,° sir—Oh, well-painted passion![3]

—I am commanded home.—Get you away;

I'll send for you anon.—Sir, I obey the mandate

Get away And will return to Venice.—Hence! Avaunt!° 260

[**Desdemona** *exits.*]

Cassio shall have my place. And, sir, tonight

I do entreat that we may sup together.

You are welcome, sir, to Cyprus. —Goats and monkeys![4]

He exits.

Lodovico

Is this the noble Moor whom our full senate

Call all in all sufficient?[5] Is this the nature 265

Whom passion could not shake, whose solid virtue

The shot of accident nor dart of chance[6]

Could neither graze nor pierce?

1   *He's that he is; I may not breathe my*
    censure / What he might be.
    He is what he is (i.e., mentally
    unsound). I am not in a position to
    whisper my opinion about what he
    may be.

2   *If what he might he is not, / I would to*
    Heaven he were!
    A difficult line. Either "If he is not
    as mentally sound as he could be, /
    I wish to God he were," or "If he's
    not insane, I wish to God that he
    were" (because only madness
    could excuse his actions).

3   *work upon his blood*
    Upset him

Iago

                                        He is much changed.

Lodovico

sound   Are his wits safe?° Is he not light of brain? *crazy?*

Iago

what   He's that° he is; I may not breathe my censure   270
What he might be.[1] If what he might he is not,
I would to Heaven he were![2]

Lodovico

                              What? Strike his wife?

Iago

were sure   'Faith, that was not so well. Yet would I knew°
That stroke would prove the worst!

Lodovico

habit   Is it his use?°
Or did the letters work upon his blood[3]   275
And new-create his fault?

Iago

                              Alas, alas!

loyalty   It is not honesty° in me to speak
What I have seen and known. You shall observe him,
actions / depict   And his own courses° will denote° him so
That I may save my speech. Do but go after   280
And mark how he continues.

Lodovico

about   I am sorry that I am deceived in° him.   *They exit.*

1 *Lay down my soul at stake*

Risk my soul as my bet

2 *abuse your bosom*

Mislead you (the *bosom*, or breast,
was thought to be the seat of inner
feelings)

3 *the serpent's curse*

I.e., a curse like that with which
God punished the serpent that
tempted Eve in the Garden of Eden
(see Genesis 3:14)

context: Othello and Emilia are ~~a~~ talking about Desdemona and Cassio. ~~a~~ Emilia is defending Desdemona. Before Locl. just talked to Iago and thinks Othello is crazy. Desd. is also slapped

Act 4, Scene 2

Enter **Othello** and **Emilia**.

Othello

You have seen nothing, then?   *asks if Emilia has seen or heard anything but she declines*

Emilia

Nor ever heard, nor ever did suspect—

Othello

Yes, you have seen Cassio and she together.

Emilia

But then I saw no harm, and then I heard   *she saw*
Each syllable that breath made up between them.   *no* 5 *wrong and heard what she said*

Othello

What, did they never whisper?

Emilia

Never, my lord.

Othello   *they never whispered or made her leave them alone*

Nor send you out o' th' way?

Emilia

Never.

Othello   *Desd. never asked Emilia to get any of he belongings*

To fetch her fan, her gloves, her mask, nor nothing? 10

Emilia

Never, my lord.

Othello

That's strange. → *This contradicts what Iago tells Othello*

Emilia   *Emilia says Desdemona is faithful and is not what ~~she~~ he thinks she is*

would dare / faithful   I durst,° my lord, to wager she is honest,°
otherwise   Lay down my soul at stake.[1] If you think other,°
    Remove your thought; it doth abuse your bosom.[2] 15
    If any wretch have put this in your head,
~~metaphor~~ *Allusion* →   Let Heaven requite it with the serpent's curse,[3]
    For if she be not honest, chaste, and true,

275

1   *She says enough, yet she's a simple bawd /*
    That cannot say as much.

    What she says seems satisfactory,
    but the simplest proprietor of a
    brothel could concoct a similar
    story.

2   *This*

    Probably refers to Emilia (who in
    lines 29–32 is similarly charged
    with conspiring with Desdemona),
    but possibly to Desdemona

3   *A closet, lock and key*

    A closed room, complete with lock
    and key

4   *Some of your function, mistress.*

    Othello continues to insist that
    Emilia is a procuress and that
    Desdemona is one of her
    prostitutes. He orders Emilia to
    perform the functions of her job
    (i.e, leave the room and signal if
    anyone approaches).

5   *mystery*

    Profession (as a procuress)

There's no man happy. The purest of their wives
Is foul as slander.   *If shes cheated then*
Othello   *theres no such thing as*
                    Bid her come hither. Go. *a pure₂₀ wife*

Emilia *exits.*

She says enough, yet she's a simple bawd
That cannot say as much. [1] This [2] is a subtle whore,
A closet, lock and key, [3] of villainous secrets.
And yet she'll kneel and pray—I have seen her do 't.

Enter **Desdemona** *with* **Emilia**.

Desdemona
My lord, what is your will?   25
Othello
dear   Pray you, chuck,° come hither.
Desdemona
wish   What is your pleasure?°
Othello
                                    Let me see your eyes;
Look in my face.
Desdemona
                                What horrible fancy's this?
Othello
[*to* **Emilia**] Some of your function, mistress. [4]
sexual partners   Leave procreants° alone and shut the door;   30
Cough or cry "hem" if anybody come.
hurry   Your mystery, [5] your mystery! Nay, dispatch!°

Emilia *exits.*

Desdemona
mean   [*kneeling*] Upon my knee, what doth your speech import?°
I understand a fury in your words,
But not the words.

1   *An instrument of this your calling back*

    I.e, of being responsible for the
    order for you to return to Venice

2   *try me with affliction*

    Possibly an allusion to the biblical
    story of Job. With God's
    permission, Satan severely tested
    the pious and righteous Job;
    though his children were killed, his
    property destroyed, and his body
    ravaged by disease, Job refused to
    curse God and, consequently, God
    restored his happiness.

Othello

                          Why, what art thou?   35

Desdemona

Your wife, my lord, your true and loyal wife.

Othello

Come, swear it, damn thyself,

seeming   Lest, being° like one of Heaven, the devils themselves

Should fear to seize thee. Therefore be double damned:

Swear thou art honest!

Desdemona

                     Heaven doth truly know it.   40

Othello

Heaven truly knows that thou art false as Hell.

Desdemona

To whom, my lord? With whom? How am I false?

Othello

Ah, Desdemon, away, away, away!

Desdemona

sorrowful   [*rising*] Alas the heavy° day! Why do you weep?

cause   Am I the motive° of these tears, my lord?   45

by any chance   If haply° you my father do suspect

An instrument of this your calling back, [1]

Lay not your blame on me. If you have lost him,

I have lost him too.

Othello

                  Had it pleased Heaven

To try me with affliction, [2] had they rained   50

All kinds of sores and shames on my bare head,

Steeped me in poverty to the very lips,

greatest   Given to captivity me and my utmost° hopes,

I should have found in some place of my soul

A drop of patience. But, alas, to make me   55

1 *The fixèd figure for the time of scorn / To point his slow and moving finger at*
I.e., to make me an object of unending scorn. Othello imagines himself as paralyzed by Desdemona's betrayal, unable to move as scorn points him out with its *slow and moving finger*.

2 *there, where I have garnered up my heart*
There, where I have stored my most deep-seated feelings (i.e., in Desdemona)

3 *knot and gender*
Intertwine and procreate

4 *Turn thy complexion there, / Patience, thou young and rose-lipped cherubin. / Ay, here look grim as Hell!*
Othello addresses Patience, personified as a cherub, and asks him to turn and look at Desdemona; the sight, Othello says, will cause the youthful and red-lipped angel's face to turn as black as Hell. (The form *cherubin* obviously is singular here but is a variant of the plural form (*cherubim*) of the Hebrew *cherub*.)

5 *That quicken even with blowing*
That come to life as soon as the flies' eggs are deposited in the carcasses

6 *paper, this most goodly book*
Depicting the beloved as a page or book was a conventional literary metaphor.

7 *Committed*
Othello's reiteration of this word (also lines 75, 78, and 82) stems from the fact that it could mean "committed adultery."

8 *I should make very forges of my cheeks / That would to cinders burn up modesty / Did I but speak thy deeds.*
I.e., if I were to put what you have done into words, my breath would fan the fire and incinerate chastity itself.

9 *the hollow mine of Earth*
According to Greek mythology, the winds lived imprisoned in a cave until the gods required their services.

The fixèd figure for the time of scorn
To point his slow and moving finger at [1]—
Yet could I bear that too, well, very well;
But there, where I have garnered up my heart, [2]
Where either I must live or bear no life,   60
source The fountain° from the which my current runs
Or else dries up—to be discarded thence!
cesspool Or keep it as a cistern° for foul toads
face To knot and gender[3] in! Turn thy complexion° there,
Patience, thou young and rose-lipped cherubin.   65
Ay, here look grim as Hell. [4]

Desdemona
believes I hope my noble lord esteems° me honest.

Othello
slaughterhouse Oh, ay, as summer flies are in the shambles,°
That quicken even with blowing. [5] O thou weed,
Who art so lovely fair and smell'st so sweet   70
That the sense aches at thee, would thou hadst ne'er
    been born!

Desdemona
unwitting Alas, what ignorant° sin have I committed?

Othello
Was this fair paper, this most goodly book, [6]
Made to write "whore" upon? What? "Committed?" [7]
prostitute "Committed?" O thou public commoner!°   75
bellows I should make very forges° of my cheeks
That would to cinders burn up modesty
Did I but speak thy deeds. [8] What? "Committed?"
shuts its eyes Heaven stops the nose at it and the moon winks;°
promiscuous The bawdy° wind that kisses all it meets   80
Is hushed within the hollow mine of Earth [9]
And will not hear 't. What? "Committed?"
Impudent strumpet!

1   *as I shall be saved*

    **As I believe my soul will be saved
    when I die (i.e., I'm innocent)**

2   *cry you mercy*

    Beg your pardon (sarcastic)

3   *keep our counsel*

    Be discreet.

Desdemona

By Heaven, you do me wrong!

Othello

Are you not a strumpet?   85

Desdemona

No, as I am a Christian.

body If to preserve this vessel° for my lord

i.e., other's From any other° foul unlawful touch

Be not to be a strumpet, I am none.

Othello

What, not a whore?

Desdemona

                        No, as I shall be saved. [1]   90

Othello

Is 't possible?

Desdemona

Oh, Heaven forgive us!

Othello

                        I cry you mercy, [2] then;

I took you for that cunning whore of Venice

That married with Othello.—[*calls*] You, mistress,

Enter **Emilia**.

That have the office opposite to Saint Peter   95

And keeps the gate of Hell! You, you, ay, you!

business We have done our course.° There's money for your

            pains. [*hands her coins*]

I pray you, turn the key and keep our counsel. [3]

                                                He exits.

Emilia

imagine Alas, what does this gentleman conceive?°

How do you, madam? How do you, my good lady?   100

1   *But what should go by water*

     I.e., except that which can be
     expressed by tears

2   *How have I been behaved that he might*
     stick / The small'st opinion on my least
     misuse?

     What have I done that he could be
     angry with even my worst fault?

Desdemona

dazed Faith, half-asleep.°

Emilia

Good madam, what's the matter with my lord?

Desdemona

With who?

Emilia

Why, with my lord, madam

Desdemona

Who is thy lord?   105

Emilia

He that is yours, sweet lady.

Desdemona

I have none. Do not talk to me, Emilia.
I cannot weep, nor answers have I none,
But what should go by water.[1] Prithee, tonight
Lay on my bed my wedding sheets. Remember,   110
And call thy husband hither.

Emilia

Here's a change indeed!   *She exits.*

Desdemona

fitting (ironic) / treated 'Tis meet° I should be used° so, very meet.
How have I been behaved that he might stick
The small'st opinion on my least misuse?[2]   115

                    Enter **Iago** and **Emilia**.

Iago

What is your pleasure, madam? How is 't with you?

Desdemona

I cannot tell. Those that do teach young babes
reprimands Do it with gentle means and easy tasks;°

1   *a child to chiding*

   I.e., new to being rebuked

2   *bewhored her*

   Called her a whore

3   *A beggar in his drink / Could not have*
   laid such terms upon his callet.

   A drunken beggar could not have
   described his harlot in such
   (vulgar) terms.

4   *noble matches*

   Opportunities for advantageous
   marriages

scolded He might have chid° me so, for, in good faith,

I am a child to chiding. ¹   120

Iago

What is the matter, lady?

Emilia

Alas, Iago, my lord hath so bewhored her, ²

abuse / angry Thrown such despite° and heavy° terms upon her,

That true hearts cannot bear it.

Desdemona

Am I that name, Iago?   125

Iago

What name, fair lady?

Desdemona

Such as she said my lord did say I was.

Emilia

He called her "whore." A beggar in his drink

Could not have laid such terms upon his callet. ³

Iago

Why did he so?   130

Desdemona

I do not know. I am sure I am none such.

Iago

Do not weep; do not weep. Alas the day!

Emilia

forsaken Hath she forsook° so many noble matches, ⁴

Her father, and her country, and her friends,

To be called "whore"? Would it not make one weep?   135

Desdemona

It is my wretched fortune.

Iago

Curse / delusion Beshrew° him for 't! How comes this trick° upon him?

1 *cogging, cozening slave*
Deceiving, double-crossing rascal

2 *Why should he call her "whore"? Who keeps her company? / What place? What time? What form? What likelihood?*
Beginning with John Wilson in 1850, critics have noted in Othello a "double-time scheme" composed of two separate modes of time elapse—"short time" and "long time." Certain sequences of events require more time than the play supplies, most notably the time required for Cassio and Desdemona to commit multiple acts of adultery, but also the time necessary to explain remarks like Bianca's to Cassio: *What, keep a week away? Seven days and nights? . . . More tedious than the dial eightscore times!* (3.4.165–167). These sorts of inconsistencies exist throughout Shakespeare's works, but in *Othello* the illogic of double time helps to support the theme of jealous irrationality. Emilia's urgent questions remind the audience of the play's temporal inconsistencies, and the audience's suspension of disbelief in regard to these inconsistencies is associated here with Othello's irrational belief in Desdemona's many *stolen hours of lust* (3.3.342) and his assertion that *she with Cassio hath the act of shame / A thousand times*

committed (5.2.209–210), assertions that are not credible given a realistic time frame for the play's action.

3 *that such companions thou'dst unfold*
If only you would expose such knaves

4 *Even from the east to th' west*
All the way from one end to the other

5 *Speak within door.*
Lower your voice.

6 *turned your wit the seamy side without*
I.e., turned your mind inside out, so that the underside appeared (with a play on the word *seamy*, which can both describe the rough side of a garment on which the seam shows or mean "sordid, degrading")

Desdemona

i.e., only Heaven   Nay, Heaven° doth know.

Emilia

damned   I will be hanged if some eternal° villain,

meddling   Some busy° and insinuating rogue,   140

position   Some cogging, cozening slave,[1] to get some office,°

Have not devised this slander. I will be hanged else!

Iago

Fie, there is no such man. It is impossible.

Desdemona

If any such there be, Heaven pardon him!

Emilia

noose   A halter° pardon him, and Hell gnaw his bones!   145

Why should he call her "whore"? Who keeps her

company?

arrangement   What place? What time? What form?° What likelihood?[2]

The Moor's abused by some most villainous knave,

despicable   Some base notorious knave, some scurvy° fellow.

O Heaven, that such companions thou'dst unfold,[3]   150

And put in every honest hand a whip

To lash the rascals naked through the world

Even from the east to th' west![4]

Iago

Speak within door.[5]

Emilia

fine fellow (ironic)   Oh, fie upon them! Some such squire° he was

That turned your wit the seamy side without[6]   155

And made you to suspect me with the Moor.

Iago

You are a fool. Go to!

Desdemona

Alas Iago,

What shall I do to win my lord again?

1   *Delighted them in any other form*
    I.e., found delight in any other
    man's appearance

2   *shake me off / To beggarly divorcement*
    I.e., abandon me to the destitution
    that might come with divorce

3   *Comfort forswear me*
    May I lose all hope of comfort (if
    what I say is false).

4   *Not the world's mass of vanity could
    make me*
    All the useless riches in the world
    could not make me (do those
    deeds that would earn me the title
    of "whore").

5   *If 'twere no other.*
    I.e., I wish that were all.

6   *stays the meat*
    Wait to dine

Good friend, go to him, for, by this light of Heaven,
I know not how I lost him. [*kneeling*] Here I kneel: 160
sin   If e'er my will did trespass° 'gainst his love,
process   Either in discourse° of thought or actual deed,
if   Or that° mine eyes, mine ears, or any sense
Delighted them in any other form, [1]
still   Or that I do not yet°—and ever did,   165
And ever will, though he do shake me off
To beggarly divorcement [2]—love him dearly,
Comfort forswear me! [3] Unkindness may do much,
destroy   And his unkindness may defeat° my life,
But never taint my love. I cannot say "whore."   170
It does abhor me now I speak the word;
title   To do the act that might the addition° earn
Not the world's mass of vanity could make me. [4]

Iago
passing mood   [*helping her rise*] I pray you, be content; 'tis but his humor.°
causes / distress   The business of the state does° him offense,°   175
And he does chide with you.

Desdemona
If 'twere no other. [5]

Iago
guarantee   It is but so, I warrant.°   [*Trumpets sound.*]
Hark how these instruments summon to supper.
The messengers of Venice stays the meat. [6]   180
Go in and weep not. All things shall be well.

Desdemona *and* **Emilia** *exit*

Enter **Roderigo**.

How now Roderigo!

Roderigo
I do not find that thou deal'st justly with me.

1   *Every day thou doff'st me with some device*
     Every day you put me off with some trick.

2   *advantage of*
     Occasion for

3   *put up in peace*
     Quietly put up with

4   *your words and performances are no kin together*
     Your words and your actions bear no relation to one another.

5   *wasted myself out of my means*
     Bankrupted myself

6   *would half have corrupted a votaress*
     Would have gone halfway to seducing a nun

7   *comforts of sudden respect and acquaintance*
     Hope of immediate favor and access to her

Iago

To   What? In° the contrary.

Roderigo

Every day thou doff'st me with some device, [1] Iago, and   185
rather, as it seems to me now, keep'st from me all
opportunity   conveniency° than suppliest me with the least
advantage of [2] hope. I will indeed no longer endure it,
nor am I yet persuaded to put up in peace [3] what already
I have foolishly suffered.   190

Iago

Will you hear me, Roderigo?

Roderigo

Faith, I have heard too much, and your words and
performances are no kin together. [4]

Iago

You charge me most unjustly.

Roderigo

nothing   With naught° but truth: I have wasted myself out of my   195
means. [5] The jewels you have had from me to deliver
Desdemona would half have corrupted a votaress. [6] You
have told me she hath received them and returned me
expectations and comforts of sudden respect and
acquaintance, [7] but I find none.   200

Iago

Well, go to. Very well.

Roderigo

"Very well," "go to"! I cannot go to, man, nor 'tis not
rotten   very well. Nay, I think it is scurvy,° and begin to find
deceived   myself fopped° in it.

Iago

Very well.   205

1   *protest intendment of doing*
    Assure you I intend to do

2   *hast taken against me a most just exception*
    Have justifiably criticized me

3   *It hath not appeared.*
    I haven't seen any evidence of it.

4   *engines*
    Instruments of torture

5   *within reason and compass*
    **Reasonable and within the bounds
    of possibility**

Roderigo

I tell you 'tis not very well. I will make myself known to
Desdemona. If she will return me my jewels I will
up   give over° my suit and repent my unlawful solicitation.
repayment   If not, assure yourself I will seek satisfaction° of you.

Iago

had your say   You have said° now.   210

Roderigo

Ay, and said nothing but what I protest intendment of
doing.[1]

Iago

spirit   Why, now I see there's mettle° in thee, and even from
this instant do build on thee a better opinion than ever
before. Give me thy hand, Roderigo. Thou hast taken   215
against me a most just exception,[2] but yet I protest I
straightforwardly   have dealt most directly° in thy affair.

Roderigo

It hath not appeared.[3]

Iago

I grant indeed it hath not appeared, and your suspicion
is not without wit and judgment. But, Roderigo, if thou   220
hast that in thee indeed, which I have greater reason to
believe now than ever—I mean purpose, courage, and
valor—this night show it. If thou the next night
following enjoy not Desdemona, take me from this
world with treachery and devise engines[4] for my life.   225

Roderigo

Well, what is it? Is it within reason and compass?[5]

Iago

Sir, there is especial commission come from Venice to
appoint   depute° Cassio in Othello's place.

1   *abode be lingered*
    Stay is prolonged

2   *fashion to fall out*
    Contrive to take place

3   *fall between us*
    **I.e., be undone by us working
    together**

4   *grows to waste*
    Is almost over

5   *About it!*
    Let's get going!

Roderigo

Is that true? Why, then, Othello and Desdemona return
again to Venice.   230

Iago

Oh, no. He goes into Mauritania and taketh away with
him the fair Desdemona unless his abode be lingered[1]
nothing   here by some accident—wherein none° can be so
decisive   determinate° as the removing of Cassio.

Roderigo

How do you mean "removing" him?   235

Iago

of taking   Why, by making him uncapable of° Othello's place:
knocking out his brains.

Roderigo

And that you would have me to do?

Iago

Ay, if you dare do yourself a profit and a right. He sups
harlot / there tonight with a harlotry,° and thither° will I go to him.   240
He knows not yet of his honorable fortune. If you will
watch his going thence (which I will fashion to fall out[2]
between twelve and one) you may take him at your
aid   pleasure. I will be near to second° your attempt, and he
shall fall between us.[3] Come; stand not amazed at it,   245
but go along with me. I will show you such a necessity
inflict   in his death that you shall think yourself bound to put°
well into   it on him. It is now high° suppertime, and the night
grows to waste. " About It![3]

Roderigo

I will hear further reason for this.   250

Iago

convinced   And you shall be satisfied.°   *They exit.*

1 *be returned forthwith*

Return to you in a moment

2 *incontinent*

Literally means "immediately" but can also mean, appropriately here, "lacking self-restraint"

Act 4, Scene 3

Enter **Othello**, **Lodovico**, **Desdemona**, **Emilia**, *and attendants.*

Lodovico

I do beseech you, sir, trouble yourself no further.

Othello

Oh, pardon me, 'twill do me good to walk.

Lodovico

Madam, good night. I humbly thank your Ladyship.

Desdemona

Your honor is most welcome.

Othello

       Will you walk, sir?

O Desdemona—

Desdemona

    My lord?

Othello

       Get you to bed   5

On th' instant. I will be returned forthwith. [1]

i.e., Emilia / see that   Dismiss your attendant° there; look° 't be done.

Desdemona

I will, my lord.

     Othello [*with* **Lodovico** *and attendants*] *exits.*

Emilia

How goes it now? He looks gentler than he did.

Desdemona

He says he will return incontinent, [2]   10

And hath commanded me to go to bed

And bid me to dismiss you.

Emilia

      Dismiss me?

299

1 *nightly wearing*

Bed clothes

2 *So would not I.*

I.e., I don't share your wish.

3 *doth so approve him*

Judges him so worthy

4 *unpin me*

May refer to either Desdemona's dress or her hair

5 *All's one.*

I.e., it doesn't matter.

6 *You talk!*

I.e., what nonsense!

7 *proved mad*

Turned out to be insane

8 *expressed her fortune*

Prefigured her fate (i.e., Barbary's life resembled the story related in "Willow")

9 *I have much to do / But to go hang my head*

It's all I can do to keep from hanging my head.

Desdemona

It was his bidding; therefore, good Emilia,

Give me my nightly wearing, [1] and adieu.

We must not now displease him.   15

Emilia

wish   I would° you had never seen him!

Desdemona

So would not I. [2] My love doth so approve him [3]

reproofs   That even his stubbornness, his checks,° his frowns—

Prithee, unpin me [4] —have grace and favor.

Emilia

I have laid those sheets you bade me on the bed.   20

Desdemona

All's one. [5] Good faith, how foolish are our minds.

If I do die before thee, prithee, shroud me

In one of these same sheets.

Emilia

                                        Come, come, you talk. [6]

Desdemona

My mother had a maid called Barbary.

he that   She was in love, and he° she loved proved mad [7]   25

And did forsake her. She had a song of "Willow";

An old thing 'twas, but it expressed her fortune, [8]

And she died singing it. That song tonight

Will not go from my mind. I have much to do

But to go hang my head [9] all at one side   30

hurry   And sing it like poor Barbary. Prithee, dispatch.°

Emilia

Shall I go fetch your nightgown?

Desdemona

                                        No, unpin me here.

admirable   This Lodovico is a proper° man.

1   *The poor soul sat sighing by a sycamore*
    tree, / Sing all a green willow. . . .

    The sycamore (punning on "sick-
    amour") and willow tree were
    traditional emblems of grief for
    unrequited love or the death of a
    loved one. There are several other
    versions of this ballad extant, in
    which the gender of the singer is
    male (for example, "My love she is
    turned, untrue she doth prove / O
    willow, willow, willow!"). The song
    was probably well known before
    Shakespeare wrote *Othello*.
    Desdemona misremembers one
    line as *Let nobody blame him; his scorn*
    I approve, when the original was
    "Let nobody blame me, her scorns
    I do prove." This slip foreshadows
    her later attempt to protect
    Othello from blame for her
    murder.

2   *Lay by these*

    Put these things away.

3   *'Tis neither here nor there.*

    I.e., It means nothing.

[Handwritten annotations: "her own death"; "she knew she was going to die somehow."; "trying to prove that Othello didn't kill her even tho he will."]

Emilia

A very handsome man.

Desdemona

                        He speaks well.

Emilia

I know a lady in Venice would have walked barefoot to   35

lower   Palestine for a touch of his nether° lip.

Desdemona

        [*sings*] The poor soul sat sighing by a sycamore tree,
        Sing all a green willow. ¹
        Her hand on her bosom, her head on her knee,
        Sing willow, willow, willow.   40
        The fresh streams ran by her and murmured her moans,
        Sing willow, willow, willow.
        Her salt tears fell from her and softened the stones,
        Sing willow—
Lay by these ²— [*sings*] willow, willow.   45

hurry   Prithee, hie° thee; he'll come anon
        [*sings*] Sing all a green willow must be my garland.
        Let nobody blame him; his scorn I approve—
Nay, that's not next. Hark! Who is 't that knocks?

Emilia

It's the wind.   50

Desdemona

        [*sings*] I called my love false love, but what said he then?
        Sing willow, willow, willow.

sleep   If I court more women, you'll couch° with more men.
So, get thee gone; good night. Mine eyes do itch.

portend   Doth that bode° weeping?

Emilia

                        'Tis neither here nor there. ³   55

1   *In such gross kind*

   In such a disgusting way

2   *joint-ring*

   A finger ring made in two
   separable halves, symbolizing the
   union of husband and wife, and
   often presented as a gift at the time
   of betrothal.

3   *lawn*

   A kind of fine, white linen

Desdemona

I have heard it said so. Oh, these men, these men!

truth   Dost thou in conscience° think—tell me, Emilia—

That there be women do abuse their husbands

In such gross kind?[1]

Emilia

                    There be some such, no question.

Desdemona

Wouldst thou do such a deed for all the world?   60

Emilia

Why, would not you?

Desdemona

                 No, by this heavenly light!

Emilia

Nor I neither, by this heavenly light.

I might do 't as well i' th' dark.

Desdemona

Wouldst thou do such a deed for all the world?

Emilia

The world's a huge thing; it is a great prize   65

For a small vice.

Desdemona

faith   In troth,° I think thou wouldst not.

Emilia

In troth, I think I should, and undo 't when I had done.

Marry, I would not do such a thing for a joint-ring,[2] nor

quantities   for measures° of lawn,[3] nor for gowns, petticoats, nor

gift   caps, nor any petty exhibition.° But for all the whole   70

i.e., God's   world? 'Ud's° pity, who would not make her husband a

risk going to   cuckold to make him a monarch? I should venture°

purgatory for 't.

Desdemona

Let evil befall   Beshrew° me if I would do such a wrong

1   *to th' vantage*

    In addition

2   *fall*

    Fall from virtue

3   *pour our treasures into foreign laps*

    I.e., spend the money that
    rightfully belong to us (their wives)
    on other women. There may also
    be a bawdy meaning here, with
    treasures a euphemism for semen.

4   *Throwing restraint upon us*

    Curtailing our freedom

5   *scant our former having in despite*

    Reduce what money was
    previously given to us out of spite

6   *galls*

    Capacities for anger

7   *sense*

    I.e., sense organs, but the word
    also means "reason," "judgment,"
    "intuition," as well as "the ability
    to respond to physical sensation."

8   *The ills we do, their ills instruct us so*

    The sins we commit, we learn from
    their example.

9   *God me such uses send, / Not to pick
    bad from bad, but by bad mend.*

    May God grant me the ability not
    to emulate the bad behavior I see
    but to improve myself through
    seeing what to avoid.

For the whole world. 75

Emilia

Why the wrong is but a wrong i' th' world, and, having
the world for your labor, 'tis a wrong in your own
world, and you might quickly make it right.

Desdemona

I do not think there is any such woman.

Emilia

Yes, a dozen, and as many to th' vantage [1] as would 80
populate | store° the world they played for.
But I do think it is their husbands' faults
neglect | If wives do fall. [2] Say that they slack° their duties
And pour our treasures into foreign laps, [3]
irritable | Or else break out in peevish° jealousies, 85
Throwing restraint upon us. [4] Or say they strike us,
Or scant our former having in despite. [5]
mercy | Why, we have galls, [6] and though we have some grace,°
Yet have we some revenge. Let husbands know
Their wives have sense [7] like them. They see, and smell, 90
And have their palates both for sweet and sour,
i.e., husbands | As husbands have. What is it that they° do
exchange / amusement | When they change° us for others? Is it sport?°
desire | I think it is. And doth affection° breed it?
I think it doth. Is 't frailty that thus errs? 95
It is so too. And have not we affections,
Desires for sport, and frailty, as men have?
treat | Then let them use° us well, else let them know,
The ills we do, their ills instruct us so. [8]

Desdemona

Good night, good night. God me such uses send, 100
Not to pick bad from bad, but by bad mend. [9]

They exit.

1   *bulk*

A rack or stall jutting out from the
front of a shop, used for
displaying wares. Probably Iago
and Roderigo stand in the
discovery space or behind one of
the pillars (see figures on pages
376–377).

2   *put it home*

I.e., thrust it in deep

3   *I may miscarry in 't*

I.e., I may be unsuccessful.

4   *'Tis but a man gone.*

I.e., (if I kill Cassio) it only means
that there is one fewer man in the
world.

5   *to the sense*

Raw

6   *Live Roderigo*

If Roderigo lives

7   *calls me to a restitution large*

Will want me to return the
considerable quantity

8   *daily*

The word here probably has the
sense of "easy" or "effortless."

9   *There stand I in much peril.*

There I run a great risk.

Act 5, Scene 1

Enter **Iago** *and* **Roderigo**.

Iago

Straightaway   Here, stand behind this bulk. [1] Straight° will he come.

drawn   Wear thy good rapier bare° and put it home. [2]

Quick, quick! Fear nothing. I'll be at thy elbow.

It makes us or it mars us. Think on that,

And fix most firm thy resolution.   5

Roderigo

Be near at hand; I may miscarry in 't. [3]

Iago

Here at thy hand. Be bold and take thy stand.

                                       [*withdraws*]

Roderigo

commitment   [*aside*] I have no great devotion° to the deed,

And yet he hath given me satisfying reasons.

'Tis but a man gone. [4] Forth, my sword; he dies!   10

Iago

pimple   [*aside*] I have rubbed this young quat° almost to the sense, [5]

And he grows angry. Now, whether he kill Cassio

Or Cassio him, or each do kill the other,

works to   Every way makes° my gain. Live Roderigo, [6]

He calls me to a restitution large [7]   15

swindled   Of gold and jewels that I bobbed° from him

As gifts to Desdemona.

It must not be. If Cassio do remain,

He hath a daily [8] beauty in his life

That makes me ugly. And, besides, the Moor   20

expose   May unfold° me to him. There stand I in much peril. [9]

so be it   No, he must die. But so.° I hear him coming.

Enter **Cassio**.

1 *had been mine enemy*
   Would have harmed me

2 *coat*
   Either Cassio wears a reinforced
   undercoat or else his outer coat is
   of a leather thick enough to
   deflect Roderigo's sword.

3 *make proof of*
   Test

4 *Minion*
   I.e., darling (here sarcastic and
   addressed to the absent
   Desdemona)

5 *your unblessed fate hies*
   I.e., your death and damnation are
   fast approaching.

Roderigo

I know his gait; 'tis he.—Villain, thou diest!

[*attacks* **Cassio**]

Cassio

That thrust had been mine enemy[1] indeed

But that my coat[2] is better than thou know'st.   25

I will make proof of [3] thine.

[*draws and wounds* **Roderigo**]

Roderigo

Oh, I am slain!

[**Iago** *stabs* **Cassio** *in the leg and exits.*]

Cassio

I am maimed forever. Help, ho! Murder! Murder!

Enter **Othello**.

Othello

[*aside*] The voice of Cassio. Iago keeps his word.

Roderigo

Oh, villain that I am!

Othello

[*aside*] It is even so.   30

Cassio

Oh, help, ho! Light! A surgeon!

Othello

[*aside*] 'Tis he. O brave Iago, honest and just,

That hast such noble sense of thy friend's wrong!

Thou teachest me. —Minion,[4] your dear lies dead,

And your unblessed fate hies.[5] Strumpet, I come,   35

from   For, of° my heart, those charms, thine eyes, are blotted.

Thy bed, lust-stained, shall with lust's blood be spotted.

Othello *exits*.

Enter **Lodovico** *and* **Gratiano**.

Cassio

watchmen / passersby   What, ho! No watch?° No passage?° Murder! Murder!

Gratiano

calamity / dreadful   'Tis some mischance.° The voice is very direful.°

Cassio

Oh, help!   40

Lodovico

Hark!

Roderigo

O wretched villain!

Lodovico

dark   Two or three groan. 'Tis heavy° night;

tricksters   These may be counterfeits.° Let's think 't unsafe

toward   To come in to° the cry without more help.   45

Roderigo

Nobody come? Then shall I bleed to death?

Enter **Iago**.

Lodovico

Hark!

Gratiano

nightshirt   Here's one comes in his shirt,° with light and weapons.

Iago

out   Who's there? Whose noise is this that cries on° "murder"?

Lodovico

We do not know.

Iago

              Do not you hear a cry?   50

Cassio

Here, here! For Heaven sake, help me!

1   *spoiled*

    Seriously wounded

2   *What are you there?*

    I.e., who is there? The idiom is the
    same as in lines 54 and 66.

Iago

                                        What's the matter?

Gratiano

ensign   [*to* **Lodovico**] This is Othello's ancient,° as I take it.

Lodovico

The same indeed, a very valiant fellow.

Iago

Who   [*to* **Cassio**] What° are you here that cry so grievously?

Cassio

Iago? Oh, I am spoiled,¹ undone by villains!   55
Give me some help.

Iago

O me, lieutenant! What villains have done this?

Cassio

I think that one of them is hereabout

get   And cannot make° away.

Iago

                                    O treacherous villains!

[*to* **Lodovico** *and* **Gratiano**] What are you there?² Come
   in and give some help.   60

Roderigo

Oh, help me there!

Cassio

That's one of them.

Iago

                            O murd'rous slave! O villain!

                                        [*stabs* **Roderigo**.]

Roderigo

O damned Iago! O inhuman dog!   [*He dies.*]

Iago

Kill men i' th' dark? Where be these bloody thieves?
How silent is this town!—Ho! murder! murder!   65
—What may you be? Are you of good or evil?

1   *As you shall prove us, praise us.*

   Value us as you find us to be.

2   *I cry you mercy.*

   I.e., I beg your pardon.

3   *may you suspect / Who they should be*

   **Do you have any idea who they
   were**

Lodovico

As you shall prove us, praise us. [1]

Iago

Signior Lodovico?

Lodovico

He, sir.

Iago

I cry you mercy. [2] Here's Cassio hurt by villains.   70

Gratiano

Cassio?

Iago

How is 't, brother!

Cassio

                    My leg is cut in two.

Iago

Marry, Heaven forbid!

Light, gentlemen! I'll bind it with my shirt.

Enter **Bianca**.

Bianca

What is the matter, ho? Who is 't that cried?   75

Iago

Who is 't that cried?

Bianca

                    Oh, my dear Cassio!

My sweet Cassio! O Cassio, Cassio, Cassio!

Iago

well known   O notable° strumpet! Cassio, may you suspect

Who they should be[3] that have thus mangled you?

Cassio

No.   80

1   *garter*

A sash or band, here to be used as a
tourniquet

2   *chair*

I.e., litter or stretcher to carry
Cassio

Gratiano

I am sorry to find you thus. I have been to seek you.

Iago

Lend me a garter.¹ So.—Oh, for a chair²

To bear him easily hence!

Bianca

Alas, he faints! O Cassio, Cassio, Cassio!

Iago

i.e., Bianca   Gentlemen all, I do suspect this trash°   85

To be a party in this injury.

—Patience awhile, good Cassio.—Come, come,

Lend me a light. Know we this face or no?

Alas, my friend and my dear countryman

Roderigo! No. Yes sure! O Heaven, Roderigo.   90

Gratiano

What, of Venice?

Iago

               Even he, sir. Did you know him?

Gratiano

Know him? Ay.

Iago

Signior Gratiano? I cry your gentle pardon.

These bloody accidents must excuse my manners

That so neglected you.

Gratiano

             I am glad to see you.   95

Iago

How do you, Cassio?—Oh, a chair, a chair!

Gratiano

Roderigo!

Iago

done   He, he, 'tis he. [*A litter is carried in.*] Oh, that's well said°—the

chair!

1   *man*

This is the reading in both the
Quarto and the Folio text, though
the situation would make "men"
more logical (to carry the litter
with Cassio in it).

2   *Save you your labor*

Don't trouble yourself (i.e., to
feign distress). Iago continues to
pretend he suspects Bianca in the
attack on Cassio.

3   *bear him out o' th' air*

I.e., bring him inside.

4   *gastness of*

Terror in

5   *if you stare, we shall hear more anon*

I.e., if you stare (a sign of guilt),
we will make you confess.

6   *out of use*

Not used

Some good man¹ bear him carefully from hence.   100

As for I'll fetch the General's surgeon.—[*to* **Bianca**] For° you,
          mistress,

Save you your labor.²—He that lies slain here, Cassio,

Was my dear friend. What malice was between you?

Cassio

None in the world, nor do I know the man.

Iago

[*to* **Bianca**] What? Look you pale? [*to attendants*] Oh, bear
          him out o' th' air.³   105

                    [**Cassio** *and* **Roderigo** *are carried off.*]

[*to* **Lodovico** *and* **Gratiano**]

Stay you, good gentlemen.—Look you pale, mistress?

—Do you perceive the gastness of⁴ her eye?

[*to* **Bianca**] Nay, if you stare, we shall hear more anon.⁵

—Behold her well. I pray you, look upon her.

Do you see, gentlemen? Nay, guiltiness   110

even if Will speak, though° tongues were out of use.⁶

                    [*Enter* **Emilia**.]

Emilia

Alas, what is the matter? What is the matter, husband?

Iago

Cassio hath here been set on in the dark

By Roderigo and fellows that are 'scaped.

He's almost slain, and Roderigo quite dead.   115

Emilia

Alas, good gentleman! Alas, good Cassio!

Iago

This is the fruits of whoring. Prithee, Emilia,

find out Go know° of Cassio where he supped tonight.

          [*to* **Bianca**] What? Do you shake at that?

1   *I therefore shake not*

    I don't tremble because of it (i.e.,
    I have nothing to hide).

2   *fie*

    An exclamation of disgust,
    meaning something like "I spit"

3   *Cassio dressed*

    Cassio's wounds treated

4   *tell 's another tale*

    Come up with a better story

Bianca

He supped at my house, but I therefore shake not. [1]   120

Iago

command   Oh, did he so? I charge° you, go with me.

Emilia

Oh, fie [2] upon thee, strumpet!

Bianca

I am no strumpet, but of life as honest

As you that thus abuse me.

Emilia

As I? Fie upon thee!   125

Iago

Kind gentlemen, let's go see poor Cassio dressed. [3]

—Come, mistress, you must tell 's another tale. [4]

—Emilia, run you to the citadel

happened   And tell my lord and lady what hath happed.°

ahead   —Will you go on afore?° [*aside*] This is the night   130

destroys / utterly   That either makes me or fordoes° me quite.°

                                        They exit.

1 *It is the cause; it it the cause, my soul. / Let me not name it to you, you chaste stars; / It is the cause.*

The cause is literally the legal ground for action in a lawsuit, but here it also refers to the legal principle that, once guilt has been proven and judgment made, the law must be enforced by punishing the guilty party. The *cause* here is the act of adultery, apparently too foul a crime to be named before the *chaste stars*. In this passage Othello presents his killing of Desdemona as the disinterested enactment of a just punishment rather than a case of personal vengeance. Nonetheless, Othello's ritualistic triple repetition of *It is the cause* suggests that Othello still needs to convince himself to carry through with the killing.

2 *whiter skin of hers than snow*

Skin of hers, which is whiter than snow

3 *monumental*

I.e., used in the building of monuments

4 *light, and then put out the light*

The first *light* Othello refers to is literal (a torch or candle); the second figurative (the *light* of Desdemona's life)

5 *flaming minister*

I.e., the torch or candle

6 *thy light*

Here, addressing Desdemona (i.e., your life force)

7 *Thou cunning'st pattern of excelling nature*

I.e., you most exquisite example of nature's most perfect handiwork

8 *Promethean*

I.e., life-giving. Prometheus is a figure from Greek mythology. In one version of the story, he creates humans by breathing life into clay; in another, he gives man the power of fire by stealing it for them from the gods. George Peele, in *England's Holidays* (1595), refers to "Prometheus' life-infusing fire."

9 *I'll smell thee on the tree*

I.e. I'll smell you once more before I kill you; i.e., while her *rose* is still *on the tree* (bush).

10 *Justice to break her sword*

The figure of Justice has long been represented as a blindfolded woman bearing a sword in one hand (as a symbol of the right to punish) and a pair of scales in the other (for weighing the evidence).

Act 5, Scene 2

*Enter **Othello**, and **Desdemona** in her bed.*

Othello

It is the cause; it is the cause, my soul.
Let me not name it to you, you chaste stars;
It is the cause.[1] Yet I'll not shed her blood,
Nor scar that whiter skin of hers than snow[2]
And smooth as monumental[3] alabaster.

or else   Yet she must die, else° she'll betray more men.
Put out the light, and then put out the light.[4]
If I quench thee, thou flaming minister,[5]
I can again thy former light restore

if I once   Should I repent me. But once° put out thy light,[6]
Thou cunning'st pattern of excelling nature,[7]
I know not where is that Promethean[8] heat

rekindle   That can thy light relume.° When I have plucked thy rose
I cannot give it vital growth again;

inevitably   It needs° must wither. I'll smell thee on the tree.[9]

fragrant   [*kisses her*] O balmy° breath that dost almost persuade
Justice to break her sword![10] One more, one more. [*kisses her*]
Be thus when thou art dead, and I will kill thee
And love thee after. One more, and that's the last.
[*kisses her*] So sweet was ne'er so fatal. I must weep,

i.e., without pity   But they are cruel° tears. This sorrow's heavenly;
It strikes where it doth love. She wakes.

Desdemona

Who's there? Othello?

Othello

           Ay, Desdemona.

Desdemona

Will you come to bed, my lord?

1   *bethink yourself of any crime*

    Remember any sin

2   *Solicit for it straight*

    Ask for forgiveness right away.

3   *walk by*

    **Stand aside (to afford you some
    privacy)**

4   *Humh!*

    **An indication for the actor to make
    some angry sound**

Othello

Have you prayed tonight, Desdemon?

Desdemona

                              Ay, my lord. 25

Othello

If you bethink yourself of any crime[1]

Unreconciled as yet to Heaven and grace,

Solicit for it straight.[2]

Desdemona

Alack, my lord, what may you mean by that?

Othello

Well, do it and be brief. I will walk by.[3] 30

I would not kill thy unprepared spirit.

forbid No, heavens forfend,° I would not kill thy soul!

Desdemona

Talk you of killing?

Othello

                    Ay, I do.

Desdemona

                            Then Heaven

Have mercy on me!

Othello

                        Amen, with all my heart.

Desdemona

If you say, I hope you will not kill me. 35

Othello

Humh![4]

Desdemona

deadly And yet I fear you, for you're fatal° then

When your eyes roll so. Why I should fear I know not,

Since guiltiness I know not. But yet I feel I fear.

Othello

Think on thy sins.

1   *loves I bear to you*

Perhaps a reference to her
elopement or to the intensity of
her love for him

2   *conception*

Idea (referring either to Othello's
certainty of Desdemona's guilt or
to his intention to kill her)

3   *groan withal*

Groan with. The phrase was used of
a woman in labor, thus picking up
on the word *conception* in the
previous line.

Desdemona

               They are loves I bear to you. [1]   40

Othello

Ay, and for that thou diest.

Desdemona

That death's unnatural that kills for loving.

lower   Alas, why gnaw you so your nether° lip?

violent   Some bloody° passion shakes your very frame.

These are portents, but yet I hope — I hope   45

They do not point on me.

Othello

               Peace, and be still.

Desdemona

do so   I will so.° What's the matter?

Othello

                That handkerchief

Which I so loved and gave thee, thou gav'st

To Cassio.

Desdemona

       No, by my life and soul!

Send for the man and ask him.

Othello

                Sweet soul, take heed;   50

Take heed of perjury. Thou art on thy deathbed.

Desdemona

Ay—but not yet to die!

Othello

right away   Yes, presently;°

Therefore confess thee freely of thy sin,

accusation   For to deny each article° with oath

stifle   Cannot remove nor choke° the strong conception [2]   55

That I do groan withal. [3] Thou art to die.

1   *such general warranty of Heaven / As I*
    might love
    I.e., except in the sense that God
    authorizes us to love all mankind.

Desdemona

Then Lord have mercy on me!

Othello

                    I say "amen."

Desdemona

And have you mercy too! I never did

Wrong   Offend° you in my life, never loved Cassio

But with such general warranty of Heaven   60

As I might love.¹ I never gave him token.

Othello

By Heaven, I saw my handkerchief in 's hand.

turn to stone   O perjured woman, thou dost stone° my heart,

And mak'st me call what I intend to do

A murder, which I thought a sacrifice.   65

I saw the handkerchief.

Desdemona

                    He found it then.

I never gave it him. Send for him hither;

hear witness to   Let him confess° a truth.

Othello

                    He hath confessed.

Desdemona

What, my lord?

Othello

              That he hath used thee.

Desdemona

i.e., Sexually   How? Unlawfully?°

Othello

             Ay.

Desdemona

              He will not say so.   70

1   *interprets*

    Has guessed correctly

2   *Had all his hairs been lives*

    If he'd had as many lives as he has hairs

3   *had stomach for*

    Would have had appetite to consume

4   *Out*

    An exclamation of disgust

5   *Being done, there is no pause.*

    I.e., having been decided, there can be no hesitation

6   (at the door)

    Emilia calls from offstage.

Othello

No, his mouth is stopped. Honest Iago

steps   Hath ta'en order° for 't.

Desdemona

                    Oh! My fear interprets. [1]

What? Is he dead?

Othello

                    Had all his hairs been lives [2]

My great revenge had stomach for [3] them all.

Desdemona

ruined   Alas, he is betrayed, and I undone.° [*weeps*]   75

Othello

Out, [4] strumpet! Weep'st thou for him to my face?

Desdemona

Oh, banish me, my lord, but kill me not!

Othello

Down, strumpet!

Desdemona

Kill me tomorrow. Let me live tonight!

Othello

struggle   Nay, if you strive°—   80

Desdemona

But half an hour!

Othello

               Being done, there is no pause. [5]

Desdemona

But while I say one prayer!

Othello

               It is too late. (*smothers her*)

Emilia

(*at the door*) [6] My lord , my lord! What, ho! My lord, my lord!

Othello

What noise is this?—Not dead? Not yet quite dead?

1 *globe*

Earth (but Shakespeare's audience must also have heard "Globe" as the name of the theater in which they saw the play)

2 *Should yawn at alteration*

I.e., should split open in response to this change (i.e., the eclipses and that which occasioned them: the death of Desdemona)

3 *yonder's foul murders done*

Foul murder has been committed out there.

I that am cruel am yet merciful,   85
I would not have thee linger in thy pain.
So, so. [*smothers her again*]

Emilia

(*within*) What ho! My lord, my lord!

Othello

                                        Who's there?

Emilia

[*within*] O good my lord, I would speak a word with you!

Othello

Yes; 'tis Emilia.—[*to* **Emilia**] By and by.—She's dead.   90

likely   'Tis like° she comes to speak of Cassio's death;

loud   The noise was high.° Ha! No more moving?

i.e., Emilia   Still as the grave. Shall she° come in? Were 't good?

i.e., Desdemona I think she° stirs again. No. What's best to do?

If she come in, she'll sure speak to my wife—   95
My wife! My wife! What wife? I have no wife.

sad   O insupportable, O heavy° hour!

Methinks it should be now a huge eclipse

terrified   Of sun and moon, and that th' affrighted° globe[1]

Should yawn at alteration.[2]

Emilia

                            [*within*] I do beseech you   100
That I may speak with you. O good my lord—

Othello

I had forgot thee. Oh, come in, Emilia.

Wait / bed curtains Soft;° by and by. Let me the curtains° draw.
Where art thou? What's the matter with thee now?

Enter **Emilia**.

Emilia

O my good lord, yonder's foul murders done![3]   105

1   *the very error of the moon*

Only the wandering of the moon
out of its normal orbit. The
Elizabethans believed one cause
of madness was the deviation of
the moon from its regular course
(thus giving rise to the word
lunacy).

Othello

What? Now?

Emilia

Just   But° now, my lord.

Othello

It is the very error of the moon. [1]

accustomed   She comes more nearer Earth than she was wont°

And makes men mad.

Emilia

                   Cassio, my lord, hath killed   110

A young Venetian called Roderigo.

Othello

Roderigo killed? And Cassio killed!

Emilia

No, Cassio is not killed.

Othello

             Not Cassio killed!

Then murder's out of tune, and sweet revenge grows

    harsh.

Desdemona

unjustly   Oh, falsely,° falsely murdered.   115

Emilia

Alas, what cry is that?

Othello

That? What?

Emilia

Out and alas, that was my lady's voice.

                       [*opens the bedcurtains*]

Help! Help, ho, help! O lady, speak again.

Sweet Desdemona! O sweet mistress, speak!   120

Desdemona

A guiltless death I die.

Emilia

               Oh, who hath done this deed?

1   *how should she be murdered*

I.e., how could this have come about?

2   *false as water*

The proverbial notion of water as *false* (unfaithful) comes from Genesis 49:4, when Jacob accuses his sons of being "light (i.e., flighty) as water."

3   *rash as fire*

I.e., furious and uncontrollable

4   *else*

I.e., if you don't believe me

5   *extremity*

Extreme measure; most severe punishment

Desdemona

Nobody. I myself. Farewell.

Commend me to my kind lord. Oh, farewell!   [*dies*]

Othello

Why, how should she be murdered?[1]

Emilia

                                        Alas, who knows?

Othello

You heard her say herself it was not I.   125

Emilia

necessarily She said so. I must needs° report the truth.

Othello

She's like a liar gone to burning Hell:

'Twas I that killed her.

Emilia

Oh, the more angel she, and you the blacker devil!

Othello

wickedness She turned to folly,° and she was a whore.   130

Emilia

slander Thou dost belie° her, and thou art a devil.

Othello

She was false as water.[2]

Emilia

                              Thou art rash as fire[3]

To say that she was false. Oh, she was heavenly true!

Othello

have sex with Cassio did top° her; ask thy husband else.[4]

would be Oh, I were° damned beneath all depth in Hell,   135

Except But° that I did proceed upon just grounds

To this extremity.[5] Thy husband knew it all.

1   *Had she been true, / If Heaven would*
    make me such another world / Of one
    entire and perfect chrysolite, / I'd not
    have sold her for it.

    **If Desdemona had been faithful,
    even had I been offered a second
    Earth made entirely out of pure
    chrysolite (a gemstone), I would not
    have traded her for it.**

2   *made mocks with*

    Made a mockery of

3   *half a grain a day*

    I.e., very slowly

4   *to th' heart*

    **Down to his very heart
    (i.e., completely)**

5   *her most filthy bargain*

    **Her disgusting contract (i.e., her
    marriage to Othello); *filthy* is
    Emilia's judgment here and is a
    response to his use of the word in
    line 145.**

Emilia

My husband?

Othello

     Thy husband.

Emilia

        That she was false?

To wedlock?

Othello

     Ay, with Cassio. Had she been true,

If Heaven would make me such another world   140

Of one entire and perfect chrysolite,

I'd not have sold her for it. [1]

Emilia

       My husband?

Othello

about Ay, 'twas he that told me on° her first.

An honest man he is and hates the slime

That sticks on filthy deeds.

Emilia

       My husband?   145

Othello

repetition What needs this iterance,° woman? I say "thy husband."

Emilia

O mistress, villainy hath made mocks with [2] love!

My husband say she was false?

Othello

       He, woman.

I say "thy husband"—dost understand the word?

My friend, thy husband, honest, honest Iago.   150

Emilia

evil If he say so, may his pernicious° soul

Rot half a grain a day! [3] He lies to th' heart. [4]

She was too fond of her most filthy bargain. [5]

1   *Peace, you were best.*

    You'd do best to keep quiet.

2   *Thou hast not half that power to do me*

    harm / As I have to be hurt.

    I.e., I can endure much more pain
    than you are capable of inflicting.

3   *I care not for*

    I am not afraid of

4   *I'll make thee known / Though I lost*

    twenty lives

    I'll make what you've done
    publicly known even if it costs me
    twenty lives.

Othello

[*drawing his sword*] Ha!

Emilia

Do thy worst.   155

worthy of This deed of thine is no more worthy° Heaven

Than thou wast worthy her.

Othello

                                               Peace, you were best. ¹

Emilia

Thou hast not half that power to do me harm

dupe As I have to be hurt. ² O gull!° O dolt

As ignorant as dirt! Thou hast done a deed—   160

I care not for ³ thy sword; I'll make thee known

Though I lost twenty lives. ⁴—Help! Help, ho! Help!

The Moor hath killed my mistress! Murder, murder!

Enter **Montano**, **Gratiano**, *and* **Iago**.

Montano

What is the matter? How now, General?

Emilia

Oh, are you come, Iago? You have done well   165

i.e., head That men must lay their murders on your neck.°

Gratiano

What is the matter?

Emilia

[*to* **Iago**] Disprove this villain, if thou be'st a man.

He says thou told'st him that his wife was false.

I know thou didst not; thou'rt not such a villain.   170

Speak, for my heart is full.

Iago

I told him what I thought, and told no more

1   *set the murder on*

    Incited the murder

likely   Than what he found himself was apt° and true.

Emilia

But did you ever tell him she was false?

Iago

I did.   175

Emilia

You told a lie, an odious, damnèd lie.

Upon my soul, a lie, a wicked lie!

She false with Cassio? Did you say with Cassio?

Iago

subdue   With Cassio, mistress. Go to! Charm° your tongue.

Emilia

obligated   I will not charm my tongue. I am bound° to speak.   180

My mistress here lies murdered in her bed—

All

forbid   Oh, heavens forfend!°

Emilia

[*to* **Iago**] And your reports have set the murder on. [1]

Othello

Nay, stare not, masters. It is true, indeed.

Gratiano

'Tis a strange truth.   185

Montano

Oh, monstrous act!

Emilia

Villainy, villainy, villainy!

I think upon 't; I think I smell 't. O villainy!

I thought so then. I'll kill myself for grief.

O villainy, villainy!   190

Iago

order   What? Are you mad? I charge° you, get you home.

Emilia

permission   Good gentlemen, let me have leave° to speak.

1 *uncle*

I.e., Gratiano (Brabantio's brother); see 1.1.176.

2 *Shore his old thread in twain*

I.e., cut the thread of his aged life. In classical mythology, the three Fates spun lengths of thread which were measured to correspond to individual human lives; when the time came for a person to die, the Fates clipped (*shore*) his or her thread.

3 *do a desperate turn*

Commit suicide (an act of despair, thus literally *desperate*)

4 *It was a handkerchief, an antique token / My father gave my mother*

Compare the earlier (and different) account of the handkerchief Othello gives at 3.4.50–70.

'Tis proper I obey him, but not now.
—Perchance, Iago, I will ne'er go home.
Othello
Oh! Oh! Oh! [*falls on the bed*]
Emilia

          Nay, lay thee down and roar,   195
For thou hast killed the sweetest innocent
That e'er did lift up eye.
Othello

          [*standing*] Oh, she was foul!
—I scarce did know you, uncle. [1] There lies your niece,
Whose breath indeed these hands have newly stopped.
appears   I know this act shows° horrible and grim.   200
Gratiano

Poor Desdemon, I am glad thy father's dead;
fatal   Thy match was mortal° to him, and pure grief
Shore his old thread in twain. [2] Did he live now,
This sight would make him do a desperate turn, [3]
guardian   Yea, curse his better° angel from his side   205
damnation   And fall to reprobance.°
Othello

nonetheless   'Tis pitiful, but yet° Iago knows
That she with Cassio hath the act of shame
A thousand times committed. Cassio confessed it,
reward / acts   And she did gratify° his amorous works°   210
token   With that recognizance° and pledge of love
Which I first gave her. I saw it in his hand;
It was a handkerchief, an antique token
My father gave my mother. [4]
Emilia

O God! O heavenly God!   215

1 *'Twill out*
The truth will come out.

2 *as liberal as the north*
As freely as the north wind blows

3 *cry shame against me*
**Condemn me (for disobeying my
husband)**

Iago

Zounds, hold your peace.

Emilia

keep silent   'Twill out;¹ 'twill out. I, peace?°

No, I will speak as liberal as the north.²

Let Heaven and men and devils, let them all,

All, all cry shame against me,³ yet I'll speak.   220

Iago

[*drawing his sword*] Be wise and get you home.

Emilia

I will not.

Gratiano

        Fie! Your sword upon a woman?

Emilia

stupid   O thou dull° Moor! That handkerchief thou speak'st of

chance   I found by fortune° and did give my husband,

For often, with a solemn earnestness   225

More than indeed belonged to such a trifle,

He begged of me to steal 't.

Iago

              Villainous whore!

Emilia

She give it Cassio? No, alas, I found it,

And I did give 't my husband.

Iago

             Filth, thou liest!

Emilia

By Heaven, I do not; I do not, gentlemen.   230

fool   [*to* **Othello**] O murd'rous coxcomb!° What should such
    a fool

Do with so good a wife?

1 *Are there no stones in Heaven / But what serves for thunder?*

Aren't there any thunderbolts (to strike Iago dead) in Heaven, or are they all reserved for accompanying thunder?

2 *But why should honor outlive honesty?*

Othello realizes that his *honor* will not *outlive* the death of Desdemona, and he begins to contemplate his suicide.

3 *play the swan*

According to legend, a swan sings its most beautiful song just before dying.

Othello

                          Are there no stones in Heaven

extreme   But what serves for the thunder? [1]—Precious° villain!

                       *[He charges **Iago** and is stopped;*

                          Iago *stabs **Emilia**.]*

Gratiano

The woman falls! Sure he hath killed his wife.

Emilia

Ay, ay. Oh, lay me by my mistress' side.   235

                           *[**Iago** exits.]*

Gratiano

He's gone, but his wife's killed.

Montano

out-and-out   'Tis a notorious° villain. Take you this weapon,

taken away   Which I have recovered° from the Moor.

from the outside Come; guard the door without.° Let him not pass,

               But kill him rather. I'll after that same villain,   240

               For 'tis a damnèd slave.   *He [and **Gratiano**] exit.*

Othello

                        I am not valiant neither,

whipper-snapper But every puny whipster° gets my sword.

               But why should honor outlive honesty? [2]

               Let it go all.

Emilia

portend   What did thy song bode,° lady?

               Hark, canst thou hear me? I will play the swan [3]   245

               And die in music. *[sings]* Willow, willow, willow.

               —Moor, she was chaste; she loved thee, cruel Moor.

               So come my soul to bliss, as I speak true.

               So speaking as I think, alas, I die.   *[dies]*

1   *ice-brook's temper*

I.e., tempered (hardened) in ice-cold brook water after being heated red hot

2   *your stop*

I.e., the obstacle that you constitute

3   *butt*

Target (a term from archery)

4   *very sea-mark of my utmost sail*

exact destination of my final voyage

5   *go back dismayed*

Pull back in alarm

6   *Man but a rush against Othello's breast*

I.e., brandish even a flimsy reed (*rush*) in my direction

7   *at compt*

On the day of Judgment

Othello

I have another weapon in this chamber.   250

from It was a sword of° Spain, the ice-brook's temper. ¹

Oh, here it is—Uncle, I must come forth.

Gratiano

[*within*] If thou attempt it, it will cost thee dear.

necessarily Thou hast no weapon and perforce° must suffer.

Othello

Look in upon me then and speak with me,   255

unarmed Or, naked° as I am, I will assault thee.

[*Enter* **Gratiano**.]

Gratiano

What is the matter?

Othello

                         Behold, I have a weapon;

A better never did itself sustain

Upon a soldier's thigh. I have seen the day

That with this little arm and this good sword   260

I have made my way through more impediments

Than twenty times your stop. ² But, O vain boast,

Who can control his fate? 'Tis not so now.

Be not afraid, though you do see me weaponed.

Here is my journey's end; here is my butt ³   265

And very sea-mark of my utmost sail. ⁴

unwarranted Do you go back dismayed? ⁵ 'Tis a lost° fear.

Man but a rush against Othello's breast, ⁶

withdraws And he retires.° Where should Othello go?

[*to* **Desdemona**] Now, how dost thou look now? O   270

ill-fated   ill-starred° wench,

Pale as thy smock! When we shall meet at compt, ⁷

This look of thine will hurl my soul from Heaven,

1   *steep-down gulfs*
    Steep gorges

2   *look down towards his feet*
    **I.e., look for cloven hooves (one of
    the devil's distinguishing
    characteristics)**

devils And fiends° will snatch at it. Cold, cold, my girl,

Even like thy chastity. O cursèd, cursèd slave!

Whip me, ye devils,   275

From the possession of this heavenly sight!

Blow me about in winds, roast me in sulfur,

Wash me in steep-down gulfs¹ of liquid fire!

Oh, Desdemon! Dead, Desdemon! Dead! Oh! Oh!

> *Enter* **Lodovico**, **Cassio** [*carried in a litter*],
> **Montano**, *and* **Iago**, *with officers.*

Lodovico

Where is this rash and most unfortunate man?   280

Othello

That's he that was Othello. Here I am.

Lodovico

Where is that viper? Bring the villain forth.

> [**Iago** *is brought forward.*]

Othello

I look down towards his feet,² but that's a fable.

If that thou be'st a devil, I cannot kill thee.

> [*stabs* **Iago**]

Lodovico

Wrench his sword from him.

> [*They take* **Othello**'*s sword.*]

Iago

I bleed, sir, but not killed.   285

Othello

I am not sorry neither. I'd have thee live,

mind For in my sense° 'tis happiness to die.

Lodovico

O thou Othello, that was once so good,

1 *naught*

   Nothing (but the word can also
   mean "wickedness")

2 *consent in*

   Conspire to bring about

3 *ope your lips*

   I.e., make you talk

plot Fall'n in the practice° of a cursèd slave,
What shall be said to thee?

Othello

Why, anything: 290
An honorable murderer, if you will,
For naught¹ I did in hate, but all in honor.

Lodovico

i.e., Iago/partly This wretch° hath part° confessed his villainy.
Did you and he consent in² Cassio's death?

Othello

Ay.   295

Cassio

Dear General, I never gave you cause.

Othello

I do believe it, and I ask your pardon.

i.e., Iago Will you, I pray, demand that demi-devil°
Why he hath thus ensnared my soul and body?

Iago

Ask Demand° me nothing. What you know, you know.   300
From this time forth I never will speak word.

Lodovico

What, not to pray?

Gratiano

Torture Torments° will ope your lips.³

Othello

Well, thou dost best.

Lodovico

happened Sir, you shall understand what hath befall'n,°   305
Which, as I think, you know not. Here is a letter
Found in the pocket of the slain Roderigo,
concerns And here another. The one of them imports°
The death of Cassio to be undertook
By Roderigo.   310

1 *discontented paper*

   Letter expressing his grievances

2 *satisfied him*

   I.e., answered his complaints

3 *wrought to his desire*

   Achieved his goal

4 *whereon it came / That I was cast*

   I.e. whereupon it came about that I was dismissed

5 *taken off*

   Withdrawn

Othello

Oh, villain!

Cassio

barbaric / outrageous   Most heathenish° and most gross!°

Lodovico

Now here's another discontented paper[1]

Found in his pocket too, and this, it seems,

Roderigo meant to have sent this damnèd villain,

probably   But that, belike,° Iago in the interim   315

Came in and satisfied him.[2]

Othello

villain   O thou pernicious caitiff!°

—How came you, Cassio, by that handkerchief

That was my wife's?

Cassio

I found it in my chamber,

And he himself confessed it but even now,   320

That there he dropped it for a special purpose

Which wrought to his desire.[3]

Othello

O fool! fool! fool!

Cassio

There is besides in Roderigo's letter,

reproaches   How he upbraids° Iago, that he made him

Provoke   Brave° me upon the watch, whereon it came   325

i.e., Roderigo   That I was cast,[4] and even but now he° spake,

After long seeming dead: Iago hurt him;

Iago set him on.

Lodovico

leave   [to **Othello**] You must forsake° this room and go with

us.

Your power and your command is taken off,[5]   330

i.e., Iago   And Cassio rules in Cyprus. For this slave,°

1 *Soft you*

Wait a moment.

2 *Nothing extenuate*

Don't minimize the seriousness of what I have done.

3 *Then*

I.e., if you grant this request

4 *wrought*

The word means both "agitated" and "worked upon."

5 *Like the base Judean*

Judean is the reading of the 1623 Folio; the 1622 Quarto reads "Indian." We have no way of knowing whether the discrepancy is due to a copyist's or printer's error, to authorial revision, or to other causes. Both words make sense, but in quite different ways. "Base Indian" would allude to the many tales about ignorant barbarians (in either the East or West Indies) who possessed precious pearls, gems, or gold but were unaware of their value: for example, George Gascoigne, in *The Steel Glass* (1575), asks, "How live the Moors that spurn at glistering pearl, / And scorn the costs, which we hold so dear." Thus the *base* Othello throws away Desdemona because he fails to see her true value as a wife. *Base Judean*, on the other hand, would be an allusion to Judas Iscariot, the betrayer of Christ and the only disciple who was a Judean. This comparison of Othello to Judas would play upon the biblical image of Christ as "the pearl of great price," and it would associate Othello's kissing of the dead Desdemona with the way that Judas betrayed Christ with a kiss in the garden of Gethsemane. The analogy makes further sense because both Judas and Othello commit suicide in despair at what they have done.

6 *subdued eyes*

Eyes overcome with emotion

7 *Arabian trees*

Probably either the balsam or myrrh tree, each of which can be found in Arab countries and has gum with medicinal qualities.

8 *Aleppo*

A city in northern Syria under Turkish rule; it served as an important center of international trade.

cleverly devised   If there be any cunning° cruelty

him alive   That can torment him much and hold him° long,

closely guarded   It shall be his. You shall close° prisoner rest

Till that the nature of your fault be known   335

To the Venetian state.—Come, bring away.

Othello

Soft you;[1] a word or two before you go.

I have done the state some service, and they know 't.

No more of that. I pray you, in your letters,

When you shall these unlucky deeds relate,   340

Speak of me as I am. Nothing extenuate,[2]

anything   Nor set down aught° in malice. Then[3] must you speak

Of one that loved not wisely, but too well;

Of one not easily jealous, but being wrought,[4]

Bewildered   Perplexed° in the extreme; of one whose hand,   345

worthless   Like the base° Judean,[5] threw a pearl away

Worth more   Richer° than all his tribe; of one whose subdued eyes,[6]

i.e., weeping   Albeit unusèd to the melting° mood,

Drop tears as fast as the Arabian trees[7]

secretions   Their medicinable gum.° Set you down this,   350

And say besides that in Aleppo[8] once,

malevolent   Where a malignant° and a turbaned Turk

betrayed   Beat a Venetian and traduced° the state,

I took by th' throat the circumcisèd dog

And smote him, thus.   *[stabs himself]*   355

Lodovico

conclusion   Oh, bloody period!°

Gratiano

All that is spoke is marred.

1 *Spartan dog*
   Proverbially savage bloodhound

2 *anguish*
   Excruciating pain

3 *succeed on you*
   Will be inherited by you (as he is Desdemona's uncle)

Othello

before   [*to* **Desdemona**] I kissed thee ere° I killed thee. No way
     but this,

   Killing myself, to die upon a kiss.

                       [*kisses* **Desdemona**, *and*] *dies.*

Cassio

   This did I fear, but thought he had no weapon,

   For he was great of heart. [Shits on Othello]

Lodovico

                      [*to* **Iago**] O Spartan dog, [1]   360

savage   More fell° than anguish, [2] hunger, or the sea,

   Look on the tragic loading of this bed.

scene   This is thy work. —The object° poisons sight.

guard   Let it be hid.—Gratiano, keep° the house

   And seize upon the fortunes of the Moor,   365

i.e., Cassio   For they succeed on you. [3]—To you, Lord Governor,°

   Remains the censure of this hellish villain:

   The time, the place, the torture. Oh, enforce it!

immediately / embark   Myself will straight° aboard,° and to the state

   This heavy act with heavy heart relate.   *They exit.*   370

АНАНАЦ

Longer Notes

PAGE 135

2.1.291   *the lusty Moor*

The stereotype of the Moors or Africans as a people with potentially unruly passions is emphasized in one of Shakespeare's source texts, John Pory's 1600 translation of Leo Africanus's *History and Description of Africa*, which includes this passage describing the Moors of Barbary: "What vices the foresaid Africans are subject onto. Never was there any people or nation so perfectly endued with virtue, but that they had their contrary faults and blemishes: now therefore let us consider whether the vices of the Africans do surpass their virtues and good parts. Those which we named the inhabitants of the cities of Barbary are somewhat needy and covetous, being also very proud and high-minded, and wonderfully addicted unto wrath; insomuch that (according to the proverb) they will deeply engrave in marble any injury be it never so small, and will in no wise blot it out of their remembrance. So rustical they are and void of good manners, that scarcely can any stranger obtain their familiarity and friendship. Their wits are but mean, and they are so credulous, that they will believe matters impossible, which are told to them. So ignorant are they of natural philosophy, that they imagine all the effects and operations of nature to be extraordinary and divine. They observe no certain order of living nor of laws. Abounding exceedingly with choler, they speak always with an angry and loud voice. Neither shall you walk in the daytime in any of their streets, but you shall see commonly two or three or them together by the ears. By nature they are a vile and base people, being no better accounted of by their governors then if they were dogs. They have neither judges nor lawyers, by whose wisdom and counsel they ought to be directed. . . . Their minds are perpetually possessed with vexation and with strife, so that they will seldom or never show themselves tractable to any man."

PAGE 197

3.3.169–171 *Oh, beware, my lord, of jealousy! / It is the green-eyed monster which doth mock / The meat it feeds on.*

Green was considered a "bilious hue, indicative of fear or jealousy" (*OED*). According to Thomas Wright's *The Passions of the Mind in General* (1604), "the passions not unfitly may be compared to green spectacles, which make all things resemble the color of green; even so, he that loveth, hateth, or by any other passion is vehemently possessed, judgeth all things that occur in favor of that passion." The passion of jealousy that afflicts Othello is also explored by Shakespeare's contemporary Ben Jonson in his play *Every Man in His Humour*, the original production of which in 1598 included Shakespeare as one of the actors. The following speech from that play (2.3.58–68) encapsulates the early modern understanding of jealousy as a process of mental deterioration. A character named Thorello experiences a jealousy that may well be called poor mortals' plague:

For, like a pestilence, it doth infect
The houses of the brain. First it begins
Solely to work upon the fantasy,
Filling her seat with such
    pestiferous air,
As soon corrupts the judgment; and
    from thence
Sends like contagion to the memory:
Still each to other giving the infection.
Which, as a subtle vapor, spreads itself
Confusedly through every sensive part,
Till not a thought, or motion, in the
    mind,
Be free from black poison of suspect.

In *Othello*, that the monster
Jealousy *doth mock the meat it
feeds on* suggests two possible
meanings: either the jealous
husband becomes the prey of a
monster (Jealousy personified)
that toys with (*or mocks*) its victim
as it consumes him, or alternatively, the jealous lover becomes
a monster himself, a monster
feeding on *fresh suspicions*
(3.3.183), the *meat* required
to sustain jealousy.

THE TRAGEDIE OF

Othello, the Moore of Venice.

Actus Primus. Scœna Prima.

Enter Rodorigo, and Iago.

Rodorigo.

Euer tell me, I take it much vnkindly
That thou (*Iago*) who hast had my purse,
As if ý strings were thine, should'st know of this.
    Ia. But you'l not heare me. If euer I did dream
Of such a matter, abhorre me.
    Rodo. Thou told'st me,
Thou did'st hold him in thy hate.
    Iago. Despise me
If I do not. Three Great-ones of the Cittie,
(In personall suite to make me his Lieutenant)
Off-capt to him: and by the faith of man
I know my price, I am worth no worsse a place.
But he (as louing his owne pride, and purposes)
Euades them, with a bumbast Circumstance,
Horribly stufft with Epithites of warre,
Non-suites my Mediators. For certes, saies he,
I haue already chose my Officer. And what was he?
For-sooth, a great Arithmatician,
One *Michaell Cassio*, a Florentine,
(A Fellow almost damn'd in a faire Wife)
That neuer set a Squadron in the Field,
Nor the deuision of a Battaile knowes
More then a Spinster. Vnlesse the Bookish Theoricke:
Wherein the Tongued Consuls can propose
As Masterly as he. Meere pratle (without practise)
Is all his Souldiership. But he (Sir) had th'election;
And I (of whom his eies had seene the proofe
At Rhodes, at Ciprus, and on others grounds
Christen'd, and Heathen) must be be-leed, and calm'd
By Debitor, and Creditor. This Counter-caster,
He (in good time) must his Lieutenant be,
And I (blesse the marke) his Mooreships Auntient.
    Rod. By heauen, I rather would haue bin his hangman.
    Iago. Why, there's no remedie.
'Tis the curffe of Seruice;
Preferment goes by Letter, and affection,
And not by old gradation, where each second
Stood Heire to'th'first. Now Sir, be iudge your selfe,
Whether I in any iust terme am Affin'd
To loue the *Moore?*
    Rod. I would not follow him then.
    Iago. O Sir content you.
I follow him, to serue my turne vpon him,
We cannot all be Masters, nor all Masters

Cannot be truely follow'd. You shall marke
Many a duteous and knee-crooking knaue;
That (doting on his owne obsequious bondage)
Weares out his time, much like his Masters Asse,
For naught but Prouender, & when he's old Casheer'd.
Whip me such honest knaues. Others there are
Who trym'd in Formes, and visages of Dutie,
Keepe yet their hearts attending on themselues,
And throwing but showes of Seruice on their Lords
Doe well thriue by them.
And when they haue lin'd their Coates
Doe themselues Homage.
These Fellowes haue some soule,
And such a one do I professe my selfe. For (Sir)
It is as sure as you are *Rodorigo*,
Were I the Moore, I would not be *Iago*:
In following him, I follow but my selfe.
Heauen is my Iudge, not I for loue and dutie,
But seeming so, for my peculiar end:
For when my outward Action doth demonstrate
The natiue act, and figure of my heart
In Complement externe, 'tis not long after
But I will weare my heart vpon my sleeue
For Dawes to pecke at; I am not what I am.
    Rod. What a full Fortune do's the Thicks-lips owe
If he can carry't thus?
    Iago. Call vp her Father:
Rowse him, make after him, poyson his delight,
Proclaime him in the Streets. Incense her kinsmen,
And though he in a fertile Clymate dwell,
Plague him with Flies: though that his Ioy be Ioy,
Yet throw such chances of vexation on't,
As it may loose some colour.
    Rodo. Heere is her Fathers house, Ile call aloud.
    Iago. Doe, with like timerous accent, and dire yell,
As when (by Night and Negligence) the Fire
Is spied in populus Citties.
    Rodo. What hoa: *Brabantio*, Siginor *Brabantio*, hoa.
    Iago. Awake: what hoa, *Brabantio*: Theeues, Theeues.
Looke to your house, your daughter, and your Bags,
Theeues, Theeues.
    Bra. Aboue. What is the reason of this terrible
Summons? What is the matter there?
    Rodo. Signior is all your Familie within?
    Iago. Are your Dobres lock'd?
    Bra. Why? Wherefore ask you this?
    Iago. Sir, y'are rob'd, for shame put on your Gowne,

Your

Editing *Othello*
by David Scott Kastan

thello was written sometime between 1601 and 1604, but it was not published in Shakespeare's lifetime. The earliest text of *Othello* was published six years after Shakespeare died, in 1622, by Thomas Walkley in an inexpensive Quarto edition (Q). The following year it appeared as the third play from the end in the First Folio (F), among the tragedies that make up the volume's third and final section. The Folio version has about 160 lines absent from the 1622 Quarto; the Quarto has about fifteen lines not present in the Folio. A second quarto (Q2) was published in 1630 and combines readings from both early editions, as well as introducing some emendations of its own. This Barnes & Noble edition of the play uses the Folio text as its base text, as the Folio seems to present the play as Shakespeare wrote it. Walkley's Quarto text seems not to be the original of the Folio, but rather appears to reflect someone's (perhaps Shakespeare's) reduction of the play, abridging it, especially in the final two acts, for some later performance. Nonetheless, in places the Quarto does seem to be closer to Shakespeare's intentions than the Folio, especially in regard to the play's many oaths and profanities, which appear in Q but are absent from F, and which this edition, like most modern editions, restores. In 1606, an Act against Abuses was passed, banning various kinds of profanity from the performances of plays, and it is likely the manuscript from which the Folio was printed reflects an expurgation in response to this order.

In general the editorial work of this present edition is conservative, a matter of normalizing spelling, capitalization, and punctuation, removing superfluous italics, regularizing the names of characters, and rationalizing entrances and exits. A comparison of the edited text of 1.1.1–86 with the facsimile page of the Folio (on p. 368) reveals some of the issues in editing the play. The mild oaths, "Tush" (in line 1) and "'Sblood" (in line 4), are here restored, as are all the expurgations of the Folio. Otherwise, the changes from the Folio are for the most part less substantial. The Folio's speech prefixes are expanded and normalized for clarity, so that "*Rod.*" or *Rodo.* becomes **Roderigo**, and "*Bra.*" becomes **Brabantio**. Spelling, capitalization, and italicization here regularly follow modern practices rather than the habits of the Folio's printers. As neither spelling nor punctuation in Shakespeare's time had yet been standardized, words were spelled in various ways that indicated their proximate pronunciation, and punctuation, which then was largely a rhythmical pointer rather than predominantly designed, as it is now, to clarify logical relations, was necessarily far more idiosyncratic than today. In any case, compositors were under no obligation to follow either the spelling or punctuation of their copy. Since the copy for *Othello* originated with a script prepared by a scribe (probably Ralph Crane), the spelling and punctuation of the Folio text is probably at several removes from Shakespeare's own hand; for most readers, then, there is little advantage in an edition that reproduces the spelling and punctuation of the Folio text. It does not accurately represent Shakespeare's writing habits, and it makes reading difficult in a way Shakespeare could never have anticipated or desired.

Therefore "heare" in line 4 becomes the familiar "hear," and "Cittie" in line 7 becomes "city." In the first line, "vnkindly" becomes "unkindly," though it is interesting to see that "v" was often used where we would use a "u," and "u" where we would use a "v," as in "louing" (for "loving") in line 11. Similarly, "i" was often used for "j," as in "Ioy" in line 71, which is here printed "joy," regularizing both the spelling and the capitalization. The intrusive "literary" capitalizations of nouns (e.g., "Circumstance" in line 12 and "Mediators" in line 15) are changed to reflect modern practice, as is the punctuation. The Folio's colon after "theoric" ("Theoricke") in line 23 and the semicolon after "knave" ("knaue") in line 45 respectively mark a heavy and a slightly less heavy pause rather than define a precise (and different) grammatical relation as they would in modern usage, and in this text the punctuation, or its absence, accords with modern practices. In all these cases, modernizing clarifies rather than alters Shakespeare's intentions. Thus, 1.1.44–54 reads in the Folio:

> You shall marke
> Many a dutious and knee-crooking knaue;
> That (doting on his owne obsequious bondage)
> Weares out his time, much like his Masters Asse,
> For naught but Prouender, & when he's old Cafheer'd.
> Whip me fuch honeft knaues. Others there are
> Who trym'd In Formes, and vifages of Dutie,
> Keepe yet their hearts attending on themfelues,
> And throwing but the fhowes of Seruice on their Lords
> Doe well thriue by them.
> And when they haue lin'd their Coates
> Doe themfelues Homage.

Modernized this reads:

> You shall mark
> Many a duteous and knee-crooking knave
> That (doting on his own obsequious bondage)
> Wears out his time, much like his master's ass,
> For naught but provender, and, when he's old, cashiered.
> Whip me such honest knaves. Others there are

> Who, trimmed in forms and visages of duty,
>
> Keep yet their hearts attending on themselves
>
> And, throwing but shows of service on their lords,
>
> Do well thrive by them and, when they have lined their coats,
>
> Do themselves homage.

No doubt there is some loss in modernization. Clarity and consistency are admittedly gained at the expense of expressive detail, but normalizing spelling, capitalization, and punctuation allows the text to be read with far greater ease than the original, and essentially as it was intended to be understood. We lose the archaic feel of the text in exchange for clarity of meaning. Old spellings are consistently modernized here, but old forms of words (i.e., "hast" in line 2) are retained. If, inevitably, in modernization we do lose the historical feel of the text Shakespeare's contemporaries read, it is important to note that Shakespeare's contemporaries would not have thought the Folio in any sense archaic or quaint, as these details inevitably make it for a reader today. The text would have seemed to them as modern as this one does to us. Indeed, many of the Folio's typographical peculiarities are the result of its effort to make the printed page look up to date for potential buyers.

The following list records all substantive departures in this edition from the Folio text of 1623. It does not record the modernizations of spelling, normalization in the use of capitals, corrections of obvious typographical errors, adjustments of lineation, minor repositioning of stage directions, or rationalizations of speech prefixes. The adopted reading in this edition is given first in boldface and followed by the original, rejected reading of the Folio, or noted as being absent from the Folio text. Where the adopted reading comes from one of the early quartos, this is indicated by a bold **Q** or **Q2** within bold brackets. Editorial stage directions are not collated but are enclosed within brackets in the text. Latin stage directions are translated (e.g., "They all exit" for *Exeunt omnes*), and the Latin act and scene designation of the Folio are similarly translated (e.g., Act One, scene one for *Actus primus, scena prima*).

Textual Notes

1.1.1 Tush! [Q] [not in F]; **1.1.4 'Sblood** [Q] [not in F]; **1.1.14 And in conclu-**
sion [Q] [not in F]; **1.1.24 toga'd** [Q] Tongued; **1.1. 28 other** [Q] others; **1.1.**
32 God [Q] [not in F]; **1.1. 66 full** [Q] fall; **1.1. 86 Zounds** [Q] [not in F]; **1.1.**
110 Zounds [Q] [not in F]; **1.1.155 Hell-pains** :Q hell pains; F: hell apines;
1.1.183 night [Q] might; **1.2.34 Duke** [Q] Dukes; **1.2. 70 darlings** [Q] Dearel-
ing; **1.2. 89 I** [Q] [not in F]; **1.3.61SP All** [Q] Sen.; **1.3. 92 unvarnished** [Q]
vn-varnish'd u; **1.3.101 maimed** [Q] main'd; **1.3.108SP Duke** [Q] [not in F];
1.3.109 overt [Q] ouer; **1.3.112SP First Senator** Sen.; **1.3.124 till** [Q] tell;
1.3.131 battles [Q] Battaile; **1.3.131 fortunes** [Q] Fortune; **1.3.142 heads**
[Q] head; **1.3.144 other** [Q] others; **1.3.146 Do grow** [Q] Grew; **1.3.156**
intentively [Q] instinctiuely; **1.3.229 couch** Coach; **1.3.247 did** [Q] [not in
F]; **1.3.277 SP First Senator** Sen.; **1.3.290 SP First Senator** Sen.; **1.3.299 the**
[Q] the the; **1.3.324 beam** [Q] braine; **1.3.328 our unbitted** [Q] or vnbitted;
1.3.370–373 [Q] [not in F]; **1.3.377 such a snipe** [Q] such Snpe; **1.3.380 He's**
[Q Ha's] She ha's; **2.2.9SP Second Gentlmean** [as Q] 2; **2.1.19SP Third**
Gentleman [as Q] 3; **2.1.33 prays** [Q] praye; **2.1.40SP Third Gentleman** [as
Q] Gent.; **2.1.42 arrivance** [Q] Arriuancie; **2.1.43 this** [Q] the; **2.1.52 SP A**
Voice [not in F]; **2.1.54SP Second Gentleman** [as Q] Gent. (throughout);
2.1.65 ingener Ingeniuer; **2.1.82 And bring all Cyprus comfort!** [Q] [not
in F]; **2.1.88 me** [Q] [not in F]; **2.1.94SP A Voice** [not in F]; **2.1.95 But, hark,**
a sail. [in F after l. 93]; **2.1.96 their** [Q] this; **2.1. 169 gyve** giue; **2.1.176**
clyster-pipes [Q] Cluster-pipes; **2.1. 213 hither** [Q] thither; **2.1.226 again**
[Q] a game; **2.1. 241 has** [Q] he's; **2.1.259 mutualities** [Q] mutabilities; **2.1.**
289 accountant [Q] accomptant; **2.1.302 rank** [Q] right; **2.1.303 night-cap**
[Q] Night-Cape; **2.2.10 Heaven** [Q] [not in F]; **2.3.54 to put** [Q] put to;
2.3.58 God [Q] heaven; **2.3.68 God** [Q] heauen; **2.3.73 Englishman** [Q]
Englishmen; **2.3.89 'Fore God** [Q] Why; **2.3.92 God's** [Q] heu'ns;
2.3.100 God [Q] [not in F]; **2.3.133 Zounds!** [Q] [not in F]; **2.3.144**
God's will [Q] Alas; **2.3.148 God's will** [Q] Fie, fie; **2.3.150 Zounds** [Q]
[not in F]; **2.3.193 Zounds... stir** [Q] If I once stir; **2.3.204 leagued** league;
2.3.247 God [Q] Heauen; **2.3.274 God** [Q] [not in F]; **2.3.301 denote-**

ment deuotement; **2.3.325 were 't** [Q] were; **2.3.359 By th' Mass** [Q] Introth; **2.3.366 the while** a while; **3.1.24 General's wife** [Q] Generall; **3.1.28SP Cassio** [Q] [not in F]; **3.1.28 Do, good my friend.** [Q] [not in F]; **3.1.47 To take the safest occasion by the front** [Q] [not in F]; **3.3.51 Yes, faith** [Q] I sooth; **3.3.59 or** [Q] on; **3.3.73 By'r Lady** [Q] Trust me; **3.3.94 you** [Q] he; **3.3.109 By Heaven** [Q] Alas; **3.3.139 that all slaves are free to** that: All slaues are free; **3.3.143 Where no** Wherein; **3.3.151 oft** [Q] of; **3.3.158 Zounds** [Q] [not in F]; **3.3.166 By Heaven** [Q] [not in F]; **3.3.179 God** [Q] Heauen; **3.3.206 God** [Q] Heauen; **3.3.208 keep 't** [Q2] kept; **3.3.220 I' faith** [Q] Trust me; **3.3.254 hold** [Q] [not in F]; **3.3.264 qualities** [Q] Quantities; **3.3.290 Faith** [Q] Why; **3.3.316 faith** [Q] but; **3.3.342 of** [Q] in; **3.3.390 Her** [Q2] My; **3.3.399 supervisor** [Q] super-vision; **3.3.427 lay** laid; **3.3.444 any that** any, it; **3.4.50 faith** [Q] indeed; **3.4.70 I' faith** [Q] Indeed; **3.4.72 God** [Q] Heauen; **3.4.76 Heaven** [Q] [not in F]; **3.4.90 I' faith** [Q] Insooth; **3.4.91 Zounds** [Q] Away; **3.4.163 I' faith** [Q] Indeed; **3.4.179 by my faith** [Q] in good troth; **4.1.32 Faith** [Q] Why; **4.1.35 Zounds** [Q] [not in F]; **4.1.50 No, forbear** [Q] [not in F]; **4.1.76 unsuiting** [Q] result- ing; **4.1.95 clothes** [Q] Cloath; **4.1.101 construe** [Q conster] conserue; **4.1.107 power** [Q] dower; **4.1.111 i' faith** [Q] indeed; **4.1.123 Faith** [Q] Why; **4.1.130 beckons** [Q] becomes; **4.1.159 Faith** [Q] [not in F]; **4.1.161 Faith** [Q] Yes; **4.1.211 God** [Q] [not in F]; **4.1.233 By my troth** [Q] Trust me; **4.1.246 an** [Q] [not in F]; **4.2.32 Nay** [Q] May; **4.2.35 But not the words** [Q] [not in F]; **4.2.71 ne'er** [Q] neuer; **4.2.83 Impudent strumpet!** [Q] [not in F]; **4.2.150 Heaven** [Q] Heauens; **4.2.164 them in** [Q2] them: or; **4.2.176 And he does chide with you** [Q] [not in F]; **4.2.192 Faith** [Q] [not in F]; **4.3. 16 I would** [Q] I, would; **4.3. 21 faith** [Q] Father; **4.3.22 thee** [Q] [not in F]; **4.3.37 sighing** [Q2] singing; **4.3.71 'Ud's pity** [Q] Why; **4.3.100 God** [Q] Heauen; **5.1. 1 bulk** [Q] Barke; **5.1.22 hear** [Q] heard; **5.1.90 O Heaven** [Q] Yes, 'tis; **5.1.105 out** [Q] [not in F]; **5.2.52 Yes** [Q] [not in F]; **5.2.57 Then Lord** [Q] O Heauen; **5.2. 64 mak'st** [Q makest] makes; **5.2.100 Should** [Q] Did; **5.2.125 heard** [Q] heare; **5.2.215 God** [Q] Heauen; **5.2.215 heavenly God** [Q] heauenly Powres; **5.2.216 Zounds** [Q] Come

Othello on the Early Stage
by Daniel Vitkus

T he first recorded performance of Shakespeare's *Othello* took place in 1604 at the court of King James I. An entry in the accounts of Edmund Tilney, the Master of the Revels, reads as follows:

By the King's Majesty's players. Hallowmass Day, being the first of November. A play in the Banqueting House at Whitehall called the Moor of Venice. Shaxberd.

The theatrical company for whom Shakespeare wrote was called the King's Men (or Players) because they were licensed to perform under the official patronage of the monarch (there were competing companies with other patrons, such as Queen Anne's Men). The King's Men were occasionally hired, as they were on that November 1, to put on a show before the King, but they usually performed at their own commercial, open-air playhouse, the Globe, where they made most of their money.

The role of Othello was first taken up by Richard Burbage, who had recently been the first actor to portray Hamlet. Iago may have been portrayed by John Lowin, an actor known for playing military roles. Burbage's performance as the "Grieved Moor" was remembered as one of his best roles, and several decades after his death, Burbage was described as a "delightful Proteus, so wholly transforming

Fig 1. In the large London playhouses, the balcony above the stage could be used for staging, seating, or to house musicians.

Fig 2. English Renaissance drama made minimal use of sets or backdrops. In the absence of a set, the stage pillars could be incorporated into the action, standing in for trees and other architectural elements.

Fig 3. The discovery space, located in the middle of the backstage wall, could be used as a third entrance as well as a location for scenes requiring special staging, such as in a tomb or bedchamber.

Fig 4. A trapdoor led to the area below the stage, known as "Hell" (as contrasted with the painted ceiling, known as "Heaven" or the "heavens"). Ghosts or other supernatural figures could descend through the trap, and it could also serve as a grave.

himself into his part, as he never (not so much as in the tiring-house) assumed himself until the play was done."

In a letter written in 1610, Henry Jackson, a member of Corpus Christi College at Oxford University, described a performance of *Othello* that he witnessed there. The King's Men were touring in the provinces because of a prolonged closure of the London playhouses due to an outbreak of the plague. Jackson reported that the King's Men staged several tragedies at Oxford, "which they acted with propriety and fitness. In which tragedies, not only through speaking, but also through acting certain things, they moved the audience to tears." One of these tragedies was *Othello*, and Jackson gives this account of the bedroom scene: "truly the celebrated Desdemona, slain in our presence by her husband, although she pleaded her case very effectively throughout, yet moved us more after she was dead, when, lying in her bed, she entreated the pity of the spectators by her very countenance."

As we can see from Jackson's reportage, early modern spectators were moved by the tragedy of Othello and the murder of Desdemona, just as we are today, but we should bear in mind that their theatrical experience was quite different from ours. If we can reconstruct something of what those early performances were like, it will help us to grasp the full complexity of a play like *Othello*, which was neither completely naturalistic nor entirely symbolic but combined both modes of signification. First, it is important to recall that there was no curtain or "fourth wall" separating the audience from the action of the play—that is to say, characters in Renaissance drama acknowledged the audience members sitting in the playhouse. Costuming was elaborate, but aside from the supporting columns, the flat thrust stage with its two flanking entrances at the back, a recessed "discovery space" between them in the center of that back wall, and an upper stage balcony, the structure of the performance space was fairly limited. The five-foot-high platform stage was rather bare, and so in order to evoke a sense of place, Shakespeare's company called upon the audience to participate imaginatively in the action.

The Globe was an outdoor, open-air theater, and plays were put on in the afternoon. Scenes taking place at night, like the opening scene in *Othello*, were indicated by actors carrying torches or by the dialogue. The few objects and props that were used on stage were often deployed symbolically and with great economy. Audiences were not presented with the sort of illusion produced by a modern proscenium stage, with its curtain, electric lighting, naturalistic acting style, and passive audience sitting comfortably in the shadows. The actors performing in Shakespeare's company sometimes used conventional or stylized gesture, and they frequently employed an artificial poetry or rhetoric that was often quite unlike "real" speech. Shakespeare's theater often operated in a symbolic or emblematic mode, and not in a fully realistic manner.

This did not prevent spectators from identifying with the characters on stage—after all, early modern playgoers were used to the way things were done, and their imaginative participation and suspension of disbelief were freely given as their half of the unwritten contract between players and audience. For example, in *Othello*, at the beginning of Act Two, as Montano anxiously awaits the arrival of the Moor at Cyprus, he calls up to a Gentlemen who is standing on the upper stage and looking out over the heads of the groundlings, asking, "What from the cape can you discern at sea?" (2.1.1). The audience is asked to imagine a furious tempest that has destroyed the Turkish armada and now threatens the Venetian fleet. And yet there are no special effects, except perhaps offstage a cannonball rolled on a sheet of metal to produce the sound of rolling thunder. Instead, the playgoers are instructed by the dialogue to use their minds' eyes to see what the First Gentleman sees: "Nothing at all. It is a high-wrought flood" (2.1.2). The ensuing description of the "wind-shaked surge" (2.1.13) uses high-sounding poetic language to invoke a sense of danger and suspense. This is followed by a series of entrances from the doors at the rear of the stage: first a Third Gentleman enters, then Cassio arrives, then voices cry out from "within" (i.e., from the tiring-house behind the entry doors), "A sail, a sail, a sail!" (2.1.52), then—boom—a cannon shot is fired as a salute from Iago and

Desdemona's vessel. The Second Gentleman goes out, returns, then Iago, Desdemona, Roderigo, and Emilia enter. Another sail is descried, another shot fired, and after some comic banter between Iago and Desdemona, Othello enters at last and embraces Desdemona. All this without any water, boat, dock, or seaside scenery—the audience sees "nothing at all," except for the frantic entrances and exits of various characters, punctuated by shouting and the sound of loud cannon shots. Meanwhile, the spectators themselves were not sitting passively or silently. Beer and bread were for sale, and the auditors standing on the ground could move about and observe each other in the daylight.

The intimacy between players and spectators would be all the more significant in a play like *Othello*, in which the character with the most lines, Iago, frequently moves forward onto the outer area of the thrust stage to communicate directly with members of the audience. Rather than ignoring the audience and pretending that they were not there (as a character in a play by Shaw or Pinter would do), the actor playing Iago would have engaged audience members quite directly, sometimes in the form of an aside. By soliciting their attention, their confidence, and at times their laughter, Iago implicates the audience in the play's tragedy. When Iago speaks his soliloquies at the end of Act Two, scene one ("Knavery's plain face is never seen till used"), and again in Act Two, scene three ("And what's he, then, that says I play the villain. . . ?"), he would have communicated directly with the groundlings standing in the yard and looked up at the wealthier customers sitting in the galleries. (Even those farthest from the stage were only thirty-five feet away).

The tragic intensity of *Othello*, acknowledged today, was accelerated and focused by the conditions of performance in Shakespeare's day. The play begins in the middle of an animated exchange between Iago and Roderigo, and the action moves forward with breathless rapidity, outrunning any realistic sense of time's passage as Othello is quickly turned from a confident commander and loving newlywed to a deeply disturbed murderer. Without extensive cuts, the play takes much longer to put on today than it did in the early seventeenth century. The King's Men would have needed little more than two hours, including the dancing of a jig that traditionally signaled the end of the afternoon's entertainment. The performance went so quickly because there were no intervals, scene or act breaks, and no sets to change. The actors probably spoke more rapidly than actors performing Shakespeare today: now actors need to speak more slowly and enunciate more distinctly so that twenty-first century audiences can have a chance to follow the seventeenth-century language. Even in Shakespeare's day, scenes and lines may have been cut from the script in performance. Rather than giving the audience a break by pausing the action, plays like *Othello* flowed from scene to scene without interval. A two-hour play was no strain for Londoners, who often stood to hear preaching from the pulpit for three hours at a time and enjoyed it. Shakespeare's plays were performed with a carefully crafted modulation of tone and seriousness, however, moving from long set speeches, to rapid-fire dialogue or comic banter, to mirthful or melancholy song, and frequently punctuated with flashes of violent action.

In contrast to the hurly-burly of the play's opening scene, or of Act Two, scene one, discussed earlier, there are portions of *Othello* that are paced quite differently, such as Act Five, scene two, which begins slowly and ominously and then builds gradually to protestation and violence. A playgoer attending one of the early performances of this scene would see, before Othello enters, a curtained bed being pushed out from behind the tiring-house façade by stage keepers onto the stage platform, a bed already laden with the body of a boy actor, dressed in a long white nightgown and wearing a wig, with his face made up to accentuate Desdemona's white skin and blood-red lips in contrast to Othello's black skin and "thick-lips" (1.1.66). Burbage would enter, his face and hands evenly blackened with soot, bearing a flaming lamp, its candle flickering dimly in the daylight at the Globe. Both of these cosmetic devices would be accepted and understood as conventional and symbolic: the audience would not interpret them as racist caricature or disturbing preadolescent transvestitism.

The play's final scene utilizes a few symbolic objects to provide a visual focus for the climactic action—a lamp, a bed, and later a sword. Black curtains or hangings covered part of the tiring-house façade to indicate that the afternoon's play was a tragedy, and that black backdrop stood in contrast to the white wedding sheets on the fatal bed, which Desdemona had requested in the previous scene. The upper stage was decorated with stars and planets to form the "heavens," and a trapdoor was built into the platform, allowing access to the "Hell" beneath the stage, and so the playhouse space represented the cosmic framework that contained and defined Othello's fall from bliss into damnation. After intoning, "It is the cause; it is the cause" (5.2.1), Othello extinguishes the lamp, and the light of Desdemona's life is "put out" (5.2.7) as the black Othello smothers the white Desdemona using their nuptial bedclothes. Soon a figurative and imaginary darkness (an "eclipse," according to the Moor) fills the bedroom.

At the Globe Theatre, this intimate, primal scene would have been powerfully spare and striking in the way that it conveyed and emphasized the binary oppositions of black and white, light and darkness, Hell and Heaven, life and death, wrong and right, guilt and innocence. At the end of the performance, the bed and its "tragic loading" (5.2.362) became an "object [that] poisons sight" (5.2.363). "All that is spoke is marred" (5.2.356): the tragedy achieves closure by directing the audience toward silence and toward an inward acknowledgment of the unknowable and the hideous, which are evil and its abhorrent effects. "Let it be hid," (5.2.364) says Lodovico, who has the last word, and the bed curtains are drawn on the tableau of death. This final concealment, along with the last scene's invocation of silence and inexpressible grief, is consistent with Jackson's experience, in 1610, of a play that, "not only through speaking, but also through acting certain things, . . .moved the audience to tears."

Significant Performances
by Daniel Vitkus

1604   The original production of *Othello* is staged by the King's Men, with Richard Burbage as Othello and probably John Lowin as Iago.

1660   *Othello* is one of the first plays performed by Thomas Killigrew's new company, the King's Men, when the London stage reopens at the time of the Restoration. Therefore *Othello* may be the first of Shakespeare's plays to be performed with a woman in the heroine's role. (See *Stage Beauty*, Richard Eyre's 2004 film about the reopening of the theaters and the first women actors on the English stage.) On October 11, the diarist Samuel Pepys attended a performance of *Othello* and noted that "a very pretty lady" seated near him "called out to see Desdemona smothered."

1682–1709   Thomas Betterton took on the role of the Moor at the Drury Lane Theatre. Richard Steele, writing in *The Tatler* in 1710, recalled "the wonderful agony which [Betterton] appeared in when he examined the circumstances of the handkerchief."

1746   David Garrick, often thought to be the greatest tragic actor on the London stage at that time, played Othello in London at the Drury Lane, then took the role to Dublin, with Spranger Barry as Iago. While still in Dublin, they exchanged roles, and Garrick played Iago to Barry's Othello. Then they both went to London. Barry was considered the better Othello, and Garrick never performed the role again. Garrick's usual acting style, which relied heavily on facial expression, was hampered by the heavy blackface makeup, and the large turban he wore to increase his height was ridiculed.

1752   The governor of colonial Virginia invited the leader of the Iroquois people to attend a performance of *Othello*. The play was interrupted, however, when the chief intervened in the action of the play, ordering his men to prevent Othello from killing Desdemona.

1785–1805   John Philip Kemble played Othello at the Drury Lane, with his sister Sarah Siddons in the role of Desdemona. Kemble portrayed Othello with cold, dignified, neoclassical grandeur.

1814–1833   Edmund Kean, who first took on the role in 1814, was widely praised for his passionate, Romantic portrayal of Othello's jealousy and grief. He was the first to play Othello as a "tawny," light-skinned Moor, using a light brown makeup that did not mask his facial expressions. On March 25, 1833, he appeared for the last time on stage, collapsing into the arms of Iago (played by his son, Charles) after delivering the "Farewell" speech.

Early 1830s   *Othello Travestie, An Operatic Burlesque Burletta*, an American minstrel show parody of *Othello*, was successfully exported to the London stage. It was probably the first time that an American blackface minstrel performance was brought to England.

1852–1866   After failing to obtain support in his own country or in Britain, the African-American actor Ira Aldridge toured as Othello on the Continent, where he met with acclaim in Germany and Russia, following the liberal revolutions of 1848. Aldridge eventually settled in Russia, where he performed in the provinces.

1856–1884 In 1856, Tommaso Salvini began appearing as the Moor in Italian productions of *Othello*. At first, because he interpreted the role in a highly physical manner that violated audience expectations for decorum in tragic drama, he met with mixed success, but eventually his raging, tearful performances won over audiences. He went on to tour successfully in Britain (1875 and 1884) and America, performing in Italian.

1881 The American actors Edwin Booth and Henry Irving exchanged the parts of Othello and Iago in a series of performances at the Lyceum Theatre. Irving wore a turban, sported an ornate oriental costume, and both actors were accused of excessive ranting and raving. Ellen Terry played Desdemona.

1889 Verdi's opera *Otello* came to London, prompting the playwright George Bernard Shaw to remark that "*Othello* is a play written in the style of an Italian opera."

1930 Paul Robeson played the part of Othello in a London production. Peggy Ashcroft interpreted the part of Desdemona. Audiences were shocked when they witnessed, for the first time on the modern stage, a black actor passionately kissing a white woman.

1943 A more confident Paul Robeson takes on the role of Othello again, this time in New York City, in a production that still holds the record for the longest Broadway run for a play by Shakespeare. Uta Hagen played Desdemona. The production then toured in the northern states and Canada—Robeson refused to perform in segregated theaters in the South.

1952   A black-and-white film version directed by Orson Welles and starring Welles in the title role was released. It took several years for Welles to complete the production, which was filmed in Italy and Morocco. Due to a shortage of financial support, he was forced to halt production and then start up again several times.

1956   Richard Burton and John Neville exchanged the roles of Iago and Othello at the Old Vic in London.

1965   A film version is released starring Laurence Olivier and directed by Stuart Burge. This was based on a stage production that took place at the Old Vic for the National Theatre of Great Britain in London. Olivier attempted to transform himself into a "Moor" by wearing dark makeup and altering his hair and facial features. This was the last blackface performance of Othello by a major actor.

1972   Charles Marowitz's adaptation, *An Othello*, took on the message and appearance of the Black Power movement. His Iago, played by a black actor, is a revolutionary Black Panther to Othello's Uncle Tom, urging Othello to avenge himself on "whitey" in recompense for "all the wrongs of the past."

1981–1982   James Earl Jones played Othello and Christopher Plummer Iago in a stage production that began at the Canadian Stratford festival and then moved to the Winter Garden Theater in New York City.

1983   A film version featuring Anthony Hopkins as Othello and Bob Hoskins as Iago was released. It was directed by Jonathan Miller, who had Hopkins play the role as a light-skinned Arab with a beard. It was produced as part of the complete Shakespeare series that was filmed for BBC Television.

1985–1986   Ben Kingsley as Othello and David Suchet as a homosexual Iago appear in a Royal Shakespeare Company production directed by Terry Hands. Kingsley's Othello is an East Indian Muslim in caftan with Indian accent.

1990   Trevor Nunn directed the play for the Royal Shakespeare Company at the Other Place (one of the RSC's smaller performance venues) in 1989, and a film version of the production was made the next year. Ian McKellen played Iago, and Imogen Stubbs was Desdemona.

1995   Oliver Parker's film version of *Othello* was the first to cast a black Othello in a major commercial movie. Laurence Fishburne appeared as Othello, and the role of Iago was played by Kenneth Branagh.

1997   The Shakespeare Company in Washington, DC, staged a "photo-negative" production, starring Patrick Stewart as Othello, and a cast of black actors taking all of the other speaking parts. Directed by Jude Kelly.

2001   An American film called *O*, directed by Tim Blake Nelson, is released. The film is an adaptation of Shakespeare's story, set at a private high school in the South, where Odin (nicknamed *O*) is an African-American basketball player who is persuaded to murder his white girlfriend, Desi, by his teammate Hugo.

Inspired by *Othello*

Film

The first productions of *Othello* in Elizabethan England would have starred a white man as the black hero and a young boy playing his beautiful wife. It is therefore not surprising that many adaptations of the play explore the nature of an actor's relationship to the role he performs. In these films the main characters, usually participants in a production of *Othello*, are forced through their performances (and their on- and offstage relationships) to face the same problems of power, identity, and faith that Shakespeare's characters confront. Several early *Othello* adaptations share a similar plotline: a husband and wife are performing together in Shakespeare's play. The husband, in a jealous rage, murders (or attempts to murder) his wife onstage, and the story ends with either the death of one or both or with a marital reconciliation. In each case, the intensity of the *Othello* experience causes the actors to conflate their own emotions with those of their characters.

In *Desdemona* (1911), a silent melodrama by Danish director August Blom, a famous actor hears a rumor that his wife and co-star is having an affair with a French count. To test his wife's fidelity, the actor disguises himself as her supposed lover (whom he closely resembles). Fooled by the disguise, she responds passionately to his advances. During their performance of _Othello_ the next night, the actor is carried away with vengeful anger, and instead of simulating the murder of Desdemona (played by his wife), he actually kills her.

Another silent film, Leonce Perret's 1917 _A Modern Othello_ (also known by the alternate titles _The Lash of Jealousy_ and _The Mad Lover_) is one of the few _Othello_ adaptations with a happy ending. Othello and Desdemona become Robert and Clarice Hyde, who get married, despite Robert's sworn bachelorhood, after a car accident brings them together. After their wedding, Clarice, anxious to get pregnant, pines for Robert, who spends all of his time hunting and fishing. The conflict is resolved when Clarice's aunt brings a group of friends to the Hyde estate, where they plan to put on an amateur benefit performance of _Othello_. Count Vinzagolio's love scenes with Clarice excite Robert's jealousy, and Robert dreams that he (as Othello) has murdered Clarice (as Desdemona). Robert later catches the count making real advances on his wife, and throws him out. The incident prompts Robert to pay more attention to Clarice, who is soon happily pregnant.

Carnival (1931) similarly ends happily. In the film, Silvio and his wife Simonetta are rehearsing _Othello_ in Venice. Their friend Andrea flirts with Simonetta, and Silvio's sister convinces him that the two are having an affair. Through a series of plot twists and misunderstandings, Silvio's jealousy and suspicion escalate, while Simonetta rebuffs Andrea's continuing romantic overtures. Finally, on opening night, Silvio discovers Andrea's deceit and nearly strangles Simonetta onstage. Ultimately, the couple reconciles when Simonetta explains that her brief dalliance with Andrea meant nothing and that she was never actually unfaithful.

In Walter Reisch's _Men Are Not Gods_ (1936), Edmund Davey is a classical actor about to debut a new production of Shakespeare's _Othello_. After discovering that an important critic has written a negative review, Davey's wife Barbara (who is playing Desdemona) persuades Ann, the critic's secretary, to revise the notice. As a result of Ann's positive review, Davey's *Othello* is a great success, and after watching several of his performances, Ann falls in love with him. Davey reciprocates. Barbara discovers the affair and confronts Ann, announcing that she is pregnant. Ann writes to Davey, explaining that they cannot be together because of his wife. He interprets her letter as incitement to kill Barbara, which he nearly does during a performance of *Othello* that night. In his mind, he is the victim, persecuted by his wife's jealous nature. Sitting in the audience, Ann realizes what is about to happen and screams, halting the action. Later Davey learns that Barbara is pregnant and breaks off his affair with Ann to reunite with his wife.

Marcel Carne's *Les Enfants du Paradis* (1945) does not closely follow the plot of *Othello*, but it incorporates a scene from the play at a crucial moment. *Les Enfants du Paradis* tells the story of four men in love with the same woman, Garance. One of these men, Frederick, is an ambitious and pretentious actor who claims that he can master any role except that of *Othello*, because he has never experienced jealousy. After wooing and being rejected by Garance, he gains new insight into the character's passion and rage. During a performance of the play, he catches a glimpse of Garance in the audience, and his wounded ego erupts into an authentic and moving Othello.

George Cukor's *A Double Life* (1947) turns the play-within-a-play into a psychological thriller. The film follows the actors Tony and Brita (Tony's ex-wife) through a 300-plus performance run of *Othello* on Broadway. Already prone to losing himself in his stage roles, Tony gradually capitulates to the part of Othello. He murders his mistress but has no memory of the crime, and eventually kills himself. Ronald Colman won an Oscar for his portrayal of Tony's descent into homicidal mania.

A second category of big-screen *Othello* adaptations sets the play in new cultural contexts, amplifying and contemporizing its central relationships. Delmer Daves transforms the story into a Western and focuses on the Cassio character, recast by Daves as the transient Jubal Troop. In *Jubal* (1955), Othello and Desdemona become Shep and Mae, a couple who give Jubal a job on their ranch, eventually promoting him to foreman. The Iago character is a ranch hand who becomes jealous of Jubal and accuses him of having an affair with Mae. Daves's crucial divergence from Shakespeare's plotline is to make Mae guilty: she tries to seduce Jubal, having already committed adultery with the ranch hand himself. During the climactic bedroom scene, Mae falsely admits to having slept with Jubal, prompting Shep to attack Jubal, who then kills Shep in self-defense. The ranch hand then murders Mae. Mae is contrasted in the film with the Bianca character, a virginal girl from a Christian wagon train on pilgrimage to find the Promised Land. Her marriage to Jubal is the film's resolution.

Tim Blake Nelson's *O* (2001) transposes *Othello* to a predominantly white South Carolina prep school where O is a black basketball star, specially recruited to help the school team win a title. Hugo and Mike (Iago and Cassio) are O's teammates and friends until Hugo, jealous of O's athletic success and general popularity, begins to insinuate that Desi (O's girlfriend) has cheated on him with Mike. As O and Desi's relationship starts to deteriorate, the film engages with the contemporary issues of academic diversity, underage sex, and teenage violence. After he murders Desi, O repudiates the stereotype of the angry black man, condemned to a criminal life because of an underprivileged youth: "You tell 'em, where I came from didn't make me do this," he says to Hugo.

Stage

Both the power dynamics that govern the plot of *Othello* as well as the controversies surrounding its performance history have inspired contemporary playwrights to use the play to explore social and moral themes, particularly issues of race and gender.

Paula Vogel's *Desdemona: A Play About a Handkerchief* (1986) is a revision of *Othello* from the point of view of its women characters. While the action of Shakespeare's play takes place offstage, Emilia, Bianca, and Desdemona develop an alternative plot in a backroom of the palace. In Vogel's provocative drama, Desdemona is worldly, narcissistic, and sexually adventurous, filling in on certain nights for Bianca, a prostitute. Bianca herself is torn between her independent lifestyle and her desire to marry Cassio and raise a family. Emilia is simultaneously earnest and scheming: she wants to remain loyal to Desdemona but feels a duty (partly out of Christian piety) to honor her husband, whom she despises. The play consists almost entirely of conversations between the three women as they discuss their impressions of their own situations, developing a gritty backstory to Shakespeare's original text. By the time Desdemona meets her fate (which remains the same as in Shakespeare's play), her character has become so full and complex that she can no longer be seen as a simple victim of the violent male ego. Desdemona has contributed to her own destiny, as Vogel seems to suggest is the right of all women.

Ann Marie MacDonald's 1988 play *Goodnight Desdemona (Good Morning Juliet)* is another feminist take on Shakespeare, although more lighthearted and less political than Vogel's. The play tells the story of Constance Ledbelly, an academic whose own Ph.D. work gets sidelined while she performs free labor for the object of her unrequited affection, Professor Knight. After the professor runs off with a student, Constance magically lands inside the Shakespeare plays (*Othello* and *Romeo and Juliet*) that are the subject of her research. Constance traipses through the plot of each play in a search for the author himself and for the "fool" whom she believes to be the missing ingredient that would prove her thesis that the two plays were originally meant to be comedies. Along her way, she has the chance to intervene at pivotal moments in each play, correcting misunderstandings, preventing disasters, and exposing villains. Her interference comes with unintended consequences. For example, she rescues Desdemona, who turns out to be willful and proud in her own right, and who then falls victim to the same suspicion and rage (this time directed against Constance herself) that Othello did in the original play. Constance's search turns out to be a search of her own subconscious, a journey to unite the elements of her own personality and to become the author of her own life.

Harlem Duet (1997) by Djanet Sears is probably the most overt adaptation of *Othello* in terms of its advancement of a particular socio-political perspective. Sears's heroine is an inserted character, Othello's first wife Billie, a graduate student who discovers that her husband (a professor at Columbia University) has fallen in love with another woman ("Mona"). But the play supplements its setting in modern-day Harlem with flashbacks reimagining the couple in two other historical situations: as slaves considering a trip on the Underground Railroad in the 1860s, and as a vaudeville era couple struggling to pay the bills by acting in racially demeaning minstrel shows. Instead of sexual jealousy, Othello suffers from a jealousy of white privilege, while Billie tries to assemble the various pieces of her dream life: a career, a powerful husband, a family. Billie and Othello are thus ideologically unfaithful to one another, with Mona functioning only as an embodiment of that crisis. Drawing heavily on the blues tradition for its themes and its general atmosphere, the play is rhapsodic, brooding, and passionate, very much in keeping with the tragedy that inspired it.

Music and Dance

Giuseppe Verdi picked up on the rhythm and resonance of Othello when he selected it as the second of three Shakespeare plays to be adapted for opera. More critically acclaimed than either *Macbeth*, which preceded it, or *Falstaff*, which came afterward, Verdi's *Otello* (1887) is often touted by opera lovers as superior to even Shakespeare's original. The love duet between Othello and Desdemona at the end of Act One poignantly expresses the love and devotion between husband and wife, which in the play is not nearly so definite or tender. But while the whirling and sinister music evokes the poetry of the play, its dramatic structure diminishes some of the characters. By focusing on the nobility of the hero, the opera mutes the other characters considerably. Iago is less biting, Desdemona is even more passive, and Bianca is completely eliminated. The mysteriousness of Iago's malevolence is undermined by the insertion of his Credo, a solo in which he professes his allegiance to a satanic spirit. To complete the explanation, Desdemona also gets additional lines, in the form of an Ave Maria, in which she delivers a prayer to ward off evil. Her death, Verdi seems to say, is not the result of human sin, but of a supernatural assault by evil against good.

Choreographer Lar Lubovitch's 1997 *Othello*—produced in collaboration with American Ballet Theater and San Francisco Ballet, with a score by Elliot Goldenthal—uses complex and difficult choreography to mirror the predicaments of its characters. Combining traditional sets with visual projections, Lubovitch merged the modern and the classical in his staging as well as in his choreography. Of all the characters, Iago came across the most concretely. The steps in variations were, like him, meticulous and surreptitious, and they marked him clearly as the architect of Othello's crime. The production had a large budget and was televised nationally in 2002, coming about as close to Hollywood as a ballet can get.

For Further Reading
by Daniel Vitkus

Boose, Lynda. "Othello's Handkerchief: 'The Recognizance and Pledge of Love.'" *English Literary Renaissance* 5 (1975): 360–74. Boose shows how the handkerchief, which is mentioned thirty-five times and displayed repeatedly, operates as a key visual signifier in the play, functioning as a love token and as a symbol of sexual consummation.

Burke, Kenneth. "*Othello*: An Essay to Illustrate a Method." In "*Othello*": *Critical Essays*, edited by Susan Snyder, 127–68. New York and London: Garland, 1988. Burke's classic interpretation of the play describes the "cathartic functions" of Iago and focuses on the play's presentation of sexual love as property and/or ennoblement.

Daileader, Celia. *Racism, Misogyny, and the Othello Myth*. Cambridge: Cambridge University Press, 2005. Beginning with *Othello* and other early modern plays, this study offers an analysis of "the Othello myth," arguing that myths about black male sexual rapacity and the danger of racial "pollution" functioned to "protect" white women and to exorcise collective guilt.

D'Amico, Jack. *The Moor in English Renaissance Drama*. Tampa: University of South Florida Press, 1991. This study catalogues all the Moorish characters that appeared on the early modern stage in England and offers useful historical information about cross-cultural contact between England and North African cultures.

Hankey, Julie, ed. *"Othello": Plays in Performance*. Bristol: Bristol Classical Press, 1987. This book includes a chronological table of *Othello* performances, a survey of the play's performance history, and the text of *Othello*, thoroughly annotated with helpful accounts of various performances.

Hunter, G. K. "Othello and Colour Prejudice." *Proceedings of the British Academy* 53 (1967): 139–63. In this article, Hunter attempts to recover a historically accurate sense of "what the idea of a black man suggested to Shakespeare, and what reaction the appearance of a black man on the stage was calculated to produce."

Kolin, Philip C., ed. *"Othello": New Critical Essays*. NY: Routledge, 2002. This is the best recent collection of essays on *Othello*, offering a wide range of innovative readings of the play and its performance history.

Korda, Natasha. "The Tragedy of the Handkerchief: Female Paraphernalia and the Properties of Jealousy in *Othello*." Chap. 4 in *Shakespeare's Domestic Economies: Gender and Property in Early Modern England*. University of Pennsylvania Press, 2002. This insightful feminist study discusses the representation of women in *Othello* in relation to early modern England's nascent consumer culture and competing conceptions of property.

Neely, Carol Thomas. "Women and Men in *Othello*." In *The Woman's Part: Feminist Criticism of Shakespeare*, edited by Carolyn Lenz, Gayle Greene, and Carol Thomas Neely, 211–39. Urbana: University of

Illinois Press, 1980. Neely compares the men in the play to the women and comes to the defense of Desdemona, Emilia, and Bianca, arguing that they have been neglected and misread by both "Othello critics" and "Iago critics."

Neill, Michael. "Unproper Beds: Race, Adultery, and the Hideous in *Othello*." *Shakespeare Quarterly* 40 (1989): 383–412. Neill examines the shock value of *Othello*, arguing that the play "engages its audience in a conspiracy to lay naked the scene of forbidden desire, only to confirm that the penalty for such exposure is death and oblivion."

Newman, Karen. "'And wash the Ethiop white': Femininity and the Monstrous in *Othello*." In *Shakespeare Reproduced*, edited by Jean E. Howard and Marion O'Connor, 143–62. London: Methuen, 1987. Newman analyzes and links the issues of gender and racial discrimination in *Othello* and concludes that in many ways the play works to challenge the oppressive ideologies of gender and race that operated in early modern England.

Paster, Gail Kern. "Roasted in Wrath and Fire: the Ecology of the Passions in *Hamlet* and *Othello*." Chap. 1 in *Humoring the Body: Emotions and the Shakespearean Stage*. Chicago: University of Chicago Press, 2004. The second half of this chapter offers a fascinating account of Othello's descent into jealousy as it would have been understood by Shakespeare's audience—as a psychosomatic process produced by the ebb and flow of "humors" in the body and mind of the Moor.

Pechter, Edward. *Othello and Interpretive Traditions*. Iowa City: University of Iowa Press, 1999. This book provides a useful survey of critical responses to and theatrical productions of *Othello*, from the seventeenth to the late twentieth centuries, but it also puts forward an argument claiming that the interpretive traditions surrounding *Othello* are mutually dependent, reciprocally constitutive ways of talking about the same thing.

Rymer, Thomas. *A Short View of Tragedy.* London, 1693. Reprinted in *The Critical Works of Thomas Rymer*, edited by C. Zimansky. New Haven: Yale University Press, 1956. Reprinted Greenwood Press, 1971. Rymer's lively attack is the first important analysis of *Othello*, disparaging the play for its violation of neoclassical tragic decorum and declaring the drama to be "none other than a bloody farce without salt or savor."

Spivack, Bernard. *Shakespeare and the Allegory of Evil.* NY: Columbia University Press, 1958. This book discusses the influence of the earlier morality play tradition on Shakespeare's work, and it is particularly helpful in demonstrating Iago's connection to the Vice, the allegorical personification of evil who tempts Everyman and shares his devilish delight with the audience.

Vaughan, Virginia Mason. *"Othello": A Contextual History.* Cambridge: Cambridge University Press, 1994. This study places *Othello* in the context of early modern history and then traces the performance history of the play through from Shakespeare's time to the twentieth century.

Vitkus, Daniel. "Othello Turns Turk." Chap. 4 in *Turning Turk: English Theater and the Multicultural Mediterranean, 1570–1630.* New York: Palgrave, 2003. This chapter discusses Othello's "conversion" from noble, Christianized Moor to "Turkish" cruelty and violence, linking that process to English anxieties about religious conversion and the threatening power of the Ottoman Empire.